W9-DDF-694

HOLY WARS

HOLY
WARS

3,000 YEARS OF BATTLES
IN THE HOLY LAND

BY GARY L. RASHBA

CASEMATE
Philadelphia & Oxford

Published in the United States of America and Great Britain in 2013 by
CASEMATE PUBLISHERS
908 Darby Road, Havertown, PA 19083
and
10 Hythe Bridge Street, Oxford, OX1 2EW

Copyright 2011 © Gary L. Rashba

ISBN 978-1-61200-153-1
Digital Edition: ISBN 978-1-61200-019-0

Cataloging-in-publication data is available from the Library of Congress
and the British Library.

All rights reserved. No part of this book may be reproduced or transmitted in
any form or by any means, electronic or mechanical including photocopying,
recording or by any information storage and retrieval system, without
permission from the Publisher in writing.

10 9 8 7 6 5 4 3

Printed and bound in the United States of America.

For a complete list of Casemate titles please contact:

CASEMATE PUBLISHERS (US)
Telephone (610) 853-9131, Fax (610) 853-9146
E-mail: casemate@casematepublishing.com

CASEMATE PUBLISHERS (UK)
Telephone (01865) 241249, Fax (01865) 794449
E-mail: casemate-uk@casematepublishing.co.uk

CONTENTS

CONTENTS *(continued)*

MAPS

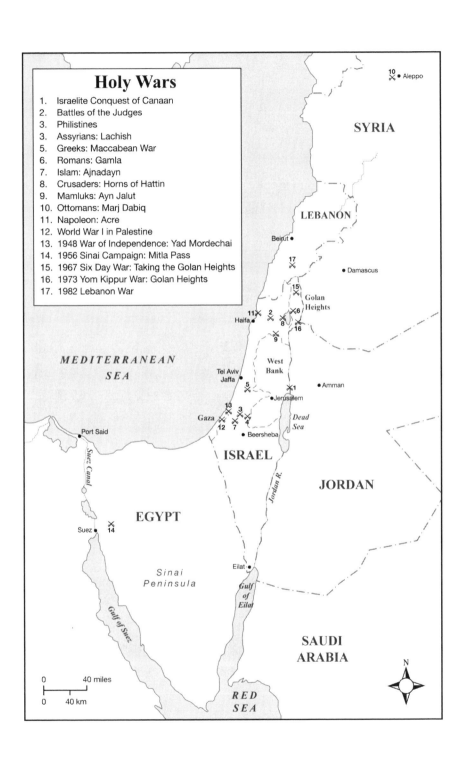

Holy Wars

1. Israelite Conquest of Canaan
2. Battles of the Judges
3. Philistines
3. Assyrians: Lachish
5. Greeks: Maccabean War
6. Romans: Gamla
7. Islam: Ajnadayn
8. Crusaders: Horns of Hattin
9. Mamluks: Ayn Jalut
10. Ottomans: Marj Dabiq
11. Napoleon: Acre
12. World War I in Palestine
13. 1948 War of Independence: Yad Mordechai
14. 1956 Sinai Campaign: Mitla Pass
15. 1967 Six Day War: Taking the Golan Heights
16. 1973 Yom Kippur War: Golan Heights
17. 1982 Lebanon War

Aleppo

SYRIA

LEBANON

Beirut

Damascus

Golan
Heights

Haifa

West
Bank

MEDITERRANEAN
SEA

Tel Aviv
Jaffa

Amman

Jerusalem

Gaza

Dead
Sea

Port Said

Beersheba

ISRAEL

Suez Canal

JORDAN

EGYPT

Suez

Sinai
Peninsula

Eilat

Gulf
of
Eilat

SAUDI
ARABIA

N

Gulf of Suez

0   40 miles

0   40 km

RED
SEA

PREFACE

Holy Wars is intended to give an overview of the Holy Land's profound military history—a history which teaches many lessons, including the importance of timing, speed, stealth, good intelligence, and the danger of complacency or letting down one's guard—issues as relevant today as they have been throughout the history of warfare. Examples of experiences and lessons from history transcending time abound. Napoleon, who was well-versed in both the Bible and Josephus' writings, opted to avoid the difficult terrain of the Judean hills, where he knew many armies had met their demise. During World War I, there was British Major Vivian Gilbert, serving in the British Commonwealth army fighting the Ottomans in Palestine. Recalling the Biblical story of King Saul's son Jonathan who, accompanied only by his shield bearer, attacked and routed a Philistine garrison at Michmas by flanking the position and attacking from an unexpected direction (see chapter 3), the British officer devised a plan replicating Jonathan's attack route to overtake an enemy position in that very spot.

I do not wish to bog the reader down with overly detailed accounts of which unit moved on a specific flank, as I find that such micro-analyses of battles tend to either lose the reader's interest or can be difficult to follow. On the other hand, overly general accounts tend to gloss over fascinating military history.

Though I aim for accuracy, I am more a storyteller than historian, striving to bring both ancient and recent events to life in an interesting and readable way. That isn't to say that writing this book did not involve extensive research: *Holy Wars* is the culmination of some twelve years of work, compiling sources and materials to piece together a coherent account of events. Working at times with ancient or archaic sources that are prone to exaggerations, such as numbers of forces that simply could not have been sustained, or Goliath's height, I have tried to qualify such points with credible modern interpretations or clarifications. Historical accounts often exaggerated the strength of one's enemy (and reduced the actual number of the victor's force) to make a victory seem all the more impressive. When possible, I consulted with experts in the field. However, this is by no means a definitive history. Both archaeology and other historical research are ongoing pursuits within which new discoveries can revise contemporary accounts of historical events.

The land stretching between the Mediterranean Sea and the Jordan River that I am calling the Holy Land has been known by different names over the millennia, its name changing with the ebb and flow of peoples, empires and civilizations. Within chapters the contemporary names for the region are used.

My stimulus for researching the topic was that I simply wanted to know more about the Holy Land's military history, yet could never find the version I wanted—one that gives a sense of the fight and the context in which it was fought. My quest ultimately resulted in my writing the account. Rather than presenting an exhaustive rendition of every battle fought during the periods covered, the focus is usually on one of the significant battles—not necessarily the best known, but one that captures the essence of the war or campaign. I wrote a chapter. Then another. And another, and it began shaping up into a book. While *Holy Wars* runs chronologically, chapters are self-contained, meaning readers can choose a specific chapter for a snapshot of a particular period of interest without having to read the previous or subsequent chapters.

I hope that you, the reader, finds the subject as fascinating as I do!

ACKNOWLEDGMENTS

The author would like to thank Professor Mordechai Gichon, professor emeritus of Military History and Archaeology at Tel Aviv University; Dr. Yehuda Dagan of the Israel Antiquities Authority for his assistance with chapters 3 and 4; Dr. Danny Syon of the Israel Antiquities Authority for his invaluable comments on chapter 7; Professor Reuven Amitai, Dean of the Hebrew University of Jerusalem Faculty of Humanities, for his comments on an early draft of chapter 9; Professor Michael Winter of the Tel Aviv University Department of the History of the Middle East and Africa, and Professor Carl Petry of Northwestern University's Department of History, for assisting me with chapter 10; the late Munio Brandvein for recounting his wartime experiences to me for chapter 13, Dr. Arieh Gilai for his assistance with chapter 14; Kibbutz Yad Mordechai Archive; and the Israel Air Force History Department. Additionally, I'd like to thank Alan Merbaum, Yossi Sorogon, Curt Fischer, Dick Osseman, Marshall Editions and Kregel Publications for the photographs and images they were kind enough to permit me to use.

I would also like to thank my wonderful wife Sigal for all her love and support; my editor Ruth Sheppard whose extensive knowledge and keen eye helped shape this work; Steve Smith, Libby Braden, Tara Lichterman and the team at Casemate; and my friends at *Military History* Magazine.

INTRODUCTION

They shall beat their swords into ploughshares, and their
spears into pruning-hooks; nation shall not lift up sword
against nation, neither shall they learn war any more.
Isaiah 2: 4

In the Holy Land, this ancient hope and prayer remains as elusive today as it was when written. Today's Arab-Israeli conflict, ever present in the news, is merely the latest iteration in an unending history of violence. While each side in the modern dispute blames the other for its origins, the truth is that the Holy Land has been contested for millennia.

Beginning with the Israelites' capture of Jericho and ending with the 1982 war in Lebanon (the last time Israel fought a nation-state), *Holy Wars* describes 3,000 years of war in the Holy Land, uniquely focusing on pivotal battles or campaigns to tell the story of a historical period. An epilogue covers the low-intensity, or asymmetric, conflicts Israel fought in the first decade of the 21st century.

Sitting at a strategic crossroads between continents, the Holy Land has been the scene of conflict for many of the world's great civilizations. The Israelites took Jericho and secured a foothold in what was to them the Promised Land. The native Canaanites resisted the newcomers, just as the Israelites would later fend off desert dwellers attracted to the land's bounty, and would counter invading powers.

Many of the world's great empires would leave their footprints in the Holy Land. Rome demonstrated its might after the Seleucids, successors to Alexander the Great—fielding one of the most modern armies of the day—met defeat at the hands of insurgents dead-set on defending their faith, a theme that resonates in wars being fought in modern times. Both the Mongols and Napoleon suffered their first defeats in this contested land.

Great stories of history took place in the Holy Land: the walls of ancient Jericho crashing down; the battle of Lachish described in detailed reliefs decorating the Assyrian palace at Nineveh; the armies of the new faith of Islam bursting out of the Arabian desert to wrest control of the Levant from Byzantium; crusaders from Europe liberating Christianity's holy sites from what they considered infidel Moslem hands; and modern Israel's legendary military victories. The fact that the land is holy to the three monotheistic faiths, with some invoking claims of divine right to the land, has helped fuel dispute. The conflicting commitments made by the British during World War I to both Jews and Arabs promising them the same territory only exacerbated the situation and almost guaranteed continued strife. Today both Palestinians and Jews consider the Holy Land their rightful home, with both sides claiming Jerusalem as their capital.

Further conflict may be predicted in the New Testament's Book of Revelation, which indicates that the war of wars will take place at Armageddon (a corruption of the Hebrew *Har Megiddo*, located not far away from the northern fringe of the Palestinian Authority's territory), where the forces of good will battle those of evil. It truly takes a great deal of optimism to believe the Holy Land may one day enjoy the blessing of peace, rather than enduring conflict.

CHAPTER 1

LATCH OF THE LAND OF ISRAEL

ISRAELITE CONQUEST OF
THE PROMISED LAND, 1400 BCE

Circling Jericho's massive walls, the Israelite men had their doubts. Armed with only knives, swords, spears, lances, and bows and arrows, the Israelites had nothing with which to knock down such walls. They also lacked equipment to scale, tunnel, or breach the ramparts. Yet their plan for the conquest of Canaan hinged on first taking Jericho. Looking up at the fortified city's defenses, some of the men became demoralized and questioned how they could possibly succeed. It was 1400 BCE, and the Israelites were following Joshua to take possession of their Promised Land after spending forty years in the desert.

Bountiful with food and water in an arid, inhospitable land, Jericho was a way-station for caravans and travelers moving between and along the two banks of the Jordan River. A lush green oasis whose palm trees contrasted with the surrounding desolate brown terrain, Jericho was accustomed to attacks by marauding nomadic tribes. The city had gone to great lengths to protect and defend itself:

Jericho was surrounded by a great earthen rampart, or embankment, with a stone retaining wall at its base. The retain-

ing wall was some four to five metres (12–15 feet) high. On
top of that was a mud brick wall two metres (six feet) thick
and about six to eight metres (20–26 feet) high. At the crest of
the embankment was a similar mud brick wall whose base
was roughly 14 metres (46 feet) above the ground level outside the retaining wall.[1]

There was no question that Jericho could hold out against the
Israelites. Secure behind its walls, the people of Jericho were confident
they could withstand any siege. They had proven it time and again.
Not only did the city have strong defenses, it was also well-
provisioned. The Israelites approached the city just after the spring
harvest, so the stores were full of wheat, dates and other foodstuffs;
and the perennial Spring of Elisha, or Ain es-Sultan, provided ample
water. Despite the obvious mismatch, morale in Jericho was low and
its people scared. It wasn't only that recent earthquakes could have
damaged the protective walls. There was something different about
this enemy. It is very likely that stories about these people who had
defied the pharaoh's power and left Egypt (the power that dominated
Canaan), of their crossing the Red Sea and later military victories
across the river were known by Jericho's citizenry, putting them on
edge.[2]

Before the Israelites had crossed the Jordan River into Canaan,
Joshua looked across the valley at the lay of the land before him, with
Jericho and its defenses visible in the distance. After succeeding
Moses, Joshua began formulating a plan for the Israelite advance,
bringing to fruition his people's aspiration to return to the Promised
Land, a longing maintained throughout the generations by oral tradition. No newcomer to the battlefield, Joshua had already made a
name for himself as a military leader, but planning an invasion was
something else. He knew the Israelites lacked the capability to attack
the Canaanites' secure stone-walled cities. His force was also at a dis-
advantage in open-country warfare against chariot-equipped and
heavily armed Canaanites regulars. The Israelites also had to consider
the Egyptian reaction, as Egypt claimed suzerainty over Canaan. But
with internal problems and troubles on its borders, Egypt could no
longer safeguard all of Canaan; its influence was hardly felt on the

frontier. The Israelites' best chance for successfully establishing themselves in Canaan lay in the sparsely populated hills in the center of the country. Later called the "latch of the Land of Israel" in ancient Jewish writings, Jericho controlled the route into the mountainous heartland of Canaan. If they could take Jericho, the Israelites would have a bridgehead west of the Jordan River, a foothold they could expand into a much larger area for permanent settlement.

Requiring intelligence on Jericho's defenses, Joshua dispatched a two-man reconnaissance team to scout out approaches and the city's defenses. Jericho's well-developed defensive network noticed the spies' arrival. Jericho's king received a report that Israelite men had come to search out the land.[3] The pair of Israelites would gain the confidence of, and lodge with, a woman named Rahab, who provided assistance. When townspeople hunted the two strangers, Rahab hid them and helped them escape. For her actions, Rahab and her family were later spared during the Israelite killing spree.

The reconnaissance report Joshua received indicated disunity in the city, and a fear of the Israelites, whose reputation had preceded them. Armed with this knowledge, Joshua conceived his plan.

United in their purpose of conquering the Promised Land, the Israelite host—ripe for action—set off from their encampment across the Jordan River. Years in the desert, often under attack by other nomadic tribes, had forged them into a hardy fighting force. Encouraged by recent military successes over the Ammonites and King Og, and motivated by their commander, the Israelite soldiers were raring to fight.

They crossed the Jordan River at an easily passable ford. The Book of Joshua states that the river was in flood, but that when the priests carried the Ark of the Covenant to the edge of the river, it stopped flowing until all the Israelites had crossed. Some scholars argue that an earthquake occurred at the time of the crossing and may have caused the steep banks to collapse, damming up the Jordan River for several hours.[4] The Israelites crossed over on dry land, until the build-up of water forced through the obstruction. Already instilled with the zeal of God, this was seen as divine intervention, reinforcing their faith.

The appearance and disappearance of the two Israelite spies had

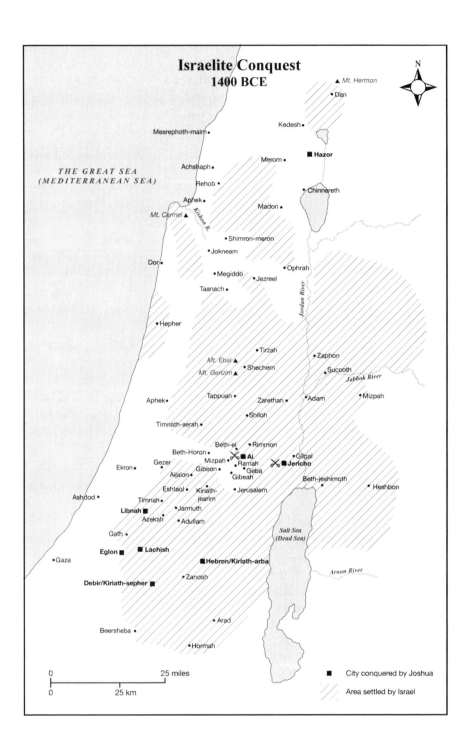

Israelite Conquest
1400 BCE

N

▲ Mt. Hermon

• Dan

THE GREAT SEA
(MEDITERRANEAN SEA)

Kedesh •

• Mesrephoth-maim

Merom •

■ **Hazor**

Achshaph •

Rehob •

• Chinnereth

Aphek •

Madon •

Mt. Carmel ▲

Kishon R.

• Shimron-meron

• Jokneam

Dor •

• Megiddo

• Ophrah

Jezreel •

Taanach •

Jordan River

• Hepher

• Tirzah

Zaphon •

Mt. Ebal ▲

• Shechem

Mt. Gerizim ▲

Succoth •

Jabbok River

Aphek •

Tappuah •

Zarethan •

• Adam

• Mizpah

• Shiloh

Timnath-serah •

Beth-el •

• Rimmon

Beth-Horon •

✗ ■ **Ai**

Gilgal •

Ekron •

Gezer •

Mizpah •

Ramah •

✗ ■ **Jericho**

Aijalon •

Gibeon •

Geba •

Gibeah •

Eshtaol •

Kiriath-jearim •

• Jerusalem

Beth-jeshimoth •

• Heshbon

Ashdod •

Timnah •

Libnah ■

• Jarmuth

Azekah •

• Adullam

Salt Sea
(Dead Sea)

Gath •

Eglon ■

■ **Lachish**

■ **Hebron/Kiriath-arba**

• Gaza

Debir/Kiriath-sepher ■

• Zanoah

Arnon River

• Arad

Beersheba •

• Hormah

0 ——————— 25 miles

0 ——————— 25 km

■ City conquered by Joshua

▨ Area settled by Israel

alerted Jericho that trouble was literally on the horizon. Walls damaged by recent tremors were hastily repaired. People living outside the city sought refuge within Jericho's protective walls, and the city gates were closed. From the vantage of their ramparts, Jericho's defenders now followed the Israelites' approach. Rumors and talk about the Israelites exacerbated the already tense situation. Morale plummeted as fear took hold in the city, and there was little will to fight. The Jordan River ceasing to flow, allowing the Israelites to cross with ease, was taken by the local people as a very bad omen.

Lacking the means with which to attack the city, Joshua put a different weapon to work: psychological warfare. Led by the Ark of the Covenant, containing the stone tablets inscribed with the Ten Commandments that Moses had received on Mount Sinai, and seven priests blowing rams' horn trumpets, the 40,000-strong Israelite host set off from their encampment and approached the city walls.

Jericho's defenses sprang into action, reinforcing defensive ramparts and towers. But the Israelites did not attack. They circled Jericho's walls, parading around the city in a huge procession. After completely circling the city once, the Israelites retired to their nearby camp.

For the next five days, the Israelites repeated this drill, marching around the walls once before returning to camp. Jericho's defenders were wary and suspicious, amused and frightened by these strange desert nomads' unusual procession around their city. There were no demands from the Israelites; the siege was anything but conventional. Blasts of the Israelite priests' rams' horns sowed fear among the besieged city's inhabitants, who were discomfited by the sight of an army laying siege to their city. Unsure how to respond, Jericho's defenders made no sallies against the Israelites.

On the seventh day of the siege, as the Israelites were completing their circuit, blasts from ram's horns signaled a change: the Israelites were to continue circling the city. The Israelites circled a second time. Then a third. And a fourth. . . . Jericho's nervous apprehension turned to fear as what had become habit veered to the unknown. With each additional lap around their city, the feeling of impending doom among the defenders grew. The noose was slowly tightening. Many prayed to Reshef, the Canaanite god of war.

After circling the city seven times, the Israelite priests blew the rams' horns, making a great noise, and the men began to shout. The ground began to shake, and a rumbling sound could be heard, growing louder and louder. The noise grew in intensity as stones and bricks began to dislodge from the wall's upper portions. Cracks appeared and grew larger, growing into large fissures until the great stones at the base broke free and rolled down the slope, kicking up a thick cloud of brown dust. In several places, the mud brick city wall collapsed down onto the retaining wall, forming a ramp. During her 1950s excavations, the late British archaeologist Kathleen Kenyon found "fallen red bricks piling nearly to the top of the revetment. These probably came from the wall on the summit of the bank."[5]

The Israelite troops rushed up the earthen embankment, over the collapsed walls and into the city. Shocked by the tumultuous collapse of the walls and their sudden vulnerability, the townspeople were overcome with terror and became paralyzed by fear.

From pessimistic doubts to what they now saw as divine intervention, the Israelites were imbued with religious fervor, faith in their mission restored. So inspired, they rushed through Jericho's streets freely killing everyone in sight. Townspeople fled among the streets and alleyways; others tried to hide. The invaders ran through the town with gusto, euphorically killing man and beast alike. Jericho's fighting men hardly resisted, and many people merely submitted themselves to slaughter by the rampaging invaders:

> They were afrighted at the surprising overthrow of the walls, and their courage was become useless, and they were not able to defend themselves; so they were slain, and their throats cut, some in the ways, and others as caught in their houses,— nothing afforded them assistance, but they all perished, even to the women and the children; and the city was filled with dead bodies, and not one person escaped.[6]

Joshua had ordered his men to completely exterminate Jericho's population, and this order was carried out without exception. Save for the pledge made to Rahab, the Israelites "utterly destroyed all that was within the city by the edge of the sword." The city was not plundered; it was destroyed and set on fire.

"The destruction was complete," wrote archaeologist Kathleen Kenyon. "Walls and floors were blackened or reddened by fire, and every room was filled with fallen bricks, timbers, and household utensils. . . ."[7] While the level of destruction and killing may seem excessive, the Israelites knew their arrival posed a true threat to all Canaanites, who might very well have taken the opportunity to wipe out this new force in their midst. And with plans to advance into, and establish themselves in, the Canaanite hinterland, their actions at Jericho were preemptive—killing off enemies who could threaten their rear while also establishing a reputation for ferocity. Jericho was left unoccupied and cursed, and the Israelites moved on.

While archaeological evidence over the last century corroborates the Bible's version of a fortified city destroyed after a short siege, its walls collapsed and the city wrecked by fire, the debate continues over when this occurred. Kenyon and others date Jericho's destruction to 1550 BCE—too early for the aggressors to have been Joshua and the Israelites. Challenging Kenyon's methodology, contemporary archaeologist Bryant Wood dates Jericho's destruction to 1400 BCE, which aligns with the timing of the Biblical account. Further debate surrounds the arrival of the Israelites to Canaan, with many scholars believing the Israelites arrived some 200 years later—in 1200 BCE—long after Jericho was destroyed.

Ai

. . . take all the people of war with thee, and arise,
go up to Ai; see, I have given unto thy hand the king
of Ai, and his people, and his city, and his land.
Joshua 8: 1

Their bridgehead west of the Jordan secured, the Israelites next set about penetrating the Judean mountains. Whether the Israelite conquest was as rapid as portrayed in the Bible is questionable. It seems they linked up with local tribes related to them—those who had not gone to Egypt and others who joined them. Thus, rather than a pure *blitzkrieg* of Canaan, it was more likely both conquest and a gradual process of encroachment and infiltration through which the

Israelites established themselves in Canaan.[8]

The mountainous areas were only lightly settled, meaning little was in the way to impede them. In planning his strategy for the initial conquest of Canaan, Joshua was careful to avoid the heavily populated, well-defended plains and valleys. The Israelites also had to steer clear of the major Egypt to Syria trade route—later known as the Via Maris, or Sea Route—to mitigate risk of Egyptian interference.

Their target along their route to Canaan's central highlands was the city of Ai. Rather than attacking the fortified city of Beth-el, Joshua set his sights on Ai, which shielded Beth-el, or may have been a fortified city in its own right. Eliminating Ai would give the Israelites access to the country beyond, central to their plan for securing the heartland of Canaan.

Buoyed by their success at Jericho, the Israelites were overconfident. When reconnaissance suggested Ai was lightly defended and could be easily taken, Joshua dispatched a force of only 3,000 men to capture the town, allowing the bulk of his men to rest. The Israelites climbed the steep trails from the Jordan Valley and attacked. The intelligence proved faulty; the Israelites met strong resistance and were forced to retreat. Ai's defenders pursued the Israelites to the descent from the heights, killing 36 Israelite men. Not only did this blow hurt the Israelites' morale, but it also tarnished their reputation of invincibility—dangerous as it could embolden their enemies. Understanding the serious consequences of this defeat, Joshua was livid. "For when the Canaanites and all the inhabitants of the land hear of it," he angrily exclaimed to his lieutenants, "they will compass us round, and cut off our name from the earth . . ."[9]

Resigned to attack again without delay, Joshua ordered a 30,000-strong ambush force to infiltrate the area and lie in wait behind Ai. Under cover of darkness, Joshua led a second force to a staging area on some heights to the city's north before moving down into the valley before Ai. Five thousand men were dispatched to serve as a blocking force concealed between Ai and nearby Beth-el to thwart any relief efforts.

When Joshua's force was spotted in the morning, the alarm was raised in Ai. Joshua led the attacking force in a feeble frontal assault, repeating their earlier folly. For a second time, the Israelites found themselves attacking Ai's well-entrenched defenders with insufficient force to oust them. Now experiencing for himself the city's fervent defense, Joshua ordered a retreat. Seeing an opportunity to annihilate these nomads who had now twice attacked his city, Ai's king rallied his forces for a counterattack. This chance for a *coup de grace* against the feared Israelites and opportunity to make a great name for himself was enticing; the king ordered his entire force to leave their posts and to pursue the retreating Israelites.

Once they were a distance away from the city, Joshua used his spear to signal the main ambush force lying in wait to move on the now undefended city. "And the ambush arose quickly out of their place, and they ran as soon as he had stretched out his hand, and entered into the city, and took it; and they hastened and set the city on fire."[10] The retreat had been part of a carefully planned ruse, and Ai's king had taken the bait.

After capturing and setting fire to the city, the Israelite ambush force attacked the Ai force's exposed rear flank. Joshua's "retreating" force stopped in its tracks and made an about face.

Believing they were chasing frightened Israelite troops fleeing from battle, the men of Ai were now confused to see their city in flames, and to find themselves being assaulted from both front and rear. Dumbfounded by the sudden change, Ai's men were decimated in a scene of great carnage. The Israelite men then set about carrying out orders that had been handed down: "do to Ai and her king as thou didst unto Jericho and her king . . ."[11] All 12,000 citizens of Ai were put to the sword, their king captured and hanged, and the city destroyed.

With each engagement, the Israelites became better fighters. Word of their skill and ferocity spread, sending shock waves through Canaan. Rulers of the Amorite cities Jerusalem, Hebron, Jarmuth, Lachish and Eglon united in a defensive coalition against the vigorous newcomers. Another bloc, a federation of four cities led by Gibeon, in the mountains north of Jerusalem, made a peace pact with the Israelites to ensure their safety.

Rather than focusing its attention on resisting the Israelites— the more pressing threat, the Amorite alliance, very angry with the Gibeon-led collaboration with the enemy invaders, moved against the federation cities to punish them. "Therefore the five kings of the Amorites . . . gathered themselves together, and went up, they and all their hosts, and encamped against Gibeon, and made war against it."[12] This split illustrated a lack of unity that would prove the Canaanites' downfall.

The besieged cities appealed to Joshua for assistance, invoking their treaty of friendship. Joshua responded to their call, which also served his purpose of weakening potential adversaries in his conquest of Canaan. Leading his force on a strenuous 15-mile (25-km) night-time march, the Israelites covertly approached besieged Gibeon. When the Israelites made a simultaneous three-pronged assault, the Amorites were caught completely unawares. Panicked, the Amorites fled towards the Beth-Horon pass, on the route down through the Ayalon Valley to the coastal plain. The Israelites pursued them, aided by a chance hailstorm that slowed the Amorites' flight and killed more fleeing soldiers than the Israelites killed. Deep in unfriendly territory and far from their base, the Israelites had to finish off the Amorites before nightfall to prevent their opponents from extricating themselves in the darkness and potentially regrouping.

Joshua beseeched the sun and moon to stand still, lengthening the day to allow the battle to continue. "'Sun, stand thou still upon Gibeon; And thou, Moon, in the valley of Aijalon.' And the sun stood still, and the moon stayed, Until the nation had avenged themselves of their enemies."[13] The Amorites were soundly defeated in what was described as "a great slaughter." The Amorite kings were captured, put to death and their corpses hung from trees. It was a complete vic-tory, which reinforced the Israelite reputation.

A string of victories followed, allowing the Israelites to further secure their position in Canaan. Their successes precipitated a show-down with a powerful combined Canaanite force led by the city of Hazor in the north. In what was considered one of Joshua's greatest victories, the Israelites defeated a chariot-equipped force by the waters of Merom. The fighting continued, with more Israelite victories. "So Joshua took all that land, the hill-country, and all the South, and all the land of Goshen, and the Low-land, and the Arabah, and the hill-country of Israel, and the Lowland of the same; . . . even unto . . . the valley of Lebanon under mount Hermon; and all their kings he took, and smote them, and put them to death."[14] "So Joshua took the whole land, according to all that the Lord spoke unto Moses; and Joshua gave it for an inheritance unto Israel according to their divisions by their tribes. And the land had rest from war."[15]

Notes

1. Bryant Wood. "The Walls of Jericho." *Creation* (21:2, March 1999), pp.36–40.
2. Joshua 2: 8–11. *The Jewish Bible: Tanakh: The Holy Scriptures* (Philadelphia: The Jewish Publication Society of America, 1985).
3. Joshua 2: 2.
4. Situated astride the Syrian–African rift fault line where two of the massive plates making up the earth's surface meet, the Jordan Valley is prone to earthquakes caused by friction as the plates move.
5. Wood, "The walls of Jericho."
6. Josephus (translator William Whiston), *Antiquities of the Jews*, Book V, Ch. I:
7. *The Complete Works of Josephus* (Grand Rapids, MI: Kregel Publications, 1981).
7. Bryant Wood. "Is the Bible accurate concerning the destruction of the walls of Jericho?"
8. Hanoch Reviv, "The Canaanite and Israelite Periods (3200–332 BC)" in Michael Avi-Yonah (ed.) *A History of the Holy Land* (Jerusalem: Steimatzky's Agency Ltd. 1969), p.49.
9. Joshua 7: 9.
10. Joshua 8: 19.
11. Joshua 8: 2.
12. Joshua 10: 5.
13. Joshua 10: 12.
14. Joshua 11: 16–17.
15. Joshua 11: 23.

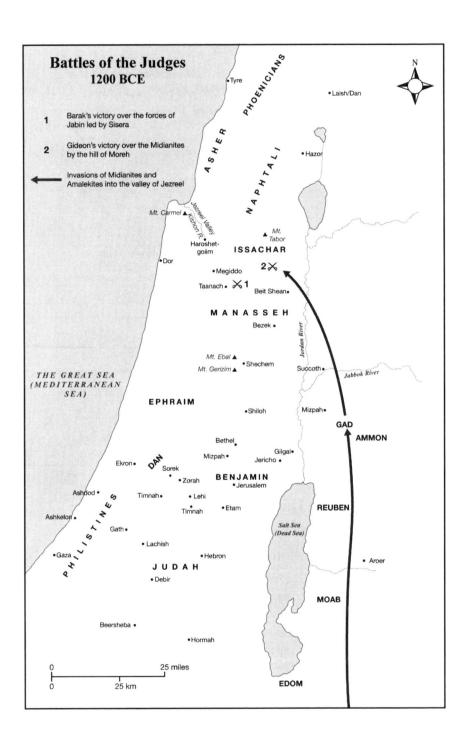

CHAPTER 2

TIMES OF TROUBLE

BATTLES OF THE JUDGES, 1200 BCE[1]

Do unto them as unto the Midianites;
as to Sisera, as to Jabin, at the brook of Kishon
Psalms 83: 9

Stung by a Bee: Deborah & Barak vs. Sisera

At first it was only harassment. Canaanite chariots constantly tormented the Israelites on the main roads of the Jezreel Valley, becoming such a menace that Israelites were forced to travel by secondary routes. Over time the situation deteriorated, with Canaanites entering Israelite villages to stir up trouble before returning to their secure walled cities. Fragmented following Joshua's death, the Israelites had no means with which to counter the Canaanites or retaliate.

When Joshua died, Canaan was still far from being in Israelite control. The coastal plain was in Philistine hands, and strong Canaanite enclaves remained. It would be another two centuries before the Israelites were securely established in Canaan. Leaving their nomadic ways behind them, the Israelite tribes divided up Canaan into areas for permanent habitation and settled down. The people busied themselves with mundane matters like working the land. With no clear successor to Joshua, the Israelites lost their cohesion, and they became a fragmented tribal society. There was no political unity;

the tribes acted completely independently, and at times even fought.

While the Israelites were weak and unorganized, Canaanite cities were thriving, following the weakening of the Egyptian hold on Canaan. The Canaanites were able to act at will against the Israelites. The harassment intensified into persecution and outright oppression. The Israelites were forced to pay such a heavy tribute that they were working mostly to pay off obligations to the Canaanites. This degrading situation went on for twenty years, so the downtrodden Israelites were almost resigned to such treatment at the hands of their much stronger neighbors.

Hazor's king Jabin particularly resented the Israelites, who had laid waste to his city under Joshua. Overcoming their traditional divisiveness, several Canaanite cities in the Jezreel Valley, including Hazor, Taanach, Megiddo and Yochneam, allied themselves under Jabin to form a league of northern Canaanite cities. Dubbing himself "king of Canaan," Jabin set out to exert his power. With his general Sisera commanding a force of 10,000 infantrymen supported by an arsenal of 900 iron chariots positioned by Haroshet-goiim, a strategic outlet from the Jezreel Valley to the coast, the Canaanites now threatened to drive a wedge between the Israelite tribes of Galilee and those in the center of the country.

Despite their independence, the Israelites' shared religion and experiences kept them united in a loose confederacy. Only the re-emergence of old enemies and the appearance of new ones led to inter-tribal cooperation. "In the absence of any central authority the Israelites had to invent some original solution to the problem of evolving a leadership and a defensive system which would ward off the threats of their enemies and the risk of foreign domination."[2] Judges were the answer. In difficult times, these divinely guided ad-hoc leaders united the people to some common cause.

Though she lived in an area removed from the Canaanite league in the north, the prophetess Deborah, whose name means "bee" in Hebrew, formulated a plan to stand up to the Canaanites, and mobilized the people to action. Deborah was already a judge, with the clout to call on Barak ben Avinoam, a leader from the tribe of Naphtali in northern Israel, and instruct him to raise a force from Naphtali and the neighboring tribe of Zebulun. "The God of Israel commanded," Deborah told him. "Go and draw toward Mount Tabor, and take with thee ten thousand men of the children of Naphtali and of the children of Zebulun. And I will draw unto thee to the brook Kishon Sisera, the captain of Jabin's army, with his chariots and his multitude; and I will deliver him into thy hand."[3] Lacking confidence in his own abilities or in the situation they faced, Barak balked and insisted Deborah go with him. She agreed, but told Barak it would cost him the glory of victory.

Barak issued a call to arms that was met with an enthusiastic response, especially by those closest to the Canaanite threat. Detachments from the tribes of Naphtali, Zebulun and Issachar in the north and from as far south as Manasseh, Ephraim and Benjamin joined in. Deborah and Barak went to Kedesh, where Barak mustered the ten thousand men before moving the force to Mount Tabor, whose steep slopes afforded protection against Canaanite chariots and a clear view of the surrounding terrain. Mount Tabor was a safe place to wait for the heavy winter rains they knew would soon come—rains with the ability to quickly turn surrounding areas into a mire that could potentially bog down the enemy force.

A Kenite man named Heber tipped off Sisera about the Israelite troop concentration. The Kenites lived in peace with both the Israelites and the Caananites. Heber had severed himself from his people and was living near Kedesh with his wife Yael. After observing the force being assembled by Barak at Kedesh, Heber reported their movements to Sisera. His motives are unclear. Maybe he was trying to ingratiate himself with the Canaanites, or perhaps the pursuit of money or other benefit motivated him. There was clearly some type of arrangement, for we are told "there was peace between Jabin the king of Hazor and the house of Heber the Kenite."[4]

The Israelite deployment on the strategic vantage point challenged Canaanite hegemony. Sisera's initial response was concern, as Mount Tabor stands between the military position at Haroshet-goiim and his patron's city of Hazor. The Israelite force—a fraction the size of Hazor's army—posed no true threat to the city that Josephus tells us "had in pay three hundred thousand footmen, and ten thousand horsemen, with no fewer than three thousand chariots."[5] But with the Via Maris travel and trade route cutting through the Jezreel Valley on its way from Egypt to Syria and Mesopotamia, the Israelites might strike at their economic lifeline by disrupting this profitable trade route. The Israelite massing of forces and deployment on Mount Tabor was more an affront than anything, but it did provide Sisera with an enticing opportunity to deal the Israelites a painful blow. Pulling out of his position at Haroshet-goiim, Sisera advanced with his chariots and infantry across the open plain towards the mountain, kicking up great clouds of dust like a sandstorm as they went. The Israelites' confidence was shaken when they saw and heard the mass of chariots and infantry approach and pitch camp near the mountain.

Sisera knew the Israelites were secure in their mountaintop deployment and that he would need to draw them onto the plain. As long as the Israelites remained on Mount Tabor, his chariots were useless. Deborah and Barak also understood this well, which was precisely the reason they had opted for this defensive posture. Sisera was confident he had the Israelite force contained on the mountain, where he could keep his eye on them. They could not remain there forever, he reasoned, and would have to come down at some point. With a large infantry force and armada of chariots under his command, Sisera had every reason to be confident. On level ground, his chariots were an excellent shock weapon against poorly organized forces like the Israelites' makeshift militia. With the chariots' speed and maneuverability, the Israelite infantry force had no possibility of escape.

Surrounded by Sisera's forces, the Israelites—civilians pressed into military service—must have been terrified when they looked at the forces massed on the plain below them. Armed with little more than bows and arrows, swords, and spears, the Israelite men felt powerless. Their apprehension grew, and many wanted to disband and slip back to their villages. With the mountain surrounded, this would not be easy, even with their familiarity with the local terrain. The two armies were in a standoff. Deborah retained the men and commanded them to remain and fight.

Deborah had devised a plan to draw Sisera's forces away from the mountain and back towards the Kishon River, which she knew the imminent rains would turn into impassable swamp. As she had earlier told Barak that she would lure Sisera's force to the Kishon River, it seems likely that Deborah had initially intended to lead a decoy force—possibly striking at Sisera's rear—but Barak's hesitation forced her to delegate its command. The decoy force skirmished with Canaanite forces in Taanach by the waters of Megiddo.[6] When word reached Sisera, his confidence was shaken. He wondered whether it was a trap, with a larger force maneuvering against him. Information on this second force was sketchy whereas the force on Mount Tabor was a known element. It certainly explained why the Israelites had deployed on such a visible position where all he had to do was wait for them to come down. Sisera quickly dispatched forces to find and engage the second Israelite force, creating some confusion and disorder in his camp as men, animals, and equipment were regrouped and moved out.

The wind was picking up, and threatening gray storm clouds overhead were a good omen for the Israelites. With the Canaanites taking the bait of the decoy force, Deborah gave the fighting men a very inspiring pep talk assuring them of divine assistance that would lead them to victory. Then she issued orders to attack. Barak and his men charged down the mountain. As if on cue, it began to rain in one of the sudden downpours common to the region. The rain intensified into a torrential downpour interspersed with hailstones, which pounded the combatants. Strong winds blew down the mountain, directing the brunt of the storm on the Canaanites, who were unable to use their arrows and slings, "nor would the coldness of the air permit the soldiers to make use of their swords."[7]

Viewing the storm as the intervention Deborah had spoken of, the Israelites drew inspiration and charged wholeheartedly into battle, slaying a great number of Canaanites. Agitated by the storm, panicky horses were soon out of control, trampling men beneath their hooves or running them over with chariots.

Withdrawing from Mount Tabor, Sisera's force ran into trouble by the Kishon River. The torrential downpour caused the normally gentle Kishon River to swell and overflow its banks. Its waters swept away men and horses, and tracts of land turned into a huge mud bath, bogging down chariots and heavily armed infantry in the suddenly muddy terrain. The Israelites came down on them with a vengeance. Horses harnessed to chariots stuck in the mud cried loudly, adding to the grunts of men fighting hand-to-hand for their lives. Canaanite charioteers abandoned their vehicles and joined infantrymen fleeing on foot, most heading west towards the safety of Horoshet-goiim or other friendly city. With flooding in this area slowing their retreat, Barak's forces harried the fleeing Canaanite soldiers all the way back to Horoshet-goiim, routing Sisera's army.

Rather than rallying his troops in the confusion of the storm and Israelite attack, Sisera panicked and fled the battlefield by foot. Heading east, away from the flooding—probably on the way to Hazor, Sisera found refuge in the tent of Yael, wife of Heber, the informant who had earlier assisted him. Yael welcomed Sisera into her tent and comforted him. Physically and mentally exhausted from the sudden turn of events and his flight, Sisera desperately needed rest. Drenched from both rain and sweat, the shivering general found the dry, warm tent very inviting. As he began to catch his breath, he asked for some water to quench his thirst before continuing on. Yael brought him some milk, which he quickly drank. Exhaustion overcame him; Sisera realized he could not yet go on and accepted Yael's hospitable offer to lie down and rest. Sisera had already been assisted by Heber, and had possibly met Yael, so he had enough faith to trust her guard and let his own down while he rested. Yael covered him with a coarse blanket and he quickly fell fast asleep.

When his deep rhythmic breathing confirmed his slumber, Yael "took a tent-pin, and took a hammer in her hand, and went softly unto him, and smote the pin into his temples, and it pierced through into the ground; . . . he swooned and died."[8] One can only speculate what motivated Yael to interfere in a conflict that was not hers and kill the Canaanite general. Perhaps Sisera had mistreated her husband or not delivered, or maybe Yael acted out of some affinity with the Israelites.

Barak, in hot pursuit of the Canaanite general, came across Yael's tent. Hearing someone approaching, Yael went outside and was relieved to see it was not a Canaanite. When Barak asked if she had seen any fleeing Canaanite soldiers, Yael replied, "Come, and I will show thee the man whom thou seekest." Barak entered the tent and, as his eyes adjusted to the smoky darkness, was shocked to find Sisera lying on the tent floor in a pool of blood. And so the glory of the *coup de grace* was stolen from him, just as Deborah had foretold when Barak had hesitated to accept her appointment. Barak went on to fight Jabin at Hazor, where he killed the so-called "king of the Canaanites" and punished the city.

The defeat of Jabin's alliance did not finish off the Canaanites, but did severely weaken them. The Israelites were freed from subjugation by the Canaanites, who no longer posed a significant threat. Barak's military force demobilized, and there were forty years of calm. With no strong, centralized Israelite leadership to step in following the collapse of Canaanite power, a power vacuum resulted, leaving the region susceptible to desert raiders.

The Sword of Gideon: Gideon vs. the Midianites

The Israelites worked the soil of the Jezreel Valley, where its wheat fields earnt it the title of the Israelites' "breadbasket." Fertile and abundant with water, the Jezreel Valley proved particularly tempting to marauding tribes from across the Jordan River, primarily the Midianites, joined by Amalakites and Arabians.

Come harvest time, these fierce desert raiders would sweep in on their camels, stealing crops, and hustling livestock and beasts of burden. With no organized defenses, the Israelites had to withdraw at the hint of danger, taking with them whatever food they could carry to their cave hideouts. Unable to harvest their crops, the Israelites began facing food shortages. It was humiliating that the little wheat they managed to spirit away had to be threshed in secret lest the Midianites steal it. Threshing yielded the flour used to bake bread, a staple of the local and neighboring Israelite tribes.

The forty years of quiet that the Israelites had enjoyed under Deborah and Barak were over, and now they found themselves in distress. Israelite submissiveness encouraged and emboldened the Midianites. This persecution went on for seven years, resulting in serious famine. Still the Israelites would sow the fields, only to have their produce taken from them in violent raids. Many people chose to forsake their livelihood and left the fertile Jezreel Valley for the safety of the mountainous hill-country.

When a huge Midianite-led force crossed the Jordan River and pitched camp in the Jezreel Valley by Gibeath-moreh (hill of Moreh), a young man named Gideon, whose brothers had been killed during a Midianite raid, took the lead in opposition. Gideon put out a call to arms to his own tribe of Manasseh and the neighboring tribes of Asher, Zebulun and Naphtali, all of whom were suffering food shortages. The Midianite threat unified the normally fragmented tribes, and the call to arms received an enthusiastic response. Thirty-two thousand men rallied to the cause and assembled by Ein Harod, the Spring of Harod, a move that did not go unnoticed by the Midianites.

Even with the large turnout, Gideon knew his force of amateurs was no match for the Midianites, who had the upper hand in terms of numbers, superior weapons and mobility. Gideon knew his only chance lay in neutralizing the Midianites' advantages. It seemed a surprise nighttime attack, when the enemy would be dismounted from their camels, would best prevent them from exploiting their edge. Such an operation would require detailed coordination, planning and execution, so the force would have to be small. Far too many men had answered his call to arms, so 22,000 men whose initial enthusiasm was greater than their actual will to fight were released, leaving Gideon with a force of 10,000 men. This was still far too many, as Gideon conceived a lightning assault by a small force rather than an attack en masse.

During the heat of day, Gideon brought the men to a spring to drink. Observing them carefully, Gideon paid close attention to those who took water with one hand as they held their spears with the other—alert to the possibility of ambush or attack by Midianite forces, exhibiting a soldierly trait. The vast majority of volunteers kneeled down on their knees to drink, without concern for the danger of their position. These latter men were dismissed.

By this method, Gideon pared his force down to 300 men. While his plan would rely on a small force initially, Gideon knew he would need all the help he could muster should his attack succeed. Careful to keep noise levels down to prevent being discovered, Gideon moved his force to high ground above the Midianite camp.

Under cover of darkness, Gideon personally reconnoitered the massive Midianite encampment, the sheer size of which awed him. They were "like locusts for multitude; and their camels were without number, as the sand which is upon the sea-shore . . ."[9] The light of fires dotted the landscape before him, illuminating tents, groups of men, camels and supplies. But Gideon was not deterred. Closing to within earshot to listen in on conversations, Gideon approached a tent where he overheard some Midianites speaking of "this Gideon and the army that was with him . . ."[10] Fear of the large Israelite force they knew had assembled seemed to be affecting their morale and was something Gideon could exploit to his advantage. Since word that he had dismissed the bulk of his volunteers had yet to reach the Midianites, Gideon knew he must attack without delay.

En route back to his camp, Gideon put together the final touches to his plan. Speaking to his men, Gideon described what he had seen and heard, and laid out his plan. He divided his 300 fighters into three companies, equipped each man with a sword, ram's horn, and a torch whose flame was hidden in a pitcher. The force stealthily approached the Midianite encampment from three directions and laid in wait by the camp perimeter for the middle of the night change in guard shift, when tired guards from the early watch had returned to their tents, where they would quickly fall asleep. New guards, still groggy from being woken up in the middle of the night, would be fighting off the nighttime chill.

Immediately after the change of guard shifts, Gideon blew his ram's horn—the sign for each of his men to do the same and to attack. Gideon's men exposed their torches and converged on the camp. The sudden commotion of 300 men attacking and blowing horns and the light of their torches startled man and beast alike. Encouraged by the sound of the rams' horns, the men howled excitedly as they set upon the Midianite camp. Coming from three directions, the Israelite attack had the appearance of an assault by an overwhelming force.

Gideon's men slew desert raiders and began setting fire to the camp, lighting up the night with flames. Confusion and panic took hold in the camp. Frightened men and animals cried out, and camels struggled to free themselves.

"A disorder and a fright seized upon the other men while they were half asleep, for it was night-time . . . so that a few of them were slain by their enemies, but the greatest part by their own soldiers. . . ."[11] The camp layout, divided by different nations, many speaking different languages and dialects, made it difficult to differentiate friend from foe. The result was utter chaos: "Once put into disorder, they killed all that they met with, as thinking them to be enemies also."[12]

The Midianites began fleeing, mostly heading eastward, toward their homes. Gideon's unscathed force chased the Midianites, but it was not large enough to finish off the fleeing army. As his men pursued the retreating Midianites, Gideon dispatched urgent messages to tribes in the vicinity to harass the retreating enemy, and to the tribe of Ephraim to block the Jordan River crossings to prevent the Midianites from escaping.

Exhausted from the attack, the killing and pursuit, Gideon and his men stopped at the settlement of Succoth for food and water, but were refused. They continued on to Penuel, where they were again turned away. Both towns refused assistance out of fear of Midianite reprisals. Though 120,000 Midianites were reported killed in the nighttime attack and subsequent pursuit, some 15,000 Midianite men—including the two Midianite kings Zebah and Zalmunna—escaped. Succoth and Penuel's hesitance illustrated the need to completely eliminate the Midianite threat, though Gideon would later return to these settlements to deal with them harshly.

The Midianites made it across the Jordan River. Believing they had finally reached safety, they stopped to rest. In relentless pursuit, Gideon's force spotted the Midianite camp and attacked. Caught unawares, Gideon's force destroyed the Midianites and captured the kings. After interrogating the kings for knowledge about his brothers, Gideon personally killed them. With revenge very much on his mind, Gideon had no problem taking spoils from his defeated enemy and allowing his men to do the same. Gideon claimed the Midianite king's royal pendants, garments and crescent symbols from their camels, and a percentage of each of his men's take.

The victory made Gideon a hero among the Israelite tribes. The people asked him to lead them, but he refused. Having avenged those responsible for his brothers' deaths and freed his people from the yoke of Midianite persecution, his work was done. There would be 40 years of rest for Israel, and for Gideon a timeless legacy. Rule by judges would continue until the system was deemed inadequate to address the threat posed by the Philistines around 1000 BCE.

Notes

1.The Bible's Book of Judges, the source for the events covered in this chapter, seems to have been written shortly after the "judges" period ended, probably around the time of the new monarchy. Josephus' *Antiquities of the Jews* is based on the Bible.

2. Reviv. "The Canaanite and Israelite Periods (3200–332 BC)," p.58.

3. Judges 4: 6–7.

4. Judges 4: 17.

5. Josephus (trans. Whiston). *Antiquities of the Jews*, Book V, Ch. V: 1.

6. Judges 5, The Song of Deborah.

7. Josephus. *Antiquities of the Jews*, Book V, Ch. V: 4.

8. Judges 4: 21.

9. Judges 7: 12.

10.Josephus. *Antiquities of the Jews*, Book V, Ch. VI: 4.

11.Josephus. *Antiquities of the Jews*, Book V, Ch. VI: 5.

12.Josephus. *Antiquities of the Jews*, Book V, Ch. VI: 5.

CHAPTER 3

TWO PEOPLES, ONE LAND

PHILISTINES AND ISRAELITES, 1000 BCE

Choose you a man for you, and let him come down to me.
If he be able to fight with me, and kill me, then will we be your
servants; but if I prevail against him, and kill him, then
shall ye be our servants, and serve us. . . . Give me
a man, that we may fight together.
I Samuel 17: 8–10

Goliath, the Philistine champion, challenged the Israelites with these words each day for forty days, inviting a man from the Israelite army to come out and fight. Goliath—a giant standing six to nine feet (2–3m) tall,[1] was decked out in a coat of mail armor and leg protectors, topped off by a brass helmet, and was armed with a spear, javelin and sword. Terrified by his massive size, impressive armor and formidable weapons, not a man among the Israelites was willing to accept the challenge.

The Philistine and Israelite armies were arrayed for battle in the Elah Valley in the Shephelah foothills, the border region between Philistia, as the Philistine areas were known, and Judah. The year was around 1000 BCE, and the Israelite army was blocking a Philistine push inland towards the hill country, the heartland of Judah. Were the Philistines to successfully cross the Elah Valley, one of the few easily passable routes inland from the coast, the Israelites' firm grip on the interior highlands would be at risk.

Conflict between the Philistines and Israelites had begun not long after the Philistines reached Canaan, roughly a century or two after the Israelites. The Philistines came from a group known as the Sea Peoples, proto-Greek seafaring invaders from the Aegean and central Mediterranean (possibly the island of Crete) uprooted by regional upheavals, which wrecked havoc in the area. The Sea People met defeat when they invaded Egypt in 1188 BCE, and the Philistines settled along the southern coastal plain in neighboring Canaan, where they established the cities of Ashkelon, Ashdod, Ekron,[2] Gath,[3] and Gaza.

With two peoples vying for the same land, it was only a matter of time before they would clash. The militarily powerful Philistines set out to enlarge the territory under their control. The Israelite tribes lacked the centralized power to deal with Philistine encroachment on their territory. There was ongoing conflict, including long periods of Philistine occupation when the Israelites were held in degrading servitude. The Philistines' well-organized military, equipped with iron weaponry and chariots, posed a very real threat to the Israelites' survival.[4]

Chariots gave the Philistines a huge advantage when operating in lowlands and on plains. But advancing inland towards the Elah Valley, the chariots lost their effectiveness as the topography changed. With the Israelites ensconced on the high ground, the Philistines feared venturing into the valley with their chariots. In these cases, the Philistines left their chariots behind and adopted a policy of establishing outposts. After conquering an area, the gains were secured and control imposed with military garrisons. Forces manning these positions also enforced the Philistine ban on ironsmithing—technology they strived to keep for themselves. The Philistines were skilled ironsmiths, providing them the best and most advanced weapons of the day, so they zealously enforced their ironsmithing monopoly to keep such weapons out of Israelite hands.

The Philistine camp was deployed on several hills on the southern side of the Elah Valley, centered around a hill known as Socoh while the Israelites were opposite, to the north, at Azekah. Both armies were arrayed defensively. Each day, the Israelite army would form up for combat but would not join battle with the Philistines. Goliath the

Philistine would then appear before the Israelite army and challenge one man to fight him. With the Israelites failing to accept Goliath's challenge, a precarious stalemate resulted. This situation was already affecting the Israelites, who could not remain mobilized indefinitely, for supplies were being depleted.

Goliath's threats, which added an element of psychological warfare designed to cause fear in the Israelite camp, only contributed to the stalemate. An adolescent named David was sent to the Israelite camp with food for his three brothers serving in the army and their officer to supplement their dwindling provisions. When David observed Goliath's daily challenge, he was embarrassed by the fear Goliath caused among his people's army and ashamed by the Israelites' failure to respond. David volunteered to fight the giant. It was not an act of reckless abandon in declaring his readiness to fight the Philistine, for the Prophet Samuel had told David that God had chosen him to become their king and "that he should overthrow the Philistines; and that against what nations soever he should make war, he should be the conqueror, and survive the fight; and that while he lived he should enjoy a glorious name, and leave such a name to his posterity also."[5] With such God-ordained invincibility, David was confident he could not lose.

When Saul heard of David's resolve, the king sent for the boy. "Thy servant will go and fight with this Philistine," David volunteered. Seeing the young boy before him, Saul dismissed the idea outright, saying, "Thou art not able to go against this Philistine to fight with him; for thou art but a youth, and he a man of war from his youth."[6] Saul had offered rewards for the man who would accept Goliath's challenge, but there had been no takers. That the Israelites did not simply decline the Philistine challenge and fight suggests there was more to the challenge than meets the eye. It may have been as it appears: an attempt to spare the death and destruction that would come from the two armies fighting. According to Goliath's challenge, the loser's side would surrender its weapons and submit themselves to be slaves. Such a challenge was a departure from the norms of warfare known to the Israelites, who had been fighting the Philistines for some time already. While foreign to the Israelites, such arrangements were an accepted tradition in the Philistine army.[7]

The challenge may also have been for a representative battle of which people's god would prevail. If this were the case, failing to send a warrior for this test of the gods would show a lack of faith in the Israelite god.[8]

In pleading his case to Saul, David cited examples of divine providence. David added: "the Lord . . . will deliver me out of the hand of this Philistine." Now that someone had come forward—albeit a boy—Saul had to accept lest he question his god's omnipotence. Acquiescing, Saul said, "Go, and the Lord shall be with thee."[9]

David had observed Goliath, noticing how cumbersome his armor was, and that the Philistine was equipped and armed solely for close-range or hand-to-hand battle; Goliath had no bow and arrows nor any other long-range weapon. But arrows were not effective against an individual mobile target wearing the armor the Philistine expected his opponent to have. It was clear to David that Goliath intended to lure his opponent in close where his advantage in size and strength could be brought to bear. Goliath would thrust his heavy spear at David when there was no time to escape the danger. The weight of the spear and iron spearhead, matched with Goliath's strength, made it likely that armor could be pierced at close range. If his opponent were wounded or if he missed his mark, Goliath had his other weapons to rely on.

Against the heavily armed and armored Philistine, David opted to go into battle without armor, armed only with a slingshot, the weapon he knew best. King Saul had offered David his armor, helmet and sword, but after trying these unfamiliar items, David declined. The sling was definitely not the weapon of choice against a single, mobile, well-armored opponent. In armies, slings were used against large targets, such as massed forces. For single combat, the user would have to be extremely skilled in its use. A shepherd, David had had ample time to practice in the fields while tending his family's flocks. Knowing that accuracy was not the sling's best feature, David collected five stones for the battle. Exposed but nimble, David set off to engage Goliath. Surprised his opponent was not fielding the same weapons and armor, and dismissing the young boy approaching him as an unworthy opponent, Goliath became angry and abusive. David's retort that he would "cut off thy head, and cast the other parts of thy body to the dogs. . . ."[10] was more than Goliath could bear.

Goliath went for the young upstart in haste but was slowed by the weight of his armor. David ran towards Goliath but stopped a safe distance away. With his target in effective range, David placed a stone in the pouch of his sling, raised it above his head and began swinging it around, harder and harder. David released the stone, which flew with great force towards the Philistine. It smashed into Goliath's face—left exposed by his helmet to provide a wide field of view—and "sank into his brain."

Mortally wounded by the blow, Goliath fell to the ground. With the heavy armor—estimated at around 125 pounds (57kg) weighing him down, Goliath was dazed, helpless and suddenly vulnerable. David rushed to him, drew the Philistine's sword from its sheath, and cut off his head. To those watching from the surrounding hilltops, the sight of David holding the Philistine champion's head aloft eliminated any doubts about the battle's outcome.

Panicked by this unexpected loss, the Philistines began fleeing en masse. If the battle had truly been an alternative to combat, then the Philistines were violating the agreement inherent in Goliath's challenge. If meant to showcase whose god would prevail, then the results were a clear harbinger of things to come. The Israelite army pursued the Philistines to the borders of their cities, killing some 30,000 and wounding double that number. Goliath's armor, weapons and kit were taken and put on display, perhaps as a tangible example of the Israelite god's power, just as the Philistines had done earlier in the conflict after capturing the Israelites' holy Ark at Eben Ezer.

The battle between David and Goliath was neither the beginning nor the end but rather the best-known event of a much larger military struggle between the Israelites and Philistines. The conflict had been going on for decades and would continue after this particular Philistine defeat.

The Israelites' first major engagement with the Philistines was the disastrous battle at Eben Ezer, near the modern town of Petah Tikva. After 4,000 Israelites were killed early in the fighting, the Ark of the Covenant was brought to the front to rally the troops. Containing the tablets inscribed with the Ten Commandments, the Ark was the most important symbol of the Israelites' faith and served as the only physical manifestation of the Israelite god. Its arrival inspired the Israelites and scared the Philistines.

As the battle continued, it went very much awry for the Israelites. In a humiliating defeat, 30,000 Israelite men were reportedly killed and, in a devastating national loss, the Ark was captured by the Philistines. This bounty would be only shortly in Philistine hands, for sickness and pestilence struck whichever Philistine city hosted the captured prize, so it was returned.

The Philistine gains from their victory at Eben Ezer were later erased, seemingly by divine intervention. When the Philistine army was poised to attack the Israelite force massed at Mitzpe, a natural disaster struck, with the ground shaking and thunder and lightning causing the Philistines to drop their weapons and flee. The Israelites pursued and killed them, and Israel recovered the cities and territory the Philistines had occupied.

In response to deprivation suffered under Philistine occupation and the on-going confrontation with the Philistines and other threats, including conflict among the tribes, pressure grew from the tribes to establish a monarchy. The Israelites were still confronting the Canaanites, but the Philistines were the more formidable enemy. At times, the Philistines occupied large swaths of Israel. The only resistance to speak of was the judge Samson's one-man war against the Philistines during a 40-year-long period of Philistine domination, yet Samson's motivation was revenge over being jilted rather than his people's freedom.

"It was necessary they should have with them one to fight their battles, and to avenge them of their enemies."[11] Responding to the will of the people, the prophet Samuel appointed a king, choosing Saul. "Be thou a king, by the ordination of God, against the Philistines, and for avenging the Hebrews for what they have suffered."[12]

Despite his mission, Saul's baptism of fire was actually against the Ammonites, east of the Jordan River. Tribes from the east were taking advantage of Israel's precarious position and the Ammonites, a neighboring tribe which had been persecuting the Israelites of Jabesh-Gilead, were laying siege to the town. With the inhabitants ready to surrender and submit to every male having his right eye put out, a call went out for help.[13] Hearing of the situation, Saul acted immediately, mobilizing a rescue force of more than 300,000 men. The speed of Saul's response allowed his force to take the Ammonites by surprise and defeat them. With the siege lifted, Saul earned a reputation for valor. This debt was later repaid following Saul's death when the men of Jabesh-Gilead risked their lives to rescue the corpses of the decapitated king and his sons, displayed ignominiously by the Philistines on the Beit Shean city wall.

Since the force he had mustered and led to the rescue of Jabesh-Gilead had been mobilized by Saul's threats, Saul saw the need for a standing army. Saul therefore established a royal army, with 2,000 men under his command and another 1,000 under his son Jonathan. There were chariots, drivers, horsemen, guards and runners. Officers commanded units of 100 and 1000, with an arms industry of skilled craftsmen making armor, chariots and other implements.

It was not long before the Philistines moved in and seized Israelite territory again, putting Saul's new force to the test. Philistine garrisons began imposing their repressive yoke over the Israelites. Jonathan's force attacked and wiped out a Philistine position at Geba, one of the hated symbols of Philistine occupation. Angered by the attack, the Philistines brought in reinforcements, amassing 300,000 infantry, 30,000 chariots and 6,000 horses, establishing a camp at Michmas. Philistine raiding parties began ravaging the countryside in reprisal. Vastly outnumbered, the Israelites were paralyzed by fear; many soldiers deserted. In an act exhibiting great courage, daring and élan (and a good measure of luck), Jonathan broke the deadlock when, accompanied only by his shield-bearer, he slipped into a Philistine position under cover of darkness and killed about 20 enemy soldiers. Alerted that something was going on, the rest of the camp reacted. Assuming they were under attack by a large force, different groups of Philistines unknowingly began fighting one another. In the ensuing melée, many Philistines were killed and a large number fled. The situation turned into a rout when an earthquake struck, causing a mass panic among the Philistine forces. Saul's force, camped nearby, took advantage of the confusion to attack, and killed some 60,000 retreating Philistines. The Philistines' hold on the center of the country had been pried open and they were chased back to the coastal plain.

Next came the Philistine thrust through the Elah Valley, which ended with the ignominious retreat following the defeat of their champion Goliath. Changing approach, the Philistines began advancing up the coast in friendly territory in an attempt to drive a wedge between the Israelite tribes in the north and center. After massing at Aphek, by a pass on the Via Maris, the Philistines cut inland to the Jezreel Valley. Monitoring their progress, Saul led his force through the highlands to reach the valley, where he deployed his men on the lower slopes of Mount Gilboa. When Saul asked God what would be, he received no answer—striking fear in the king's heart. Saul betrayed his serious concerns when he sought the services of a soothsayer before the battle. When he was told: "The Lord will deliver Israel also with thee into the hand of the Philistines; and tomorrow shalt thou and thy sons be with me; the Lord will deliver the host of Israel into the hand of the Philistines," his confidence was shattered. In what would become a self-fulfilling prophecy, the battle was doomed from the start.

The attack began the following morning at dawn. From their assembly point at the hill of Moreh, the Philistines advanced towards the Israelite camp. When they joined battle, the combat was described as a "sharp engagement" in which "the Philistines slew a great number of their enemies." The flat valley allowed the Philistines to fully employ their chariots. Saul and his sons fought "courageously and with the utmost alacrity," killing many Philistines.[14] Even when the Philistines had them surrounded, the Israelite leadership continued to fight tenaciously. In the fighting, Saul's sons Jonathan, Adinadab, and Malchishua were killed. Israelite soldiers began fleeing for their lives, hiding in the groves of the highlands. Disorder and confusion prevailed, and the Philistines slaughtered many of the fleeing Israelites.

Saul fought on, retreating up Mount Gilboa with a strong body of soldiers. The Philistines pursued them relentlessly and their archers wiped out all but a few of the Israelite force. Despite suffering from multiple wounds, Saul fought until he was too weak to continue. Rather than face capture by the Philistines, Saul committed suicide by falling on his sword. Saul had dedicated much of his energy countering the external threats to his kingdom, and died doing so. The place of his death (on Mount Gilboa) was cursed with barrenness, ironically by the young hero David, on whom Saul had expended so much effort out of spiteful jealousy: "Ye mountains of Gilboa, let there be no dew nor rain upon you, neither fields of choice fruits; for there the shield of the mighty was vilely cast away, the shield of Saul, not anointed with oil."[15]

Following his victory over Goliath, David had become a hero of Israel, receiving great acclaim—sometimes more than the king himself. David became an officer in Saul's army, where he brought more praise upon himself in further defeats over Philistines. David was held in high esteem by all the people, except for Saul, who was horribly jealous and came to hate David. Saul went as far as trying to kill David on grounds that he was a threat to the king's grip on power. Fleeing Saul's jealous wrath, David was forced into life underground. Joined by his family and others who feared the king, David became leader of a band of outlaws. With his cadre of followers, David supported himself by protecting local villages for a tribute.

Though he had opportunities to kill Saul, David refrained from doing so. But the king's relentless pursuit ironically led David to seek refuge with the Philistines. In fact, his fighting force accompanied the Philistine host on the northern offensive that culminated with the combat at Mount Gilboa until other Philistines voiced their concern and David and his force departed the area.

Following Saul's death in around 1005 BCE, David was moved by Israel's predicament. Israel's army had been decimated, civilians had fled large areas of the north and the Philistines occupied the abandoned cities. David became king, first of Judah and then of all Israel. He earned a great name for himself by unifying the Israelites into a united monarchy, through successful military campaigns and the establishment of Jerusalem as capital and religious center, where he installed the revered Ark of the Covenant. His reign was considered a golden age, and it was said that he was respected by all the peoples from the Euphrates to the Nile.

As king, David led the Israelites to defeat the Philistines, driving them back and containing them along the coastal plain. The Philistines lost their pre-eminent position in the region, although they would endure until the time of the Babylonians in the 5th century BCE. Ultimately, "in the ebb and flow of warring nations over this land it is more than probable that they were gradually absorbed and lost their identity."[16]

However, in an enduring legacy, the region continued to be called Philistia, and by this name—in the form of the word Palestine—the whole country became known. While the Philistine people may have disappeared, their name lives on with the Palestinians, the people who contend with modern-day Israel in a conflict reminiscent of the Israelite–Philistine wars, with two peoples struggling for this ancient land.

Notes

1.Moshe Garsiel's "Elements of History and Reality in the Description of the Ela Valley Warfare and the Combat Between David and Goliath (1 Samuel 17)" *Beit Mikra* (Vol. 41, 1997) has an excellent discussion of Goliath's height. Garsiel's bottom line is that "One needs to relate to the height not as an exact height, but rather as a typological number." It seems that Goliath's unusual height was further exaggerated by scribes over time who believed they were adding to the glory of Israel. Since Goliath was the Philistine champion, it stands to reason he was indeed a large, impressive figure, rejecting theories that his extreme height was the result of a growth disorder.

2. Identified as Tell Mikne, near Kibbutz Rivadim.

3. Identified as Tell Tzafit, near Kfar Menachem.

4. New archaeological evidence suggests the Philistines did not have chariots (personal interview with Yehuda Dagan, Israel Antiquities Authority, Shephelah region expert). However, chariots are mentioned in both the Bible and in Josephus' *Antiquities*, so remain in this account.

5. Josephus, *Antiquities of the Jews*, Book VI, Ch. VIII: 1.

6. I Samuel 17: 32–33.

7. Garsiel, p.299.

8. Garsiel, p.301.

9.I Samuel 17: 37.

10.Josephus, *Antiquities of the Jews*, Book VI, Ch. IX: 4.

11.Josephus, *Antiquities of the Jews*, Book VI, Ch. III: 6.

12.Josephus, *Antiquities of the Jews*, Book VI, Ch. IV: 2.

13.Putting out a man's right eye was an ancient form of "demilitarization" as it prevented the man from fighting as a soldier. Since soldiers carried shields on their left side, visibility from the left eye was obstructed, meaning the right eye was necessary to see what was happening while protected by the shield.

14.Josephus, *Antiquities of the Jews*, Book VI, Ch. XIV: 7.

15.Samuel II 1: 21.

16.Driscoll, J. F. "Philistines." *The Catholic Encyclopedia* (New York: Robert Appleton Company, 1911) http://www.newadvent.org/cathen/12021c.htm (accessed March 14, 2011).

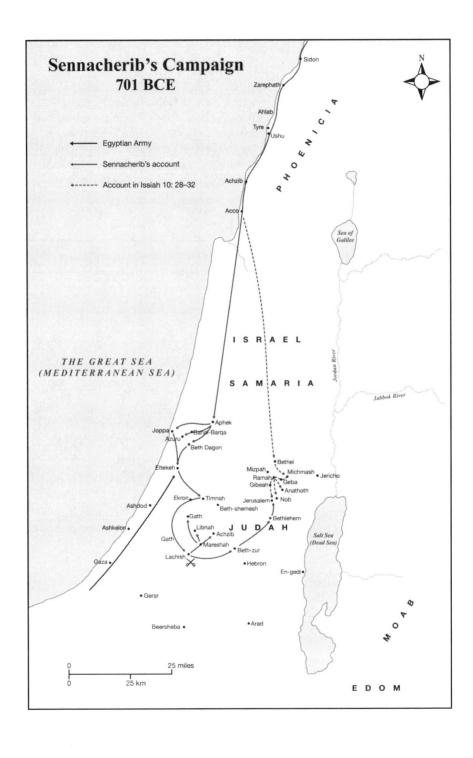

CHAPTER 4

SENNACHERIB'S CROWNING ACHIEVEMENT

ASSYRIANS AT LACHISH, 701 BCE

The Assyrians had never before seen anything like it. Of the 46 fortified towns and villages they would destroy on their 701 BCE campaign against rebellious Judah, nowhere else would they encounter such elaborate defenses as at Lachish, Judah's most important city after Jerusalem. Guardian of the southwestern approach from the lowlands (Shephelah) into the Judean mountains, Lachish was Assyrian monarch Sennacherib's first major objective during the punitive expedition.

Assyria was the Near East's strongest regime, with its empire stretching from modern-day Iraq to the Mediterranean Sea, down to the Egyptian border. The southern kingdom of Judah had been submissive to the Assyrian superpower while the northern kingdom of Israel had earlier risen up in revolt.[1] A punitive force sent by the Assyrian king laid siege to Samaria, the Northern Kingdom's capital, and the city fell in 722 BCE. The people were banished, thus beginning the saga of the ten lost tribes. At that time, Judean king Hezekiah had steered clear of anti-Assyrian activity.

But with Judah enjoying a time of prosperity that begat confidence, King Hezekiah felt the time was ripe to free Judah from the yoke of foreign subjugation and began preparing for revolt. The most illustrative example of the great lengths undertaken during these preparations is the 500m-long (1,640 foot-long) tunnel hewn from solid rock to bring the Gihon Spring's waters into Jerusalem, securing the water source for the city while denying it to invading armies. Knowing that unity and centralized leadership would be necessary if Judah were to withstand an Assyrian onslaught, Hezekiah instituted reforms designed to consolidate Jerusalem's power. Assuming the outlying areas would bear the brunt of an invasion, foodstuffs and supplies were distributed and stockpiled, and it seems the people were behind Hezekiah.

When a revolt against Assyrian rule broke out upon the death of King Sargon II in 705 BCE, Hezekiah took an active role. Babylon rebelled against Assyria, joined by Philistine Ascalon and Judah with Egyptian support, revolting against Assyrian dominance and taxation. Furious over such insubordination, Assyrian monarch Sennacherib organized and led an expedition to punish the recalcitrant lands and force payment of taxes.

The Assyrians first crushed the revolt in Babylon before setting their sights on the rebellious provinces to the west. Sennacherib's army invaded and subdued the coastal territory of the Philistines. Sennacherib recorded in his annals the capture of towns from the rebellious kingdom of Ascalon: "In the course of my campaign I besieged Beth Dagon, Joppa, Banai-Barqa, Azuru. . . . I conquered [them] and carried their spoils away."[2] When an Egyptian force rushed north to challenge the Assyrians, they were soundly defeated at the battle of Eltekeh, as Sennacherib described: "In the plain of Eltekeh, their battle lines were drawn up against me and they sharpened their weapons. Upon a trust [-inspiring] oracle [given] by Ashur, my lord, I fought with them and inflicted a defeat upon them. In the . . . battle, I personally captured alive the Egyptian charioteers with the[ir] princes and [also] the charioteers of the king of Ethiopia."[3]

Then he turned east to conquer the rebellious mountain kingdom of Judah. The Bible tells us that "In the fourteenth year of King Hezekiah, Sennacherib, king of Assyria, went on an expedition against all the fortified cities of Judah and captured them."[4] "I laid siege to 46 of his strong cities, walled forts and to the countless small villages in their vicinity," Sennacherib wrote, "and conquered [them] by means of well-stamped [earth-] ramps and battering-rams brought [thus] near [to the walls] [combined with] the attack by foot soldiers, [using] mines, breeches as well as sapper work."[5] As the largest citadel guarding the western border of the Kingdom of Judah, Lachish was Sennacherib's first major objective in Judah. More heavily fortified than all the other Assyrian objectives in Judah, it was clear to the Assyrian invaders that Lachish's formidable defenses would pose a serious challenge—even with their siege works, equipment, and experienced troops.

Sitting on high ground dominating the surrounding countryside, Lachish was a formidable citadel. Surveying their objective in hopes of finding its weak link, the Assyrian combat engineers were awed by the town's defenses. Cities and towns, generally sited along roads or trade routes, were built with thought to ensure ample water supplies and defensive considerations. To defend against the threat of invasion, cities tended to be built on high ground. A *tel* is an artificial mound created when cities were built upon the ruins of a previous city. Debris of destroyed towns was never completely cleared but merely leveled off, a base upon which the survivors or newcomers would build anew. Thus, a town originally settled on high ground continued to grow with each subsequent resettlement, resulting in easily defendable steep slopes. This was precisely the situation at Lachish, which was at such a great height that it was afforded a view of the surrounding territory for miles. Its height, and its double set of city walls, made it one well-protected city. We first learn of Lachish as a fortified Canaanite city conquered by Joshua around 1400 BCE.[6] The city was later fortified as part of a defense system based on a string of forts blocking enemy penetration into Judah.

The city was surrounded by two walls: the main defensive wall made of bricks on stone foundations standing around six meters (18 feet) high with towers protruding at regular intervals, and a stone (and in some places topped with brick) revetment wall along the middle of the slope. Though intended as a retaining wall supporting the upper wall and glacis, the revetment wall added to Lachish's defenses. The two walls joined together at a gate structure, the largest and most impressive of its kind—with massive wooden doors and flanking towers, all serving to deter assault. From their camp on the neighboring hilltop, the Assyrians could appreciate the massive scale of Lachish's palace-fort in the center of the city, which rose high above the surrounding buildings.

Fortified towns posed no real obstacle to the Assyrian military machine, with its seasoned troops and arsenal of battering rams. Its army had specialized units, including cavalry, sappers, combat engineers, snipers, and foot soldiers. The combat engineers were well versed at building siege ramps against walled cities, laying the groundwork for assault units to move battering rams into place to bash down the walls, which they did throughout Judah. But with its defensive arrangement of walls, gatehouse complex, well, and inner fort, Lachish was no ordinary adversary.

The Assyrians knew what would be in store were they to assault through the main gate complex. Cities generally had several gates through which an attacker would need to penetrate. Defenders with bows and arrows, slingshots and other weapons would be stationed on the towers, bombarding attackers to keep them at bay. From its appearance alone, the Assyrians could be certain that Lachish's gate structure would incorporate additional defenses designed to complicate an enemy attack.

The alternative was breaking through its walls. The outer wall was designed to slow an enemy's advance on the city once they were within effective range of the defenders' bows and slings, while also protecting the base of the walls from undermining and breaching. Just approaching the walls meant climbing a glacis, a protective lime-plastered ramp, while exposed to defensive fire, ruling out an assault in force to scale the barrier.

Rather than accepting the heavy casualties a direct assault on the gate structure would entail, the Assyrians opted to build a siege ramp. The southwest corner of the town was decided upon as the main attack point, for here Tel Lachish joins another hill, forming a topographical saddle. Though the city's fortifications would clearly be stronger in this area, its low height relative to other potential routes convinced the engineers that this was the best option. And so they began constructing a siege ramp, carrying boulders from the surrounding countryside to build it up. Rocks were heaped against the slope; the ramp grew larger and larger, slowly climbing over the revetment wall and up towards the main city wall. Not only was the construction physically demanding, but construction teams were constantly under fire from defensive positions on the city walls. The city's defenders constructed a counter-ramp inside the city to raise the city wall's height. This forced the Assyrians to raise the height of their ramp, as they knew their battering rams would be most successful against the upper portion of walls, as the stones at the thicker, stronger base of a wall were harder to dislodge. With the Assyrian ramp nearly complete, stones at the top were cemented together with lime-plaster, and logs laid to prepare the ground for the battering rams. Construction work became even more dangerous as building details put on the final touches, with defenders firing at near point-blank range.

Anxiety and apprehension in Lachish mounted as the Assyrian ramp grew closer to the city's main wall. Lachish was rife with a sense of helplessness and of inevitable defeat at the hands of their powerful adversary, an adversary unlikely to be merciful after suffering heavy losses during the long and difficult siege.

With the ramp complete and all preparations in order, the long-awaited attack on Lachish began. Under a hail of arrows and missiles from the defenders, armor-clad and helmeted Assyrian infantrymen—archers, sling-throwers, and shielded spearmen—advanced up the ramp. The counterfire intensified as they closed range and began rolling the feared battering rams up the ramp and into place at several locations. The defenders threw flaming torches down upon them but the Assyrians were ready with buckets of water to douse the flames. Chariots—useless in a besieged city—were set ablaze and thrown down on the battering rams, which had begun pounding the walls.

Assyrian archers took aim at the men on the parapets and in the towers. Despite the heavy suppressing fire, Lachish's defenders perched on its ramparts shot arrows and hurled stones and firebrands down on the attackers without pause. In the fierce battle, there were many casualties on both sides. Under intense fire, many of Lachish's defenders fell—the lucky ones falling back into the battlements where they could get medical treatment; others tumbling over the walls, where some were impaled and displayed by the Assyrians. Dead

Assyrian soldiers were strewn about the ground, some where they had fallen, others moved from the ramp to make room for more assault forces.

Battering rams continued pounding the walls, dislodging stones until the walls began collapsing under weight of the powerful blows, taking parts of the battlements down as the walls crumbled. With the wall breached, defenders in the towers maintained fire at the Assyrians who were now charging into the city over debris of the fallen wall. For a time, the defenders held the Assyrians at bay, but force of numbers and the Assyrians' determination after the long and difficult siege made them unstoppable. The Assyrian forces fanned out past the mud-brick shops and houses lining the main street into the town. The Assyrian calls for surrender long ago rejected, Lachish's men knew they would face the sword, and so they made for the fortified palace for a final stand. But with Assyrian soldiers now pouring through the breach, the situation was hopeless. There was no stopping the determined Assyrian war machine, and the palace was taken as well.

After securing the city, the Assyrians were amazed by the elaborate gate structure. They had been right to build a ramp as troops assaulting the gate would have been exposed to fire on their vulnerable right side (shields were typically carried with the left arm) from archers on the walls. At the top, after breaking through the outer gate, they would have found themselves channeled into a small courtyard where they would have needed to break through an inner gate while exposed to deadly crossfire from above.

Troops rounded up Lachish's frightened residents from the densely populated residential quarters. Allowed to take a few belongings, the people were forced from the city. Captives and deportees were then paraded before Sennacherib before being taken away as slaves. The city was ransacked and looted. Ceremonial symbols and other booty were carried off and displayed before the king. Corpses of some 1,500 casualties were dumped into a deep pit. The Assyrians then set fire to the town, burning Lachish to the ground.

Jerusalem

While at Lachish, Sennacherib sent a task force 30 miles (50 km) northeast to Jerusalem, perhaps to defend against the dispatch of relief forces. Jerusalem was besieged, and King Hezekiah was unable to direct the defense of his kingdom. Sennacherib gloated in this fact, writing in his official annals: "As to Hezekiah, the Jew. . . . I made a prisoner in Jerusalem, his royal residence, like a bird in a cage. I surrounded him with earthwork in order to molest those who were his city's gate."[7]

The Assyrian force pressed Hezekiah to surrender, claiming that the God of Israel had abandoned the Jews. Caged in as he was, Hezekiah apparently had time to consider all that was going on. The revolt was not going nearly as hoped. Neither the Egyptian force nor the Philistines had succeeded in standing up to Assyrian assault. And with reports reaching the king of events at Lachish and destruction throughout Judah, King Hezekiah became wary of a fate like that of the defeated northern kingdom of Israel, meaning he could be Judah's last king, a reputation history would not treat kindly.

And so Hezekiah decided to appease Sennacherib with a declaration of submission. Hezekiah sent word to Sennacherib at Lachish, saying, "I have offended; return from me; that which thou puttest on me will I bear."[8] Sennacherib demanded a large tribute, as recorded in his annals: "Hezekiah himself . . . did send me, later, to Nineveh, my lordly city, together with 30 talents of gold, 800 talents of silver, precious stones, antimony, large cuts of red stone, couches [inlaid] with ivory, nimedu-chairs [inlaid] with ivory, elephant-hides, ebony-wood, boxwood [and] all kinds of valuable treasures, his [own] daughters, concubines, male and female musicians. In order to deliver the tribute to do obeisance as a slave he sent his [personal] messenger."[9]

The tribute was evidently not enough to appease Sennacherib's anger, as the king was determined to thoroughly punish Judah for its role in the revolt. A massive Assyrian force was encamped around Jerusalem, and its citizens were subjected to demoralizing psychological warfare when Assyrian commanders speaking Hebrew denigrated the God of the Jews and King Hezekiah before his people. "Let not Hezekiah beguile you, for he will not be able to deliver you," the Assyrians called out. "Neither let Hezekiah make you trust in the Lord, saying 'The Lord will surely deliver us; this city shall not be given into the hand of the king of Assyria.'"[10] They continued their harassment, suggesting that the Lord had abandoned the Jews. With Jerusalem under siege and humiliated by the Assyrians' daily harangues, King Hezekiah prayed to God for help. The king's prayers were answered: "The angel of the Lord went forth, and smote in the camp of the Assyrians a hundred fourscore and five thousand [185,000]; and when men arose early in the morning, behold, they were all dead corpses."[11] Perhaps this was an outbreak of plague, as disease could be rampant in areas where people lived in close quarters for an extended period. Greek historian Herodotus, writing in the 5th century BCE, attributed the outbreak to field mice. Whatever its cause, the disease spread like wildfire through the Assyrian ranks, resulting in mass death.

After this horrible setback, Sennacherib, who had moved on from Lachish to besiege another objective in Judah, called off the campaign. The Assyrians broke camp and left Judah without completely subduing it, though they may have later returned to take care of unfinished business. While the Bible tells us Sennacherib returned home shamefaced, the real loser was Hezekiah. Though he survived the ordeal and retained his reign, the revolt had been a disaster. Forty-six cities, forts and villages had been destroyed, their populations taken away as slaves, and captured parts of Hezekiah's kingdom distributed to kings who had remained loyal to Assyria. Sennacherib recorded the aftermath: "I drove out [of them] 200,150 people, young and old, male and female, horses, mules, donkeys, camels, big and small cattle beyond counting, and considered [them] booty."[12] On top of these spoils, Assyria demanded an even higher annual tribute than before, meaning that Judah would now be even more subservient to Assyria.

Having failed to take Jerusalem, Sennacherib had to settle for second best: Lachish. Sennacherib considered his conquest of Lachish the crowning achievement of the campaign, as evidenced by the prominent placement of reliefs depicting events at Lachish in his palace in Nineveh, in modern-day Iraq. These reliefs, now exhibited in the British Museum in London, along with the Bible and Sennacherib's own royal annals, give us a detailed account of what transpired at Lachish. Archaeological excavations conducted under the direction of David Ussishkin of Tel Aviv University's Institute of Archaeology corroborate these accounts.

In 681 BCE, Sennacherib was murdered by his sons as he worshipped in the temple of his god Nisroch. His death ushered in a period of upheaval. Assyria's power ultimately waned and they disappeared into the history books. As for Lachish, the city was later rebuilt and fortified, only to be destroyed again in 586 BCE by the Babylonians when Judah stood up to Babylon's rising influence and authority. In a campaign of reprisal, Babylonian King Nebuchadnezzar presided over the destruction of Jerusalem and the Jews' Temple—which had been built in 957 BCE by King Solomon—followed by the forced exile to Babylon (present-day Iraq) made famous by Psalm 137: "By the rivers of Babylon, we laid down and wept, for thee, Zion." The exile was short-lived due to Babylon's defeat by Persian King Cyrus, who allowed the Jews to return home and rebuild their Temple. Work began in 538 BCE on a new Temple, whose desecration at the hands of Greek influence would usher in a new period of turmoil.

Notes

1. The monarchy established by King David and carried forward by his son Solomon unraveled when Solomon's son Rehoboam became the third king of this dynasty (reign 928–11 BCE). The northern tribes, seeking relief from excessive taxation, were rebuffed by the new king, leading to secession and establishment of the Kingdom of Israel. Relations between the two kingdoms varied from one of friendly allies to conflict.
2. Prism of Sennacherib. Retrieved at http://staff.feldberg.brandeis.edu
3. Prism of Sennacherib. Retrieved at http://staff.feldberg.brandeis.edu
4. 2 Kings 18: 13.
5. Prism of Sennacherib. Retrieved at http://staff.feldberg.brandeis.edu
6. Joshua 10: 1–32.
7. Prism of Sennacherib. Retrieved at http://staff.feldberg.brandeis.edu
8. 2 Kings 18: 14.
9. Prism of Sennacherib. Retrieved at http://staff.feldberg.brandeis.edu
10. Isaiah 36: 14–15.
11. 2 Kings 19: 35.
12. Prism of Sennacherib. Retrieved at http://staff.feldberg.brandeis.edu

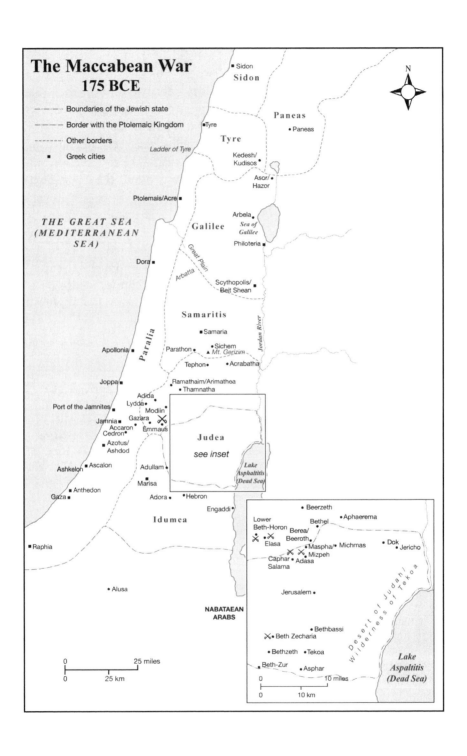

The Maccabean War
175 BCE

- – – – Boundaries of the Jewish state
- ——— Border with the Ptolemaic Kingdom
- - - - - Other borders
- ■ Greek cities

N

■ Sidon

S i d o n

P a n e a s

• Paneas

■ Tyre

T y r e

Ladder of Tyre

Kedesh/
Kudisos •

Asor/
Hazor •

Ptolemais/Acre ■

G a l i l e e

*Sea of
Galilee*

Arbela •

Philoteria •

**THE GREAT SEA
(MEDITERRANEAN
SEA)**

Dora ■

Great Plain

Arbatta

Scythopolis/
Beit Shean ■

S a m a r i t i s

■ Samaria

• Sichem
▲ *Mt. Gerizim*

Paralia

Apollonia ■

Parathon •

Tephon •

• Acrabatha

Jordan River

Joppa ■

Ramathaim/Arimathea •
• Thamnatha

Adida •
Lydda •
• Modiin

Port of the Jamnites ■

Gazara ■ ✗

Jamnia ■

Accaron •
Cedron •

Emmaus •

J u d e a

see inset

Azotus/
Ashdod •

Ashkelon ■ ■ Ascalon

Adullam •

*Lake
Asphaltitis
(Dead Sea)*

Marisa •

■ Anthedon

Gaza ■ ■

Adora •

• Hebron

I d u m e a

Engaddi •

■ Raphia

• Alusa

**NABATAEAN
ARABS**

0 ———————— 25 miles
0 ———————— 25 km

Inset

• Beerzeth

Lower
Beth-Horon
✗ •
Elasa

Bethel •

Berea/
Beeroth •

• Aphaerema

Maspha/• • Michmas

• Dok
Jericho •

Caphar •
Salama

✗ • Mizpeh
• Adasa

Jerusalem •

*Desert of Judah/
Wilderness of Tekoa*

• Bethbassi

✗ • Beth Zecharia

• Bethzeth • Tekoa

• Beth-Zur • Asphar

*Lake
Aspaltitis
(Dead Sea)*

0 ———————— 10 miles
0 ———————— 10 km

CHAPTER 5

PUSHED TOO FAR

THE MACCABEAN WAR, 175 BCE

"Avenge the wrong done to your people."
I Maccabees 2:67

With these deathbed words, Mattathias, patriarch of the priestly Hasmonean clan, bequeathed his sons responsibility to continue their struggle against the Seleucids, one of the most advanced and powerful militaries of its day.

During his conquests, Alexander the Great reached the walls of Jerusalem in 332 BCE, where he was said to have been so gratified that the Jews, led by the high priest, opened the city gates and came out in festive dress to greet him that he would not permit the city to be plundered. Following his death in 323 BCE, Alexander's generals divided the lands he had conquered, creating three main empires: the Ptolemies in Egypt, the Antigonids in Macedonia and the Seleucids in Syria, Asia Minor and the Middle East. In a process known as Hellenization, imported Greek ways and culture joined and slowly replaced the indigenous cultures of the conquered peoples. The division it would cause among the Jews, and the subsequent infighting and then war are spelled out in the Books of the Maccabees and in Josephus' *Antiquities of the Jews.*

Judea[1] lay between the Ptolemaic and Seleucid empires. It was ruled by the Ptolemies of Egypt until it was captured by the Seleucid king Antiochus III (the Great) in 200 BCE. There was tolerance towards Jewish religious practices, but many Jews, especially the urban elite, were attracted to Greek ways and willingly took to them. Hellenism, they believed, was the future, representing the modern world. Viewing Judaism as archaic, these apostate Jews embraced Hellenism with a passion, abandoning all connections to Jewish customs. Some went as far as undergoing a surgical procedure that hid their circumcision so that when they were seen naked during athletics, they would appear Greek.

The ascension to power of a new Seleucid ruler in 175 BCE brought an end to the benevolent autonomy Jews had been enjoying. The new ruler, Antiochus IV, dubbed himself "Epiphanes," or God Manifest, for he considered himself divine. His detractors called him "Epimanes," or mad-man, due to his vagaries and excesses, which he lost no time in demonstrating.

Hellenized Jews took advantage of the change in rule to advance their agenda. Approached by the apostate Jews with ideas on how to expedite the process of Hellenization in Judea, the new king was pleased to hear them out. The assimilated Jews' scheme built on the appointment of a Hellenized Jew named Jason as high priest—the spiritual leader of Jewry. With their proposal sweetened with a hefty tribute, the king consented.

Having one of their own in power gave the Hellenizers undue influence in Judea, and accelerated the pace of Hellenization. Yet when Jason's tenure failed to meet the king's expectations, the king removed him and replaced him with extreme Hellenist Menelaus, whose bribes and radical outlook pleased the king. Scorning the responsibilities of the priesthood, Menelaus opened the Jews' Temple to the worship of Greek gods and went as far as allowing the altar to be defiled by the sacrifice of pigs—an unforgivable sacrilege.[2] Menelaus' behavior was a serious affront to traditional Jewish ways and resulted in the alienation of a large proportion of the Jewish population, most of whom were simple farmers and artisans. Backlash over the Seleucid king's interference in the appointment of the high priest exacerbated the divide between the Hellenized Jews and those who continued to observe Jewish religious and cultural traditions.

The new king made two expeditions against his rivals in Egypt, the first, successful one in 170 BCE and a second a year later that was curtailed due to Roman diplomatic pressure. The Seleucids were seething from this embarrassing capitulation to Roman power and while crossing Judea en route home in 169 BCE, they found a way to reassert authority by entering Jerusalem and plundering the Temple of its holy vessels and going on an unprovoked killing spree before retiring to Antioch, their capital on the Mediterranean in northwest Syria.

Despairing of the rich and mighty Hellenizers and their powerful Seleucid backers against them, Judea's traditional Jews turned to their religion and became more observant, widening the divide. When Jason—now supported by the majority—sought to regain the high priesthood by force, a cry from the apostate Jews went out to Antioch for help. Triggered by unrest and instigation by the radical Hellenized Jews, in 167 BCE the Seleucids returned with a vengeance.

The Seleucids stole everything of value remaining in the Temple, set fire to parts of Jerusalem, leveled the city walls and wrought destruction. This time, the Seleucids established a permanent occupation presence when they built an imposing fortress overlooking the Temple. Known as the Acra, the fortress was garrisoned with troops both to intimidate and repress the local population, and to safeguard their allies among the Hellenized Jews, whose extreme views and support for the king had put them at risk. Jewish collaborators took refuge within the Acra.

From its new permanent base, the Seleucids terrorized the Jewish population, many of whom fled the city. The situation deteriorated with prohibitions on Jewish religious practice, part of a drive to unify the entire Seleucid kingdom under Greek customs. It was likely external threats to the Seleucid Empire that led the new king to accelerate the imposition of Greek religion and culture on the peoples over whom he ruled to create a loyal, uniform Hellenized population. This policy of crash Hellenization was not targeted only at the Jews; Hellenism was imposed on all Seleucid subjects. Seeing no alternative, the conquered peoples acquiesced. But the Jews of Judea mostly objected, angering the king. Considering himself a Greek god, the king expected complete submission to his commands. The Jews' obstinate rejection of Greek ways infuriated the king, bringing on more repression.

The prohibitions forbade Jewish religious practice. No longer could Jews observe the Sabbath, circumcise their children or follow their traditional way of life. Not only were Jewish rites and customs forbidden, but edicts were issued ordering the Sabbath and festivals be violated—all so that the Jews would forget their ways. Inspectors were appointed to ensure compliance with the new rules; failure to obey was punishable by death. Many Jews complied—some willingly and others out of fear of the consequences, but most refused to forsake their ways, which put their lives at risk. Thousands were martyred. Jews throughout Judea fled to the wilderness.

The Hellenizers were pleased that a mechanism was now in place to eliminate what they considered their people's antiquated customs. Knowing it was unusual for the Greeks to repress a particular religious group, the traditional Jews correctly inferred the moves came from the extremist apostate Jews, and blamed them for inviting the harsh Seleucid measures.

The Spark

Spreading throughout Judea's towns and villages, the Seleucids enforced the new edicts, epitomized by the compulsory sacrifice of pigs. When a Seleucid contingent arrived in the outlying village of Modiin, northwest of Jerusalem, they called on Mattathias, a well-respected community elder from the priestly Hasmonean family, to publicly sacrifice a pig. When the old man refused, an apostate Jew came forward and carried out the order. Mattathias' defiant refusal in itself meant a condemnation to death. Infuriated by the Jewish collaborator and with nothing to lose, Mattathias struck out, killing the Jew and the Seleucid official supervising. Mattathias' five sons led the villagers against the accompanying troops, killing them. A revolt had begun. Knowing word would soon reach the authorities and would bring on reprisals, Mattathias and his sons fled to the rugged hills of Gophna, between Jerusalem and Samaria, for refuge.

Joined by other Jews who had already fled their homes, Mattathias and his sons organized themselves and others in the hills and began training in guerilla tactics. The small group, none with military training, recruited members to its ranks. Arming themselves with farm implements and weapons they fashioned themselves, these men on the run became a people's militia. They established contacts with villages throughout the countryside, developing these relations into an effective intelligence-gathering organization. The rebels began by attacking towns where Hellenizers were strong, killing traitors and collaborators and destroying Greek idol altars—symbol of the hated Greek oppression. Next came more brazen guerilla attacks against Seleucid military patrols. Ambushing and killing the troops, the Jewish rebels supplemented their arsenal with captured weapons before melting back into the countryside.

Learning as they went along, the rebels used tactics improvised to suit each situation. Attacks on collaborators and Seleucid patrols showed that surprise and stealth worked best—they could achieve their aims and return home unscathed. Using their intimate knowledge of the countryside, the Jewish fighters struck at their enemies with near impunity, becoming known as Maccabees for the hammer-like blows they dealt their enemies. The Maccabees became the law of the land, in effect nullifying the Seleucid edicts against Jewish practice.

After a year of difficult living in the hills, Mattathias passed away, although not before delegating command to his son Judah and instructing his sons to avenge the wrongs the Seleucids were doing to the Jewish people.

The Seleucids, after encountering mainly sycophant Hellenized Jews, were amazed by the Jews' commitment to their faith, and their willingness to fight and die for their beliefs. Seleucid forces were occupying Jerusalem, a puppet government had been installed, and the Temple had been desecrated, yet the Jews would not submit. What the Seleucids did not understand was that the Maccabees were committed to a cause: fighting for religious freedom in their homeland, defending their way of life. Empowered by their passion for a cause charged with religious zeal, the Maccabees gained control of the countryside. Jerusalem and its Seleucid garrison were in danger of being isolated.

Apollonius

With rebels gaining the upper hand, word reached Antioch that authority was deteriorating throughout Judea. In 166 BCE Seleucid regional governor Apollonius set off from his base in Samaria with troops to locate and destroy the rebels.

Presumptuous and overconfident, Apollonius marched his troops along the Samaria–Jerusalem route, right into the Maccabees' stronghold, perhaps expecting that the rebels would be terrified into submission by a show of force by heavily armed Seleucid regulars. Apollonius miscalculated. Accustomed to being stationed among docile peoples, his troops were not prepared to face determined rebels.

When word reached Judah that Apollonius was on the move towards the Gophna area, he employed his knowledge of the territory to plan an attack that would not allow his powerful enemy to bring its superior numbers to bear. On the Seleucids' route of advance the logical place to attack was a long defile that Judah sensed would be perfect for an ambush.

As the Seleucids approached unawares, the rebels could not help but feel nervous in the face of the largest Greek force they had ever encountered. With Judah reassuring them, the Maccabee fighters maintained discipline as lead elements of the Seleucid force proceeded through the winding ascent, close to where the rebels lay hidden in the brush. When its vanguard rounded a bend and could not be seen by the main body, Judah signaled his troops to attack. Apollonius never even saw the attack coming. The Maccabees showered the Greeks with a deluge of arrows and rocks. Before the shocked troops could react, the Maccabees rushed them, slaying soldiers with their motley assortment of captured swords and improvised weapons. The Seleucids' heavy weapons proved useless in the restricted space of the passage. The terrain also restricted them from forming up into defensible array, leaving each man to defend himself. When Apollonius was killed in the fray, true panic broke out, with soldiers trampling one another in their haste to escape. Many of the Seleucid troops were killed, but far more were wounded and managed to flee, abandoning in the process a large quantity of weapons and gear to the Maccabees. Judah claimed Apollonius' sword as his own personal spoil, with which he would fight all subsequent battles.

Seron

With Apollonius' defeat, King Antiochus realized the situation in

Judea was far more serious than he had imagined. Embarrassed by the defeat and continued challenge to his authority, he was determined to teach this band of rebels a lesson. The king dispatched another general, Seron, who gladly accepted the mission thinking it would bring him glory. Dismissing Apollonius' expedition as a bungled mission, Seron set out in 165 BCE at the head of a strong army certain that the Jewish rebels would be no match for his professional soldiers.

Confident in the strength of his force yet careful not to repeat Apollonius' mistakes in the unfamiliar territory, Seron led his force southward along the coastal road, steering clear of the Maccabee stronghold. After turning inland on the route to Jerusalem, they were joined by Jewish collaborators familiar with the lay of the land. Seron's force pitched camp at Beth-Horon. To advance towards Jerusalem they needed to march through the adjacent pass. While navigating the narrow pass, the Seleucid force would be open to attack. Judah took men out towards the advancing Seleucid force. He could not believe a second Seleucid general was making this same critical error, which he knew would mean victory for the Maccabees. Despite their commander's confidence, the rebels were naturally intimidated by the heavily armed Seleucid force, and felt uneasy.

Summing up his plan in a talk with his men, Judah explained: "It is easy for many to be hemmed in by few"—recalling the tactic already proven successful in their victory over Apollonius. Judah reminded his men that they were fighting for their homes, families, and religious beliefs. "They come against us in great insolence and lawlessness to destroy us and our wives and our children, and to despoil us," he said. "But we fight for our lives and our laws. The Lord himself will crush them before us; as for you, do not be afraid of them."[3]

Judah deployed his men along the Beth-Horon pass, concealed along the steep slopes commanding the narrow pass. As the Seleucid force made its way up the ascent, Judah noticed large gaps between units, which he reckoned was a defensive measure allowing troops to come to the aid of any part coming under attack. The distance between the units grew as the soldiers trudged up the long, windy route, encumbered by their heavy weapons and equipment.

Maccabee slingers and archers deployed along the sides of the defile opened up with a barrage into the Seleucid ranks before Judah led his men in with swords and knives, sending the Selecuids reeling. Despite being a true combat unit, trained in Greek combat doctrine to fight in set-piece battle formations, the Seleucids were completely neutralized by the terrain, which allowed no room to maneuver. The Seleucid host was decimated, with 800 men left dead, including its commanding general. Word of Seron's death spread quickly, causing panic to break out among the Seleucid forces. Abandoning their weapons and gear, the Seleucid soldiers fled in disarray down the treacherous pass, with the Maccabees in hot pursuit.

After the rout, the Maccabees helped themselves to the weapons and equipment abandoned in the pass, putting them to use in arming the scores of new volunteers who joined their cause and in training for what they knew would be another showdown.

This second victory proved that the first was not a mere fluke. As stories of his legendary acts began to circulate, reaching as far as the palace in Antioch, Judah's reputation became well-known. Hellenized Jews and collaborators in Judea were terrified of him, and he was viewed as a true threat to the integrity of the Seleucid Empire.

The rebels in Judea were an embarrassment, but they were not the only trouble facing the Seleucid Empire. Parts of the empire were refusing to pay taxes, and the royal coffers were running low. King Antiochus was preparing for a campaign to Persia to forcibly collect taxes, but saw that more attention needed to be given to stamping out the rebellion in Judea. Before setting off on his expedition, the king appointed royal family member Lysias to act as regent for his son and to be in charge of affairs. The king allocated half his forces and elephants to Lysias with which to "wipe out and destroy the strength of Israel and the remnants of Jerusalem; . . . banish the memory of them from the place, settle aliens in all their territory, and distribute their land by lot."[4]

Taking no chances, Lysias resorted to overkill, assembling a massive force of 40,000 infantry and 7,000 cavalry under the command of three generals: Ptolemy, Nicanor and Gorgias. The force set out along the coast in 165 BCE, taking a cautious approach steering clear of the mountains, and established camp at Emmaus (near Latrun), close to where the modern road to Jerusalem begins its climb through the hills. The camp was situated on open terrain well-suited to the

Seleucid army's strengths. Various camp-followers, including slave dealers and other profiteers, descended on the Seleucid camp, waiting for action.

The Seleucid army's power centered on the phalanx. A large square-shaped tactical formation, the phalanx was a formidable array designed to smash an enemy force. The smallest building block for the formation was the 256-man syntagma, arranged in eight or 16 rows. In battle mode, a phalanx's first five ranks held their spears (sarissa) horizontally, creating an impenetrable barrier. The remaining rows rested their spears on the shoulder of the soldier in front of him, ensuring cohesion. A phalanx not only delivered a powerful punch, but was also an intimidating spectacle that had psychological impact.

Judah knew his force had no chance in a set-piece battle against a Seleucid phalanx. But he also knew the phalanx had its faults. The formation was not very mobile, it could not change its front in face of an enemy, and if penetrated it was ill-suited for hand-to-hand combat. For protection, its vulnerable flanks and rear were guarded by cavalry and light forces. In a confined area or on broken ground, a phalanx could not form up or maintain cohesion—the precise circumstances that had allowed Judah his first two victories over the Seleucids.

Given the Seleucids' cautious deployment, Judah was almost forced to allow them to take the initiative while he remained ready to immediately react to their moves. His only hope for victory lay in responding unconventionally, where advantage could be drawn from the fact that the two forces were so disparate.

With no intention of being lured into the Judean mountains where the rebels held sway and could hit them with a surprise attack, the Seleucids deliberately situated their camp on open terrain. With their overwhelming force, supplemented by reinforcements from Judea's southern neighbor Idumea and auxiliaries, the Seleucids were totally convinced of victory.

From guerilla band, the Maccabees had developed a more formal military structure, with officers commanding units of 1,000 men, companies of 100, platoons of 50 and sub-units of 10. Despite their progress and past successes, the Maccabees were still merely a militia, and thus were understandably wary of confronting such a massive fighting force, many times larger than anything they had faced before.

After initially assembling at Mitzpe, northwest of Jerusalem, Judah moved his force closer to the enemy, allowing them to observe the Seleucid camp from the hills. From the somewhat fatalistic talk to his men, it seems Judah's confidence was also shaken. Calling on his men to "be courageous," Judah told them: "It is better for us to die in battle than to see the misfortunes of our nation and of the Temple. But as the Lord's will in heaven may be, so shall He do."[5]

Knowing the Maccabees fought unconventionally, Seleucid General Gorgias tried to follow suit. Abandoning standard doctrine and tactics, he led a crack force of 5,000 infantry and 1,000 cavalry under cover of darkness against the insurgents, hoping to catch the Maccabees in their camp unawares. When Maccabee scouts reported on the preparations and departure of this force, Judah saw the opportunity to lure them away by ordering bonfires lit in the Maccabee camp to give the impression that his forces were concentrated there. Leaving behind a small decoy force, Judah evacuated the camp and led his men on an overnight march along a circuitous route down to the coastal plain.

When Gorgias' force reached the Maccabee camp, they found it empty, yet spotted what they believed was the tail end of the Maccabee army withdrawing. Gorgias immediately set off in pursuit, leading his men deeper into the hills, away from their base camp.

Reacting to the Seleucid initiative, Judah may not have had the necessary time to coordinate an ambush; it was enough to neutralize Gorgias with an aimless pursuit in the hills. With the Seleucids' best troops thus occupied, Judah led his men towards the main Seleucid encampment at Emmaus, which he hoped would have relaxed its guard in the knowledge that Gorgias' force was in the process of attacking and destroying the Maccabee camp. The Maccabee force approached the Seleucid camp at daybreak. Seeing the rebel force drawing near, the alarm was raised. Men scrambled out of their bedrolls, with the rush of adrenaline overcoming the early morning chill. Some Seleucid forces formed up into a phalanx on the plain while others scrambled to defend the camp. Exposed on the plain and with Gorgias' force in the hills, there was no option for retreat. Judah ordered an attack.

The Maccabees maneuvered and hit the Seleucid phalanx on its vulnerable flank. With the unexpected rebel attack, the Seleucids may not have fielded their full complement of light cavalry to protect the phalanx. The Maccabees penetrated, breaking up the formation's integrity.

Finding their long spears unwieldy, the Greek soldiers were hard pressed to fight off the Maccabees, who were adept in hand-to-hand combat. The Maccabees reached the Seleucid camp, and in an instant, the Seleucids' confidence deteriorated into fear, and utter confusion broke out. Horses and other animals—excited by the noise of battle—trampled soldiers in their own panic. In a chain reaction, individuals and then masses of men began fleeing, leaving 3,000 casualties in their wake. The Maccabees pursued, but Judah called off the chase as there was still the unfinished business of Gorgias' force. The massive Seleucid camp, largely destroyed by the fighting and panicked flight of so many men, was set on fire.

Gorgias' men, descending from their frustrating overnight search through the hills, saw their comrades in flight and parts of their camp on fire, and understood that something had gone very wrong. The sense that they might next fall victim set off a panicked retreat towards the coast, without even attempting to engage the Jewish rebels. Judah and his men looted what remained of the Seleucid camp, where they acquired more arms and equipment plus other booty and spoils with which to feed the needs of their growing army.

Lysias

Lysias was livid. Determined to see the Maccabees crushed, Lysias himself organized and led a force estimated at 20,000 infantry and 4,000 cavalry[6] and set out from Antioch in 164 BCE. Traveling by the safe corridor of the coastal plain, the force headed further south (towards Ashkelon) before wheeling inland, all within friendly territory. From the route they traveled, it was clear the Seleucid host was headed for Jerusalem, most likely to relieve the Acra garrison before moving against the rebels.

Judah moved to counter the Seleucids with a force some 10,000 strong. Fed with intelligence on their whereabouts by his scouts, Judah tracked the Seleucid advance, looking for an opportunity to attack. The Seleucids were slowed at Beth-Zur, a fortress on Judea's

southern border with Idumea that the Maccabees had occupied, buying time for defensive preparations.

With the Seleucids poised to drive on, Judah searched for a spot
from which to launch an ambush—resorting to the Maccabees' tried
and true tactic of attacking where the enemy would be hard-pressed
to defend itself. The Maccabees' new organization seems to have paid
off, with their large force well-coordinated to strike a blow that
inflicted heavy casualties on the Greek forces. While details of the
confrontation are scarce, it was said that Lysias observed how bold
the Maccabees were, and how ready to die nobly, such that he began
to truly appreciate what the Seleucids were up against.

What happened next came as a complete surprise to the Maccabees. The massive Seleucid army broke camp and began pulling back.
The Maccabees could not believe their eyes. Judah ordered scouts to
track the Seleucid host to ascertain what they were up to until word
reached him of King Antiochus' death, the probable reason for the
withdrawal. Indeed, when word of the king's death reached Lysias, he
decided to quit Judea and return to Antioch, where he would reign as
regent for Antiochus' son. Given the Seleucid army's withdrawal from
Judea and the mad king's death, Judah believed the Maccabees had
won a reprieve for some time, and hoped there might also be a change
in Seleucid policy. The time was ripe for a move on Jerusalem to
reclaim the Temple.

Return to the Temple

Religious freedom was finally at hand. When the city's Hellenized
Jews heard the Maccabees were making for Jerusalem, many fled.
With great joy, the Maccabees cleansed the Temple and rededicated it,
resuming religious sacrifices. Tradition has it that the sole cruse of
ritually pure olive oil found in the Temple—a one-day's supply—
miraculously burned for eight days.[7] The festivities marking the re-
dedication have been celebrated by Jews ever since as the holiday
Chanukah.

The story does not end here. The menacing Acra citadel was not
only a reminder of Seleucid authority, but its garrison actively
opposed the Jews. Additionally, in a move to frustrate upstart Judea
and ingratiate themselves with Antioch, Judea's neighbors began a

campaign of persecution against Jews living in their lands. Judah responded with punitive expeditions against the perpetrators in neighboring territories and lands. Confident from his successive victories, Judah was ready to move against the Acra fortress.

When the Jerusalem garrison pleaded for assistance, Antioch responded with an invasion on a scale that far surpassed that of all previous campaigns. Taking heed of the lessons from his earlier campaign, Lysias knew more troops were required. Leading a Greek and mercenary force of 50,000 infantry, 5,000 cavalry and a complement of war elephants, Lysias marched on Judea accompanied by his charge, the young King Antiochus V Eupator.

After marching along the same approach corridor as before, the Seleucids were again forced to invest the fortress at Beth-Zur, which the Maccabees had fortified, before continuing towards Jerusalem. Moving rapidly yet cautiously, the Seleucids advanced steadily and in good order, with their flanks protected by forces spread out in the hills. They were an impressive sight, with rank after rank of soldiers carrying golden and brass shields that flashed in the afternoon sun like flaming torches. They intentionally made a great deal of noise as they marched, with their shouts echoing through the hills causing fright among Judah's men.

Judah had mustered a fairly large force with which he tried to block the Seleucids at Beth Zecharia. The Maccabees were awed by the size of the enemy force—the most impressive the Seleucids had yet fielded in Judea—but more so by the elephants. Around "each elephant they stationed a thousand men armed with coats of mail, and with brass helmets on their heads, and five hundred picked horsemen were assigned to each beast."[8]

Seleucid forces advanced through the hilly area, carefully sending forces to secure the high ground, yet the Maccabees managed to launch an attack that hit the Seleucids hard, leaving 600 casualties. The Seleucids quickly recoiled and began rallying forces. The elephants' shock effect had its intended impression; many of the Jewish fighters were paralyzed by fear. Judah's brother Eleazar, attempting to inspire the rebels, went after an elephant he believed carried the Seleucid general. After fighting his way through the guard, Eleazar stabbed the elephant in its belly with his sword. The elephant collapsed on him, crushing him to death.

The Seleucid force far outclassed the Maccabees, who broke and retreated. Judah fell back to Jerusalem to organize its defenses before retiring to his base in the mountains of Gophna. From this safe haven, the Maccabees could return to guerilla warfare against the occupation force Lysias would undoubtedly leave. The Seleucids regained control of Jerusalem until, for a second time, the day was saved when external events forced Lysias to withdraw, this time to prevent his rival Philip from usurping power in Antioch. For the Maccabees, aided by a strong dose of luck, victory had been snatched from defeat.

Seeking quiet in Judea to free him to address domestic matters, Lysias lifted decrees forbidding religious observance, eliminating the Jews' primary grievance. The majority of the rebels were content to lay down their arms and return to their lives now that the revolt had achieved its aim of religious freedom, albeit under continued Seleucid rule. To Judah, the Seleucid concessions were not enough. Convinced that religious freedom could not be preserved under Seleucid rule, Judah wanted full political independence.

In an unexpected turn of events, the young Seleucid king Antiochus V was ousted by his cousin Demetrius, who had the deposed king and his guardian Lysias put to death. Quick to seize the opportunity presented by the new leader in Antioch, apostate Jews convinced Demetrius to intervene in Judea. To shore up the situation, Demetrius appointed a new high priest, Alcimus, who arrived in Jerusalem accompanied by a military escort under Bacchides, sent to establish and bolster the new priest's authority. The Seleucid contingent entered Jerusalem unopposed.

The new high priest and the general were quick to alienate the people through killings and other vindictive measures, proving correct Judah's skepticism. In response, the Maccabees mobilized and fought back, leading to calls for Antioch to assist. This renewed instability in Judea coincided with revolts in the Seleucid Empire's eastern satrapies, presenting a very real threat to the empire's unity.

Demetrius responded by despatching Nicanor at the head of a large force to deal with the revival of the Maccabean revolt. When the force he led was ambushed and routed at Capharsalama (Kfar Shalem), Nicanor withdrew to Jerusalem to await additional manpower. When his reinforced army resumed operations in the countryside, Judah ambushed them at Adasa, north of Jerusalem, and succeeded in killing the Seleucid general. Word of Nicanor's death in battle caused the Greek troops to panic and flee.

To counter the renewed Seleucid aggression, the Maccabees made an approach to Rome, then a regional power. Seeing an opportunity to check the Seleucids, Rome was receptive, and a treaty recognizing Judea's independence was concluded.

Angered both by the military defeats in Judea and the political maneuvering with Rome, Demetrius sent Bacchides back to Judea with a 20,000-strong infantry force backed by 2,000 cavalry. Knowing that the Maccabees lacked the strong support they had previously enjoyed, Antioch pressed its campaign to wipe out the Jewish rebels.

Death of Judah

Sources report Judah succeeded in mustering only 3,000 men with which to counter Bacchides. Seeing the Seleucid army arrayed against them on the battlefield at Elasa, the force began hemorrhaging deserters, leaving Judah with only 800 men. Given accounts of the battle, which we are told lasted from morning to night and described as severe, Judah's force was likely much greater.[9] In a brilliant maneuver, Bacchides' forces caught the Maccabees in a pincer, sandwiching them between the two flanks of his army. There were many casualties on both sides, the legendary Judah the Maccabee among them.

After recovering Judah's body from the battlefield, the Maccabees fled, taking their commander's body back to his family village of Modiin for burial. The Seleucids were back in control. Bacchides put Hellenizers in charge of the country, and they began pursuing Maccabee supporters. Judah's brothers would carry on the torch; Jonathan took on the task of breathing life back into the resistance. Bacchides returned to Antioch to help address the deteriorating situation in the east. The Maccabees' strength grew once again to the point where they were the *de facto* rulers of most of Judea. Bacchides was sent back to Judea to crush the rebellion but was himself defeated. This time, he agreed to peace terms and departed Judea for good. Demetrius was killed in battle fighting a rival for the throne. Jonathan, free to govern Judea, went on to become high priest, and purged the nation of Jewish Hellenizers. In coming to an understanding with the Seleucids, Jonathan was able to consolidate his power and expand Judea's territory until he was murdered by the treachery of Seleucid general Trypho, who feared his rising power.

Simon, the last surviving son of Mattathias,[10] stepped in to fill the void, and would go on to distinguish himself in his own right. Simon presided over the surrender of the menacing Acra, symbol of Seleucid oppression. Simon secured concessions from Antioch, chief among them freedom from taxation, which in effect was a recognition of independence. In 141 BCE, Judea was granted formal independence from Seleucid rule—the fruits of more than 30 years of resistance from the time Seleucid hostilities began. Thus began the Hasmonean Dynasty, which would rule for a century.

This is the true accomplishment, or miracle, if you will, of the Maccabees: Judea was an independent Jewish state, while the mighty Seleucid Empire slowly declined into irrelevance, all brought about by the knee-jerk reaction of a proud old man who refused to forsake his faith.

Rome, eclipsing the Seleucids as the great power in the region, granted the Hasmoneans limited authority under the Roman governor of Damascus. The Jews became hostile to the new regime, and the following years witnessed frequent insurrections. The Hasmonean dynasty's reign came to an end when Herod the Great became king of the Jews, ushering in the next chapter of foreign-domination-inspired revolt by the Jews.

Notes

1. Note the Greco-Roman spelling (formerly Judah).

2. II Maccabees 4: 24, *The Apocrypha, or Deuterocanonical Books* (New Revised Standard Version) (Cambridge UK: Cambridge University Press, 1989).

3. I Maccabees 3: 20–22.

4. I Maccabees 3: 35–36.

5. I Maccabees 3: 58–60.

6. Far less than the highly exaggerated figure of 60,000 troops reported in I Maccabees.

7. Judah ordered the Temple cleansed, a new altar built in place of the one desecrated by the sacrifice of pigs, and new holy vessels made. When the fire had been kindled anew upon the altar and the lamps of the candelabra lit, the dedication of the altar was celebrated for eight days amid sacrifices and songs in a similar fashion to the holiday Sukkot, the Feast of Tabernacles, which also lasts for eight days. (II Maccabees 10: 6)

8. I Maccabees 6: 35.

9. Bezalel Bar-Kochva. *The Seleucid Army. Organization and Tactics in the great Campaign* (Cambridge, UK: Cambridge University Press, 1979: reprinted with corrections), p.185.

10.In the period following Judah's death, younger brother Yochanan was killed by tribesmen east of the Dead Sea.

The Zealot Rebellion
67 CE

Phoenice

Gaulanitis

Ptolemais

Jotapata

Gamla

Sepphoris

Galilee

Galatis

THE GREAT SEA
(MEDITERRANEAN SEA)

Jordan River

Dekapolis

Caesarea

Samaria

Peraea

Beth-Horon

Jerusalem

Bethlehem

Herodium

Salt Sea
(Dead Sea)

Judaea

Idumea

Masada

0   25 miles

0   25 km

N

CHAPTER 6

IVDAEA CAPTA

THE RAGE OF ROME, 67 CE

Roman hegemony over Judaea had begun with Jerusalem's capture in 63 BCE by Pompey, which brought Jewish independence to an end. The province the Romans called Iudaea (Judaea) became a vassal state, and the Romans appointed Herod as King of the Jews. Initially, Rome respected some local sensibilities and granted the Jews a measure of autonomy in internal affairs. Rome generally tolerated conquered people's beliefs and ways; Roman customs were infused into conquered lands while some aspects of the conquered people's cultures might be adopted.

After enjoying a century of independence under the Hasmonean Dynasty, the Jews had a hard time accepting subjugation, which they considered a blow to national pride. While most Jews found a way to compromise between Jewish law and their new circumstances, radical Jewish nationalists, known as Zealots, virulently opposed foreign occupation. Since Rome expected complete loyalty from its subjects, the Jews did not ingratiate themselves with their new rulers. The Romans never came to understand the Jews. When Pompey captured Jerusalem, he had upset the Jews by entering the Holy of Holies—their

Temple's sacred inner sanctum entered only by the High Priest once a year—to see for himself that the Jews had no manifestation of the god they worshipped, as it was inconceivable to him, and many Romans, that the Jews worshipped an invisible god. Rome's view of the Jews deteriorated and grew into a deep-seated hatred, with Jews receiving perhaps the harshest treatment of all Rome's subjects. A hint of Rome's attitude toward the Jews can be found in Roman historian Tacitus' *Histories*, where he calls Jews "this race detested by the gods" and "the vilest of nations."[1]

Rome later moved to direct rule of Judaea by procurators: administrative officials with the power of a provincial governor. The procurators selected for Judaea were largely inept, excessively greedy, and exhibited a disregard for the Jewish people they governed. Abusing their authority to plunder for personal gain, the procurators callously bled Judaea of its wealth. Excessive taxes forced Jews from their lands and a great many into poverty, thereby alienating their subjects and increasing support for the Zealots.

Gessius Florus, who took office as procurator of the province in 64 CE, soon surpassed his predecessors with his abuses and excesses, pushing the mainstream Jews to the side of the Zealots. Josephus noted that "Gessius Florus, as though he had been sent on purpose to show his crimes to every body, made a pompous ostentation of them to our nation, as never omitting any sort of violence, nor any unjust sort of punishment."[2] Roman soldiers and locals took their cue from the procurator, who propagated incitement and violence. Intentional provocations against the Jewish community in the Roman provincial capital of Caesarea erupted into a riot that ended with the Jews' expulsion from the city, an event considered a trigger to the war. Florus' greed was so great that he raided the Temple treasury, crossing a line that inflamed the Jews' passions. When some Jews sarcastically collected alms for the procurator—a brazen insult—Florus responded with violence, unleashing his soldiers on murderous rampages that left thousands of Jews dead. His provocations and incitement worked: urged by the Zealots, the bulk of the Jews became convinced that Roman occupation was untenable; conflict was the only alternative. Florus couldn't have been happier, for war would obviate him from being called to account for his actions before Caesar. As Tacitus put it, "the Jews had patience till Gessius Florus was made procurator. Under him it was that the war began."[3]

In 66 CE, Florus left Jerusalem for Caesarea. In short order, Masada, once King Herod's desert mountain-top fortress, was seized by a band of extremist Zealots known as the Sicarii (for the daggers they carried and freely used against their enemies), who killed the Roman force stationed there and seized its arsenal. In another overt act of mutiny, the Temple priests stopped the requisite daily sacrifices for the Roman emperor, a profound move that signaled a break with Roman rule. Finally, the populace of Jerusalem rose in revolt. The local Roman garrison was massacred by revolutionaries.

Internecine fighting now broke out among the Jews, many of whom disagreed with the provocations against Rome. Aristocrats and others seeking maintenance of the status quo (with optimistic hopes that the next procurator would be better) fought the revolutionaries, who they felt were encouraging Rome to make war against them. Ill-effects of the uprising were immediate, with local populations in Judaea, Egypt and Syria attacking Jews with impunity.

Following events in Judaea with grave concern, Roman governor of Syria, Cestius Gallus—who held responsibility for Judaean affairs—marched from Antioch in November 66 CE at the head of Legion XII, supported by cohorts of infantry, troops of cavalry and auxiliaries, including many archers, to quell the Jews' uprising. Plundering and setting fire to Jewish villages en route, the Roman force reached Jerusalem and besieged the Jewish insurgents in the Temple. After undermining the Temple wall and making preparations to burn its gate, Cestius Gallus inexplicably ordered his forces to withdraw. The Jews harassed the retreating Romans and repeatedly attacked them by the Beth-Horon pass, the narrow defile where the Maccabees had defeated a Seleucid army in their fight for independence. Nearly 6,000 Roman soldiers were killed, and only by a stratagem did the governor manage to escape with some of his forces.

Though exhilarated by this victory and inspired by its symbolic location, the Jews had no illusions that Rome would tolerate such insubordination. Not only was it an embarrassment for Rome, but the Jews' insurrection threatened the important link between Alexandria in Egypt and Antioch in Syria, the Empire's greatest cities after Rome.

With its massive empire held together in a delicate balance, Rome had to send a strong message that all its ruled subjects would understand quite well—that Rome would destroy those who upset the *Pax Romana*, while also dissuading Rome's rivals, the Parthians, from intervening.

Rome's response came in the form of three legions. Burning, stealing, pillaging and murdering their way across Galilee, the Roman forces quickly subdued many Jewish towns and villages. Sepphoris (Zippori), Galilee's largest city, saved itself by pledging allegiance to Rome, siding against their own countrymen, which did not say much for the Jews' unity.

Military governors had been appointed by the aristocrats in Jerusalem organizing the war effort to prepare the country's defenses. Joseph ben Mattathias had been named to the critical post of commander of the Galilee region. It was believed the Romans would first focus their efforts in Judaea's north to conquer Galilee before moving on Jerusalem or other parts of the province. A strong stance against the invading Romans would embolden the country and might encourage intervention by the Parthians. If the Romans were to be stopped, it needed to be in Galilee.

Joseph prepared Galilee's cities and towns for defense, and assembled a force that by his account numbered 60,000 infantry, 250 horsemen, 4,500 mercenaries and 600 guards, all armed with old weapons he had collected and prepared. The force was organized according to the Roman model, with captains of tens, hundreds and thousands. Joseph trained them to "give the signals one to another, and to call and recall the soldiers by the trumpets, how to expand the wings of an army, and make them wheel about; and when one wing hath had success, to turn again and assist those that were hard set, and to join in the defense of what had most suffered."[4] He exercised them for war while impressing upon them the importance of soldiers maintaining good conscience.

Their adversary was the Roman general Titus Flavius Vespasianus (Vespasian), an experienced and well-regarded veteran of successful campaigns in Germany and Britain. Vespasian arrived at Ptolemais (Acre/Akko) with Legion XV *Apollinaris* and was joined in theater by his son Titus with Legions V *Macedonica* and X *Fretensis*. Vespasian's legions were supplemented by cohorts, troops of cavalry and thousands of auxiliaries, including cavalry, archers and infantry provided by local Roman vassal kings. In all, Vespasian commanded a force of 60,000 men with which to crush the Jews. With so many elements under his command, the Roman general needed time to organize his force before moving out in April 67 CE.

The military force Joseph had organized was quick to desert in the face of Roman legions, finding refuge in Galilee's walled cities. The training they had undergone was for naught; there would be no set battles with the Romans, only resistance in the walled cities. In effect, this acknowledged eventual defeat, for the cities and towns could not hold out against the Romans, who were masters at siegecraft. Ideas of thwarting the Romans and petitioning for a settlement would not be realized, nor would other subjected peoples join the revolt now that the Jewish War, as the revolt came to be known, was seen as a lost cause.

Joseph fled to the walled city of Jotapata (Yodfat). Roman intelligence reported the bulk of the Jewish rebels were also in the city, which was considered the strongest of the cities. Vespasian determined to demolish Jotapata and capture Joseph, thinking that the capture of the Jewish general would be a major blow to the Jews' morale and will to fight, and might frighten other cities into surrendering.

Jotapata put up a tenacious resistance throughout May 67 CE. Repeated Roman assaults were repulsed, and Roman losses were heavy, with even General Vespasian wounded in action. Only when a deserter treacherously tipped off the Romans about when the city's sentries would be sleeping were the Romans able to finally overcome the city's defenses after 47 days of siege.[5]

After convincing so many of his countrymen to give their lives for their cause, Joseph put saving himself above his ideals and turned himself over to the Romans, with whom he would collaborate. He took the Roman name Flavius Josephus and chronicled the Jewish War; his accounts are the primary source on the war. His countrymen would brand him a coward and deserter.

Gamla

After Jotapata, the Romans moved down the coastal plain to secure

Jaffa and its environs before returning north to take Tiberias and then
Taricheae (Migdal) in a land and naval battle. Intimidated by Roman
successes, most towns and villages surrendered. With Galilee almost
completely in Roman hands, the Romans turned their attention to the
city of Gamla east of the Sea of Galilee, in the Gaulanitis region, part
of what is today known as the Golan Heights.

Considered a strong and safe refuge, Gamla's population swelled
with refugees fleeing the Roman army's rampage in Galilee, and villagers from surrounding areas seeking shelter. The influx of refugees
had turned Gamla into a Zealot stronghold.

Naturally secure atop a steep hill resembling a camel's hump
(from which the city drew its name—*gamal* is Hebrew for camel),
Gamla is protected on all sides by nearly impassable ravines. The city
is approached from the east by a dip in the terrain, called a saddle,
connecting the hill to the plateau above. This was the only side protected by a defensive wall. Before going over to the Romans, Galilee
commander Joseph had helped the city to shore up its defenses. The
wall facing the approach to the city was fortified by evacuating houses
abutting the wall and filling them in with stones, entrances and gaps
between houses and other structures along the wall were filled-in or
sealed, and the wall was thickened. Trenches and underground mines
were dug across the city's approach to impede access. And for morale,
coins were minted honoring Jerusalem, perhaps as a way of reminding
citizens that their preparations were part of a greater national and
religious effort.

Confidence in the city's strength had been reinforced when Jewish
vassal King Agrippa II, a grandson of Herod the Great, who ruled a
region north of Galilee, had unsuccessfully besieged the city for seven
months earlier in the year.

Marching through difficult volcanic rock terrain cut by deep river
canyons, the Roman column comprising General Vespasian and his
guard, three legions and auxiliary forces, cavalry, siege equipment and
baggage—some 30,000 men—arrived at Gamla in September 67 CE.
The Romans established camp on a plateau overlooking the city.
Normally the Romans intentionally sited their camps to be visible
from their objective for its psychological impact on the enemy, but the
terrain around Gamla did not allow for this.[6] The ground in their

encampment was leveled and prepared, walls built and buildings erected. Sentries were posted around the city in an effort to prevent escape and block reinforcements or supplies from reaching the city.

Surveying the city wall, the Romans identified weak points where they would position battering rams. Knowing where to focus their attacks may have been made easier with the help of collaborator Josephus, who was familiar with Gamla's defenses from when he had surveyed them and advised on their improvement.

Roman engineering units quickly went to work filling in the city's defensive trench, raising a bank against the wall and preparing the ground for the siege engines. Work details set out to supply the engineers with the necessary timber, earth and rocks to build platforms for the siege engines, siege works, ramparts and lines of wooden hurdles and screens. In addition to their disciplined military drill regimen, Roman soldiers were also trained in construction.

The speed and efficiency with which the Romans went about their work shook the confidence of the defenders of Gamla. The Jews fired at the workers relentlessly, hurling rocks and projectiles, to no avail. Working behind protective screens while archers and slingers provided steady cover fire, the engineers built ramps that crept steadily towards Gamla's walls.

King Agrippa, who joined the Roman siege force at Gamla, approached the city wall calling for surrender. Gamla's response came in the form of a slinger's well-aimed rock, which sent the king reeling. Roman soldiers became apprehensive given the Jews' response to Agrippa; if the Jews would respond to one of their own this way, the Romans reasoned, they could expect a savage reception. At Jotapata, the Romans had seen how ferociously the Jews could fight, including pouring boiling oil on attacking Roman troops, proving they would resort to any means to defend themselves.

Defenders on Gamla's wall did their best to beat back the teams bringing the engines forward until cover fire became so intense that no one could oppose them from the parapet, freeing the Romans to bring up the battering rams.

Following Roman assault doctrine, the attack on Gamla began with an intense barrage. Stone balls launched from ballistae crashed down with great force. Projectiles shattered the great synagogue's roof, killing those sheltered inside. Catapults fired missiles and darts with such intensity that some reached as far as the city's western quarters, nearly 1,000 feet (300m) from the city wall. Archaeologists discovered some 2,000 basalt ballista balls and 1,600 iron arrowheads in and around the city—more than any other site in the Roman Empire, giving testimony to the intensity of the barrage.[7] Archers composed largely of auxiliary units from ethnic groups skilled with the bow, and slingers added to the fray, forcing Gamla's defenders to seek cover. The Roman artillery made a terrifying noise, both the machines' groaning and their projectiles screaming through the air.

The battering rams went to work, Gamla's wall reverberating with each blow. At Jotapata, the siege engines had been set alight several times by desperate sallies, so the Romans may have outfitted the rams with hurdles and skins to protect both their soldiers and equipment. At Gamla, they went about their work unmolested. Shaken by these huge wooden beams capped by a heavy iron tip in the shape of a ram's head, it wasn't long before the wall began giving way. Assault troops amassed behind protective screens, waiting for a breach. Soldiers equipped with ladders and hooks prepared to scale the wall in a bid to overwhelm defenses in force.

When repeated blows dislodged stones, the wall began to crumble. Led by Vespasian, the Roman assault team secured their helmets and armor, drew swords, raised protective shields and rushed forward towards the V-shaped breach in the two meter-thick section of wall just below the synagogue, shouting as they charged. Backed by archers and slingers, they climbed through the breach in the wall and penetrated the city, their assault heralded by trumpet blasts.

Gamla commanders Chares and Joseph deployed forces to the breach points, where the Jews resisted the first wave streaming in. As more and more Romans poured over and through gaps bashed through the wall, Gamla's defenders could no longer stop them. The Jews retreated, pulling back towards the upper parts of the city. In what Vespasian later described as a hasty rush to victory, the Romans pursued the retreating Jews with gusto. Following the Jews into the confusing maze of passageways and streets, the Romans were not prepared when the Jews turned around and counterattacked. With their intimate knowledge of the city, Gamla's men trapped and began repulsing the invaders while Roman soldiers continued to pour into the city.

"Jammed inextricably in the narrow alleys," Josephus described, "the Romans suffered fearful casualties."[8] The topography dictated a cramped city, with houses built nearly on top of one another. Fleeing both the Jews' counterattack and crush of their comrades' advance, Roman soldiers climbed onto rooftops for safety. Unaccustomed to such weight, the reed and packed-earth roofs and houses alike collapsed. Built so close together, the collapse of one house brought others crashing down, kicking up a huge cloud of brown dust that made it nearly impossible to see. Josephus recounted: "A great many [Roman soldiers] were ground to powder by these ruins, and a great many of those that got from under them lost some of their limbs, but still a greater number were suffocated by the dust that arose from those ruins."[9] Jews threw darts and rubble at the Romans, who struggled to extricate themselves. Those able to find their way out of the melée withdrew through the breaches in the wall; others lost in the confusion were killed by Gamla's defenders or stabbed themselves in desperation. Roman corpses littered the city; the Jews collected a bounty of metal weapons from dead and wounded Romans.

After initial euphoria over routing the Roman assault, confidence and morale plummeted as they realized their vulnerability. Gamla's defenses had been breached with ease, and now they had no hopes of any terms of accommodation. Escape or fighting to the end seemed the only options. The one bright spot was that the difficult terrain surrounding Gamla prevented the Romans from entirely encircling the city with earthworks, an omission that had allowed small groups of Jews to escape from Gamla throughout the brief siege. Those who could fled; townspeople remaining suffered from shortages of water and provisions exacerbated by the influx of refugees.

Vespasian consoled his dejected troops, reminding them that "it can never be that we must conquer without bloodshed on our own side."[10] The general assured his men that the setback was not a poor reflection of them nor related to valor among the Jews, but rather Gamla's very difficult layout. Roman over-zealousness is what had resulted in their failure to take the city, with Vespasian to blame, for he had led the way and fought himself deeply into Gamla's upper sections and only narrowly escaped. One might consider it a forgivable misstep; being in the heat of action, leading his troops into battle and withdrawing last were qualities that inspired his men.

Regrouping after the failed breach, the Romans sent sappers against Gamla's round tower, which they had determined lacked strong foundations. The sappers excavated the soft chalk on which the tower was built and managed to dislodge heavy stones, undermining the tower's integrity. Late at night, the tower, which sat prominently on the city wall, came crashing down, causing panic in the city. Gamla's defenders braced for the expected Roman assault, but the Romans waited for daylight before venturing into the city.

Having learned from the first assault, the Romans limited the number of troops penetrating. Early morning on October 20, 67 CE, Vespasian's son Titus led 200 chosen horsemen and infantry into Gamla. Sentries raised the alarm, mobilizing defenders to meet the Romans at the hastily repaired breaches. While the men resisted the attack, Gamla's non-combatants took refuge in the upper part of the city.

Jews fired arrows, threw rocks and "recycled" ballista balls, and fought hand-to-hand with the Romans who were pouring through breaches in the wall, but this time the Roman war machine plowed through the resistance. Gamla's two commanders were dead, one having been killed by a Roman dart, the other having succumbed to illness. The Jews were pushed back; panicked masses fleeing the Roman onslaught crowded the way to the upper city.

With the breach secured, Vespasian led a second Roman wave with a larger assault force. The Romans killed without respite; Josephus described the scene as a slaughter, with blood flowing down the streets from the upper part of the city. Gamla's people fled to the summit of Gamla's northern slope beyond range of Roman arrows. On the exposed bluff, powerful gusts of wind blew in the Romans' favor. Clouds of dust blown by the wind blinded the Jews, adding to their desperation. The Romans began killing the cornered Jews, including those trying to surrender. Their only remaining hope was to escape down the steep slopes away from the city. In the rush, some of the panicked people fell to their deaths, tumbling down the steep slope, while others were inadvertently trampled. As Jews reached the summit and began their descent, disappearing from sight, it appeared to some of the Romans that the trapped Jews were leaping to their deaths from the steep cliffs. Gamla was once called "the Masada of the North," with the belief that 5,000 of its citizens had thrown themselves to their deaths in a mass suicide, but modern researchers refute this. The Romans showed no mercy, sparing "not so much as the infants, of whom many were flung down by them from the citadel."[11] In all, some 9,000 Jews were killed at Gamla.

With the city finally secured, the Romans stripped Gamla of valuables, collected their dead for cremation and destroyed their camp to prevent it from being of any use to their enemies. Mules and beasts of burden were loaded with baggage, the troops formed up into marching order and left the area, leaving Gamla's survivors to trickle back to rummage through their destroyed city and bury their dead. Gamla was abandoned, left as it was after its defeat, and lost to history for 1,900 years until its rediscovery and identification.

Word of Josephus' capitulation at Jotapata had inflamed the volatile situation in Jerusalem, exploding into civil war among the Jews. The in-fighting served the Romans well; having suppressed the rebellion in nearly all of Judaea, the Romans stood down and besieged Jerusalem as they waited out the tumult in Rome following Emperor Nero's suicide. In a span of a year, Rome had three emperors in rapid succession before Vespasian returned to Rome and was proclaimed emperor in late 69 CE, as Josephus had conjectured in his life-saving pitch to the Roman general following his capture. "Thou O Vespasian," Josephus had said, "art Caesar and emperor, thou, and thy son."[12] Titus remained to continue the siege of Jerusalem, a task he carried out with relish. When the city finally fell in 70 CE after bitter fighting, the Romans perpetrated a bloodbath, destroying the Temple and carrying its sacred vessels off to Rome, never to be seen again. Jerusalem was left in ruins.

Masada

With all of Judaea—save for the desert fortress of Masada—now subdued, the Jewish extremists who had taken refuge on Masada were the last vestige of the Jews' revolt. Under Flavius Silva, then procurator of Judaea, Legion X *Fretensis* moved in to destroy them. In a demonstration of Roman resolve, the Romans completely surrounded Masada and constructed a massive assault ramp up the side of the mountain in order to deploy siege engines against the rebel compound. Hopelessly surrounded and facing certain defeat, the 967 Jewish rebels holed up on the mountain committed suicide in 73 CE, dying as free men. Masada has become part of modern Israel's national ethos, a symbol of heroism, a place where few stood against many and opted for an honorable death rather than defeat and slavery.

The results of the Jewish War were disastrous: hundreds of thousands of Jews were killed, thousands more sold into slavery and exiled, and the Temple destroyed. Josephus, who returned with the victorious Titus to Rome, may have exaggerated his account of Jewish resistance and casualties as a way of accentuating the Roman victory, thus ingratiating himself with his Roman sponsors. But the minting of Roman coins publicizing the victory with the inscription "*Ivdaea Capta*" (Judaea Captured) suggests that this was considered a very real war. The victory was celebrated in Rome with a triumphant procession, a scene captured for posterity in a frieze on the Arch of Titus, a triumphal arch erected in the forum at Rome. The Arch of Titus remains to this day, showing Roman soldiers parading the Temple's sacred vessels. At some point, a visitor etched telling graffiti in Hebrew just opposite the frieze: "*Am Yisrael Chai L'Olam va'Ed* (The Jewish People Will Live Forever)."

Several hundred years later, the Roman Empire would split into western and eastern empires. The Western Roman Empire ended in the 5th century CE, while the Eastern Empire later became known as the Byzantine Empire, lasting until the 15th century. The Holy Land remained under Roman/Byzantine rule until the armies of Islam swept through the region in the 7th century.

Notes

1.Tacitus (translators Alfred Church and William Brodribb). *Histories* (London, UK: Macmillan, 1864–77), Book 5: 1, 5: 8.

2.Josephus, (translator William Whiston). *The Complete Works of Josephus* (Grand Rapids, MI: Kregel Publications, 1981). *Antiquities*, Book 20, Ch.XI: 1.

3.Tacitus: *Histories*, 5: 10.

4.Josephus, *Wars of the Jews*, Book II, Ch. XX: 7.

5.Josephus, *Wars of the Jews*, Book III, Ch. VII: 33.

6.Josephus, *Wars of the Jews*, Book III, Ch. VII: 4.

7.Syon, Danny. "Gamla—City of Refuge." In A. M. Berlin and J. A. Overman (eds.). *The First Jewish Revolt. Archaeology, History and Ideology* (London and New York: Routledge, 2002), pp.141–2.

8.Josephus, *Wars of the Jews*, Book IV, Ch. I: 4.

9.Josephus, *Wars of the Jews*, Book IV, Ch. I: 4.

10.Josephus, *Wars of the Jews*, Book IV, Ch. I: 6.

11.Josephus, *Wars of the Jews*, Book IV, Ch. I: 10. This is understood to mean "the summit" as no archaeological evidence supports the existence of a citadel fortress, nor does the battle account refer to Gamla's defenders taking refuge in and attempting a last stand from such a fortress.

12.Josephus, *Wars of the Jews*, Book III, Ch. VIII: 9.

Visitors standing above the excavation site of ancient Jericho, the world's oldest city. The Israelites' plan for the conquest of Canaan hinged on taking this heavily fortified desert oasis. (Yaacov Sa'ar, Israel Government Press Office)

Jericho, 3,000 years later. (Courtesy of Alan Merbaum)

Above: Jews working wheat fields in the fertile Jezreel Valley in 1938. Some 3,000 years earlier, Israelites sowed these very fields, only to have their produce taken from them in violent raids by Midianites and other marauding tribes until a young man named Gideon swore to put an end to such persecution. (Kluger Zoltan, Israel Government Press Office)

Left: The Kishon River overflowing its banks following a winter rainstorm. Mount Tabor was a safe place for the Israelites to wait for the heavy winter rains which they knew could quickly turn the Jezreel Valley into a mire. (Yossi Sorogon, Kishon River Authority)

Left: Aerial View of Mount Tabor showing its prominent position over the valley below. Responding to Canaanite persecution, a call to arms went out, and 10,000 Israelites volunteered. The force deployed to Mount Tabor, whose steep slopes afforded protection against Canaanite chariots and offered a clear view of the surrounding terrain. (Moshe Milner. Israel Government Press Office)

The Philistine and Israelite armies faced off in the Elah Valley, one of the few easily passable routes inland from the coastal areas, where the Philistines were dominant. The Philistine camp was deployed on several hills on the southern side of the valley while the Israelites were opposite, to the north. (Dr. Yehuda Dagan, Israel Antiquities Authority)

Copy of Verrochio's 15th-century bronze sculpture of David with the head of Goliath at his feet. (Author's collection)

Ruins of Roman-era Beit Shean are seen before the *tel*, or archaeological mound, an area of older settlement. Following the death of Israelite King Saul in battle against the Philistines on Mount Gilboa, the men of Jabesh-Gilead risked their lives to rescue the corpses of the decapitated king and his sons, displayed ignominiously by the Philistines on the Beit Shean city wall. (Curt Fischer)

Artist rendition of Sennacherib's siege of Lachish. Under a hail of arrows and missiles from the defenders, armor-clad and helmeted Assyrian infantrymen, archers, sling-throwers and shielded spearmen advanced on the embattled city and began moving up the ramp. The counter-fire intensified as they closed range and began rolling the feared battering rams up the ramp and into place at several locations.
(Courtesy of Marshall Editions)

Tel Lachish on fire, as the city may have appeared following the Assyrian capture of the city. After ransacking and looting the city, the Assyrians set fire to the town, burning Lachish to the ground.
(Dr. Yehuda Dagan, Israel Antiquities Authority)

Aerial view of Tel Lachish. The Assyrian assault ramp is to the right, between the *tel* and the modern moshav, believed to be the site of the Assyrian camp. The Assyrian assault came from their camp. The photo clearly shows the tel's dominant position over the surrounding terrain. (Dr. Yehuda Dagan, Israel Antiquities Authority)

Hezekiah's Tunnel. Preparing for an Assyrian reaction to Judah's revolt, King Hezekiah wanted to secure the Gihon Spring's waters while denying them to enemy invaders. A 500-meter long tunnel was hewn from solid rock to bring the waters into Jerusalem. (Moshe Milner, Israel Government Press Office)

Reconstruction of the battle of Beth-Horon. Boxed in by the narrow defile, the Seleucids had no room to maneuver, leaving them vulnerable to attack. Maccabee slingers and archers deployed along the sides of the defile opened up with a barrage into the Seleucid ranks before Judah led his men in with swords and knives, sending the Selecuids reeling. (Courtesy of Marshall Editions)

Judah's brother Eleazar, attempting to inspire rebels paralyzed by fear of the Greek war elephants, went after an elephant he believed carried the Seleucid general. Eleazar stabbed the elephant in its belly; the elephant collapsed on him, crushing him to death. (Image of "Eleazar's attempt to kill Antiochus" taken from *The Complete Works of Josephus*, copyright 1981, translated by Wm. Whiston. Published by Kregel Publications, Grand Rapids, MI. Used by permission of the publisher. All rights reserved.)

Naturally secure atop a steep hill, Gamla is protected on all sides by nearly impassable ravines, with the city accessed from the east in a dip in the terrain. Note the reconstructed round tower in the photo's center. (Author's collection)

Depiction of the battle at Gamla. Boulders launched from ballistae crashed down with great force while catapults fired missiles and darts with such intensity that some reached as far as the city's western quarters. Archers swept the parapets clean, allowing the battering rams to approach and smash the city's walls. Assault troops amassed behind protective screens, waiting for a breach. (Gamla Excavation Project)

Masada, the isolated mountaintop fortress where 967 Jewish rebels held out against Roman Proconsul Lucius Flavius Silva's Legion X *Fretensis* between 72 and 73 CE, was the last vestige of the Jews' revolt against Rome. In a demonstration of their resolve, the Romans completely surrounded Masada and constructed a massive assault ramp up the side of the mountain to reach the rebel compound. Hopelessly surrounded and facing certain defeat, the Jewish rebels holed up on the mountain committed suicide, not out of desperation but rather in a conscious decision to die with dignity as free men. (Author's collection)

Wreckage from the Roman rampage. Building blocks thought by archaeologists to be from the Jews' Temple complex, toppled by the Romans following their suppression of the Jews' revolt against Roman authority. (Author's collection)

View of the lower reaches of the Yarmuk River gorge, in whose upper areas the Byzantines suffered their crushing defeat in 636 CE that left Syria in Muslim control. The area's deep gorges restricted Byzantine defensive movements, allowing the smaller Muslim force to drive a wedge between the Byzantine force, breaking their integrity and leading to total defeat in a bloody battle with heavy losses on both sides. (Moshe Milner, Israel Government Press Office)

As the Holy Land's new rulers, Muslims built the Dome of the Rock on the Temple Mount in Jerusalem as a shrine for pilgrims, but also to rival Christendom's impressive churches. The building's original dome was replaced by the current gold one in a 20th-century restoration. (Author's collection)

View towards the Sea of Galilee from the Horns of Hattin. Tightening their chokehold on the Christians, Saladin's forces set fire to the dry grass and thistle. Hot, thirsty, stressed from the incessant fire from Saladin's archers and now with smoke and heat from the brush fires adding to their misery, some Christian soldiers wandered off in a desperate search for water, only to be killed or captured. (Author's collection)

The Horns of Hattin, a barren plain in the hills above the Sea of Galilee, behind Tiberias, where the Crusaders and Muslims had their showdown. (Author's collection)

Aerial view of the Horns of Hattin (background). The shores of the Sea of Galilee can be seen along the bottom of the photograph, showing how close the thirsty Crusaders were to this fresh water lake. (Moshe Milner, Israel Government Press Office)

View overlooking Mount Gilboa to the valley below. Egypt's Mamluks dealt the Mongols their first defeat on the open ground at Ayn Jalut (Goliath's Spring) at the foot of Mount Gilboa, on September 3, 1260. The valley was an ideal battleground for the two cavalry-based forces. Two millenia prior, Israelite King Saul committed suicide on Mount Gilboa by falling on his sword, rather than face capture by the Philistines. (Moshe Milner, Israel Government Press Office)

Ruins of the Crusader castle at Atlit. Consolidating their hold on power after their victory at Ayn Jalut, the Mamluks systematically destroyed Crusader positions until all that remained was the Templar fortress at Atlit, known as Chastel Pelèrin. It was abandoned in 1291. (Teddy Brauner, Israel Government Press Office)

Ruins of Montfort Castle. After their victory at Ayn Jalut, the Mamluks viewed the remaining Crusaders not only as foreign implants and infidels, but as impediments to full Mamluk hegemony. In their systematic campaign to destroy the Crusaders, the Mamluks besieged the Teutonic Knight's fortress Montfort until it surrendered. (Author's collection)

The Temple Mount in Jerusalem during the Ottoman era. Beyond the city walls is the Dome of the Rock and behind it, to the left, the al Aqsa Mosque. The Dome of the Rock and Al-Aqsa were built following the Muslims' capture of the Holy Land. The Temple Mount is Islam's third holiest site, celebrated as the spot from which the Prophet Mohammed embarked on his night-time visit to heaven. After their victory over the Mamluks, the Ottomans rebuilt Jerusalem's walls and gates, which had been in ruins. (Photographed by The American Colony, Israel Government Press Office)

Aleppo Citadel, Aleppo, Syria. Following their defeat at the Ottoman-Mamluk clash at Marj Dabiq, most of the Mamluk recruits were allowed to flee towards Aleppo. Upon arriving there, the Mamluks found themselves locked out by local inhabitants. When Ottoman sultan Selim arrived at Aleppo, he was hailed as liberator. Selim had earlier boasted that his weakest man would take Aleppo's citadel. Keeping this vow, he sent in an aged clerk to view treasures abandoned there by the Mamluks. (Dick Osseman)

Jerusalem's Tower of David. The minaret of the mosque at the citadel was built by the Ottomans, complementing the mosque built by the Mamluks. Today the entire citadel complex is a museum of the history of Jerusalem. (Author's collection)

French General Kleber at the assault on Acre. Each time Bonaparte sent his forces to breach the walls, Acre's defenders held their ground. In one attack, the French succeeded in penetrating into the city. Acre's defenders withdrew; when the French troops advanced they found themselves in a carefully prepared ambush, where many were cut down in a hail of fire. (The Weider History Group Archive)

Situated on a peninsula jutting out into the Mediterranean Sea, Acre is protected on three sides by the sea. Napoleon's army set about taking the city, but Acre's defenses and defenders proved tenacious, and ultimately the French gave up. Its walls and dry moat can be seen in the photo slightly left and below of center. (Moshe Milner, Israel Government Press Office)

CHAPTER 7

THE KORAN, THE TRIBUTE, OR THE SWORD!

ISLAM'S CONQUEST OF THE MIDDLE EAST, 634 CE

When a lone Muslim Arab warrior reconnoitered Byzantine lines and killed 19 of the 30 men dispatched to challenge him, the Byzantine Army—successors of the great Roman Legions —saw it best to attempt buying its way out of battle. With conquest their aim, the Muslim Arab army would not be deterred. Their response was succinct:

"The Koran, the tribute, or the sword!"

It was July 30, 634 CE, and the two armies were deployed at Ajnadayn along the road between Beit Guvrin and Jerusalem. With the Byzantine offer rejected, battle was now unavoidable. As the two armies formed up for combat, champions from both sides met in duels where the Muslims proved superior by killing several Byzantine officers and champions. Byzantine archers opened the attack with a massive barrage against the Muslims. The Muslims failed to respond, giving the impression they were unprepared for battle against such a modern army. Dressed in a motley assortment of robes and armor and equipped with a range of weapons and gear, the Muslim army lacked the appearance of a serious foe. But their restraint was due not to a lack of conviction or capability but rather to Muslim General Khaled ibn al-Walid's orders not to attack. Known as "the Sword of Allah," Khaled counseled discipline and patience to his men. The Arabian tribesmen were raring to fight, yet Khaled held them back while they absorbed the Byzantine barrage. The men implicitly trusted Khaled, an experienced and highly respected commander. When he determined the timing was right, Khaled finally gave the order to attack. In only two days of battle, the Muslims would break the Byzantine juggernaut.

The prophet Mohammed himself had initiated this *jihad*, or campaign of expansion from the Arabian Peninsula via conquest, but early defeats, the prophet's unexpected death from illness in 632 and then rebellion had proved setbacks. It had all begun in 610, with Mohammed's revelation of faith in, and total submission to, a single God, Allah, who punished evildoers and rewarded the righteous. Empowered to spread God's message, Mohammed converted Arabia's tribes to Islam, and the faith spread rapidly. Following Mohammed's death and the contentious appointment of Abu Bakr as caliph, or successor, to Mohammed, a number of Arabian tribes broke with the *ummah*, or community of followers. The response was heavy-handed; the *riddah* (apostasy) against Islamic authority was crushed, resulting in a powerful, consolidated caliphate. With the rebellion suppressed, the new caliph renewed military campaigning in the name of their faith.

Caliph Abu Bakr told the men that "fighting for religion is an act of obedience to God,"[1] but it was not initially a campaign of religious warriors as the tribes were not necessarily religious at this stage. Motivation may have come from the mundane lure of plunder, as much as in the name of Islam.[2] Even legendary General Khaled seems to have been indifferent towards Islam; he reportedly had his way with captive women on the battlefield following victory, and was said to have bathed in wine—hardly examples of righteousness.[3]

After consolidating power in Arabia by force of arms, the Muslims began moving beyond the Arabian Desert in a campaign of conquest and expansion. Abu Bakr began with the Persian Sassanid Empire's province of Iraq. Under Khaled, who had made a name for himself suppressing the tribal rebellion, the Muslims won a string of victories over the Persians in 633. Confident from his army's successes, the caliph set his sights on Syria.

Palestine[4] was part of Syria, which had become "Byzantine" when the Roman Empire's center of gravity shifted eastward and became the Eastern Roman, or Byzantine, Empire. It was Emperor Constantine's personal embrace of Christianity and his instituting it as the empire's official religion during his reign of 306–337 that ushered in the Byzantine period, named for his capital Byzantium in Asia Minor, which he renamed Constantinople after himself. The Roman adoption of Christianity brought Palestine new status as the Holy Land. Palestine prospered. Great edifices, such as the Church of the Holy Sepulcher and Church of the Ascension in Jerusalem, and Church of the Nativity in Bethlehem, were built. Churches and monasteries, many with exquisite mosaics—at which the Byzantines excelled—dotted the landscape, and pilgrims from throughout the empire visited sites associated with the life of Jesus.

Focused on the Persian Sassanids, the Byzantines did not fully perceive the threat emanating from Arabia. The nomadic Arabian tribesmen were known for stealing and pillaging from settled areas before disappearing back into the desert—a reputation that no doubt contributed to Byzantine emperor Heraclius' initial dismissal of the threat they posed. The Romans had fought the Persian empires for over seven centuries, so the Byzantines maintained a wary eye on this traditional enemy and the bulk of Byzantine defenses in the region were concentrated in northern Syria. Only a few years had passed since Palestine and adjoining areas were recovered after 15 years of Persian occupation, and the Byzantines were still securing and reasserting authority in these relinquished territories. The incessant fighting had taken a toll: both empires were exhausted from years of warfare. Ironically, while the Byzantines were rolling back the Persians, Mohammed was forging the power that would burst out of remote Arabia and eventually defeat both empires.

Declaring intentions to "send the true believers into Syria to take it out of the hands of the infidels,"[5] Abu Bakr dispatched four separate forces to Palestine and Syria,[6] each with its own commander and mission. A force entered Palestine north of modern Eilat and moved up the Arava Valley before cutting inland while the other three forces advanced northward up the caravan route on the east side of the Jordan River, one towards Damascus, one intending to take Jordan, and the third advancing on Emesa (now known as Hims or Homs, in Syria). Caravans from Arabia plied the ancient trade route through Syria to Mediterranean ports, so the Arabians were well aware of Syria's fertility. The Byzantines had checked Muslim Arab encroachment in the 629 battle of Mu'ta (in today's Jordan), where a Muslim force in which Khaled commanded was defeated. The battle of Mu'ta was a harbinger of Muslim intentions. As a precaution, Heraclius ordered the fortification of towns and cities in the region, some with permanent garrisons, and appointed military commanders over cities and the surrounding regions—expenses he authorized despite his efforts to reduce defense expenditures. These steps may also have been taken to discourage cities from surrendering to the Muslims, which would bring both a loss of prestige and valuable tax revenue needed by the empire's already strained coffers.

Due to competition for troops on its empire's other exposed borders, the Byzantines faced a manpower shortage on its eastern fringe. Friendly Arab tribes—best known among them the Ghassanids—helped fill the void by guarding the desert frontiers. The Byzantines lacked the resources to maintain permanent frontier garrisons, a limitation that dictated a reactive defense. This meant an enemy would be allowed to penetrate its territory before being met by mobile forces that would expel them. Ironically, as part of Byzantine cost-saving efforts, payments to their Ghassanid allies were cut off, removing one of the first lines of defense. In around 633, the Muslim forces had easily penetrated Byzantine territory and soon had multiple forces operating deep inside. When Muslim Arabs defeated a Byzantine force in early 634 at Dathin near Gaza, Heraclius responded by mobilizing forces from throughout Syria, yet evidently not enough. Some historians say Heraclius allocated an inadequate force of 10,000 men, with heavy reliance on local troops.[7]

In contrast to his personal involvement in leading the campaign that ousted the Persians, Heraclius did not fight in this campaign, perhaps a sign of failing health. Heraclius entrusted command to his brother Theodore, who was experienced from operations against the

Persians. Command may have been shared with another experienced officer named Wardan, commander of Syria's major military base at Emesa. It took two months for the Byzantine force—cavalry and infantrymen trailed by their baggage train and followers—to assemble at Emesa and make its way south, via Palestine's main military base of Caesarea Maritima, to Palestine's hinterland.

Converging on Ajnadayn

The Byzantine army converging on Palestine threatened both the Muslim force operating in Palestine and the three other Muslim forces in Syria. Following developments from Medina, the caliph responded by calling on Khaled to quit his campaigning in Iraq and to assume command of Muslim forces in Syria. Khaled united his dispersed forces by ordering them to Ajnadayn.[8]

"Know that thy brethren the Moslems design to march to Aiznadin, where there is an army of seventy thousand Greeks, who purpose to come against us. . . . As soon therefore as this letter of mine shall be delivered to thy hands, come with those that are with thee to Aiznadin, where thou shalt find us if it please the most high God."[9] Khaled hurried his force across the desert towards Palestine, taking the Byzantine city of Busra en route in mid-July 634. Khaled also made an attempt on Damascus, but withdrew after a short siege.

Camels and horses lent the Muslim forces mobility that, along with their short logistics tail and legendary hardiness and endurance (they were said to be able to survive for weeks on only dates and water), allowed them to quickly deploy and concentrate power. The agile Arabians assembled their force at Ajnadayn by July 24, 634. Armed with lances, javelins, spears, swords, daggers and bows, the Muslims deployed with a center and two wings.

Concentrating at Ajnadayn was a departure from traditional Arab fighting tactics that centered around the desert where the Arabs found refuge. These were no desert raiders; taking on the Persians and Byzantines meant the Muslims must have been a coherent force. Its make-up of tribal units from all over the Arabian peninsula gave the Muslim army inherent structure. They were also well-led, as Khaled's skillful combination of tactics and strategy would prove. But their true strength came from Islam, the force that was forging them into a nation instilled with purpose.[10]

According to doctrine, the Byzantines should have drawn up for battle in two lines, the second a reserve to exploit successes, or alternately to provide support in the event of an enemy breakthrough.[11] Heavily armed cavalry, and infantry with lances or bows, supplemented by local allies, were about to fight the first major battle between the Byzantine Empire and the Muslims in a clash in which the ultimate outcome would change the face of the Middle East and beyond.

Looking across at the Muslim Arab army, whose appearance was anything but uniform, the Byzantines were not impressed. Limited interactions between the disparate peoples had propagated stereotypes of Arabians being primitive and backwards; the Byzantines looked down on them. Though spies had brought back information on the Muslims, and the Byzantines were aware of Muslim victories against large armies in Iraq and over their own compatriots, the Muslims remained an obscurity. Not even a contemporary Byzantine military manual known as the *Strategikon* offered advice on fighting Arabs.[12]

The Byzantines arrayed at Ajnadayn got an early taste of Arabian bravery and resolve when a young Muslim warrior named Dhiraar ibn al Azwar made an aggressive reconnaissance of the Christian camp. While many of his comrades-in-arms wore hardened leather or mail armor and head protection, Dhiraar wore none. Wearing only his loose-fitting trousers and armed with his personal weapons, Dhiraar mounted his horse and approached Byzantine lines. When thirty men were sent after him, Dhiraar hastened back towards his army's lines, with the enemy in hot pursuit. Once they chased him a distance from their camp, Dhiraar spun his horse around and went on the offensive. Fighting with lance and sword, Dhiraar killed 19 of his pursuers; the others broke off pursuit and returned to camp to tell of the fearless and invincible Arab champion who came to be known as the Naked Warrior.[13]

The Byzantines knew how to fight formally organized armies like the Persians, whereas the Muslim Arab army was less conventional. Emperor Heraclius had thus warned his brother Theodore to beware of the Arabs, and avoid engaging in open battle with them. The two sides faced off for a week—time that the Byzantines probably used attempting to divide the enemy coalition, and hoping that the Muslims might possibly tire of campaigning and return home, as they were known to do after past raids. Contemporary Byzantine military strategy counseled such caution over decisive action. When the Muslim Arab army proved unwavering, the Byzantines opted to invoke a common practice of negotiating to avoid battle.

An old bishop approached the Muslim army asking to meet their commander. The bishop pitched to Khaled the Byzantine offer to give each Muslim "a dinar, a robe and a turban; and for you there will be a hundred dinars and a hundred robes and a hundred turbans" if the Arabs would withdraw from Syria.[14] "Ye Christian dogs, you know your option," Khaled immediately responded. "The Koran, the tribute, or the sword!"[15] meaning convert to Islam, pay the submissive *jizya*[16] tribute, or war. "As for the dinars and fine clothes," Khaled reportedly added, "the Muslims would soon possess them anyway, by right of conquest!"[17]

While accounts of the battle are sketchy, the engagement was thought to be unremarkable, with none of the clever maneuvering or stratagem for which the Muslim armies would become known. The Byzantines espoused a massive opening assault with arrows raining down on the enemy to distract their foes until mounted lancers plowed through enemy lines. Apparently the Byzantines' shock assault was either thwarted or somehow failed to deliver its desired effect. After the Muslim Arabs absorbed the opening Byzantine barrage, the two sides fought a conventional battle in which casualties would have been high on both sides. Questionable Muslim sources tell us the Byzantines suffered massive casualties in the tens of thousands while the Muslims were relatively unscathed. With neither side managing to get the better of the other, the Byzantine commander attempted to break the deadlock by means of a ruse to lure Khaled into an ambush. Wardan asked under false pretenses to meet the Muslim commander to discuss peace terms—a classic Byzantine strategy of using cunning and duplicity to win battles. A Christian Arab betrayed the plan to Khaled, and it backfired; instead Wardan was said to be killed when he went to the designated meeting place. With the Byzantines reeling from the death of a senior commander, Khaled ordered his army to attack. Again, it was a physical and exhaustive exchange. When the

Muslims penetrated a gap in Byzantine defenses, Byzantine front-line troops fell back, banking on protection by their rear lines. But the Christians could not coordinate their defense, despite their training in mutual support—perhaps the reliance on local troops had come at the expense of cohesion. Fresh Muslim reserves helped penetrate Christian lines, causing a breakdown of Byzantine resistance. Troops began fleeing the battlefield towards Jerusalem, Gaza and Jaffa in disorganized flight while Muslim horsemen ran them down. Given the battle's outcome, Byzantine accounts are sparse while Muslim sources cite a serious defeat with extremely heavy Byzantine casualties. Muslim historian al-Waqidi put the Byzantine casualties at a highly exaggerated 50,000 versus 450 Muslims.

As Khaled had confidently declared before the battle, the booty—consisting of multiple banners and large crosses of gold and silver, precious stones, silver and gold chains, and suits of the richest armor and apparel—was indeed his by conquest. Adding insult to injury the Muslims offered to sell the booty back to the Byzantines. Also captured were countless weapons that the Muslims would put to use against the Byzantines in subsequent battles. The Muslim victory foreshadowed what would come two years later in the better-known Battle of Yarmuk, the outcome of which resulted in the loss of Syria to *Dar al-Islam*, the House of Islam.

Aftermath

Like so many of his troops, Theodore fled to Jerusalem before making his way north to report the defeat to Heraclius, who ordered his brother imprisoned. The defeat created a vacuum in Byzantine authority in Palestine that gave the victorious Muslims nearly free reign. With Palestine in disarray, the Byzantines assumed a defensive posture. People sought safety in walled cities and towns, which were isolated from each other, resulting in fear and a sense of insecurity.

Receiving reports of the Muslim victory, the caliph encouraged a continuation of the campaign. Khaled's army headed north, taking Tiberias and Scythopolis (Beit Shean/Beisan) before besieging and capturing Damascus. The victorious Muslims imposed only a poll tax on Damascus—these were very generous terms that likely contributed to more surrenders. While many Christians abandoned their homes and fled for safer parts of the Byzantine Empire, the Muslims' unexpected victory was embraced by the many people discontent with Byzantine rule. Syria's Christians—the majority of the population—were alienated from the official Byzantine Church over theological differences, local Arabs shared a cultural connection to the victorious Muslims, and even Jews welcomed the change, despite having brought on the Muslims' wrath when they rejected Mohammed's claim to be a prophet. The Muslims would bestow the special second-class *dhimmi* status on Jews and Christians, tolerating their religions in recognition of their shared heritage.

Seething over the defeat at Ajnadayn, Heraclius was determined to push the Muslims out of Syria. Reallocating forces, the emperor managed to assemble an army claimed to have numbered 100,000 men.[18] Units formed up into brigades and divisions and deployed to Syria intent on overwhelming and destroying the Muslims. Consolidating his forces, Khaled withdrew from Damascus and other areas and concentrated 25,000 men on the left bank of the Yarmuk River gorge where the two armies faced off. In typical Byzantine military fashion, the army did not make any decisive moves nor press its advantages but rather trod cautiously while possibly looking for ways to avoid combat. For nearly two months the two armies sparred until the Muslim Arabs took decisive action on August 20, 636. On a hot summer's day when clouds of dust limited visibility, the two armies came to blows. Muslim maneuvering seems to have split the Byzantine force, whose movements were restricted by the area's deep gorges. It was a bloody battle with heavy losses on both sides, but the smaller Muslim force succeeded in crushing the Byzantines. Only a small number of Byzantine forces survived to report the defeat to Emperor Heraclius.

The Muslims returned to all their earlier conquests vacated before the showdown at Yarmuk. As word quickly spread of the major Byzantine defeat, the Muslim Arabs took Byzantine towns in succession, leaving Syria in Muslim control, save for Caesarea and Jerusalem which both held out for some time. Jerusalem fell in 638, with the city's surrender personally received by new caliph Omar, who had assumed leadership following the death of Abu Bakr.

Heraclius had spent six difficult years the previous decade fighting the Persians to liberate the Holy Land, which he had now lost for Christianity. His desperation could be felt in his parting words: "Farewell, O Syria! What a wonderful country you are for the enemy."[19] Heraclius worked his way back to his capital of Constantinople, where he died in 641, by which time the armies of Islam had taken the Fertile Crescent, Iraq, Syria, Palestine, and Egypt. At its height, the Muslim Empire would stretch from Spain in the west, across North Africa, the Middle East and into Asia. In taking the Middle East, the Muslims destroyed the Sassanid Persian Empire and captured vast territories from the Byzantines. Byzantium regained its balance and was able to halt the Muslim advance on its territory, and its empire survived until 1453.

Over time the Muslims began changing the face of Palestine. Masterpieces such as the Dome of the Rock and Al-Aqsa mosque were built, the provincial capital city of Ramla was established and coastal areas prospered. Ultimately trade routes shifted eastward, away from Palestine, causing decline. When European Christians began to view as sacrilege that the birthplace of Jesus was under Muslim control, Europe would be galvanized to embark on a crusade to free the *terra sancta* from Muslim rule.

Notes

1. Edward Gibbon. *The History of the Decline and Fall of the Roman Empire.*
2. A. A. Vasiliev. *History of the Byzantine Empire, Volume 1, 324–1453* (Madison: University of Wisconsin Press, 1958), p.208.
3. Arthur Goldschmidt Jr. *A Concise History of the Middle East* (Boulder: Westview Press, 1979), p.51.
4. Following a Jewish anti-Roman revolt between 132–135 CE, Roman Emperor Hadrian changed the name of Judaea to Syria Palaestina, or simply Palestine.
5. Gibbon, *The History of the Decline and Fall.*
6. Historians disagree on the actual number of Muslim fighters involved as sources vary from about 1,000 men per army to 7,500.
7. There is no precise account of the size of either the Byzantine or Muslim armies, nor of the battle fought at Ajnadayn. Accounts of the battle come mostly from Arab sources recorded long after the events occurred, and tend to be biased. Arab historian al-Waqidi's descriptions of the early Islamic campaigns were written more than a hundred years later, and his works have been considered literary rather than history. For example, al-Waqidi put the Byzantine forces at 90,000. Sources provide figures that vary wildly: 10,000–45,000 Muslim combatants

versus 10,000–90,000 Byzantines. Arab sources tend to exaggerate in order to glorify the Muslim victory. See A. I. Akram. *The Sword of Allah—Khaled bin Al-Waleed*. October 1969.

8.According to Israel Antiquities Authority Shephelah region expert Yehuda Dagan, the battle site has not been precisely located. Expert assessments put the site somewhere between Beit Guvrin and Ramle.

9.Gibbon, *The History of the Decline and Fall*.

10.Fred Donner. *The Early Islamic Conquests* (Princeton: Princeton University Press, 1981).

11.*The Strategikon*, Byzantine military manual.

12.Walter E. Kaegi. *Heraclius. Emperor of Byzantium* (Cambridge, UK: Cambridge University Press, 2003).

13.Khaled was angry at Dhiraar for losing sight of his reconnaissance mission, to which Dhiraar responded that concern over upsetting his commander prevented him from taking on the 11 Byzantines who escaped.

14.Akram. *The Sword of Allah*.

15.Gibbon, *The History of the Decline and Fall*.

16.A tax levied on non-Muslims.

17.Akram. *The Sword of Allah*.

18.Bernhard Bischoff and Michael Lapidge. *Biblical Commentaries from the Canterbury School of Theodore and Hadrian* (Cambridge, UK: Cambridge University Press, 1994), p.39.

19.Moshe Sharon, "The History of Palestine from the Arab Conquest Until the Crusades (633–1099)" in Michael Avi-Yonah (ed.). *A History of the Holy Land* (Jerusalem: Steimatzky's Agency Ltd. 1969). p.196.

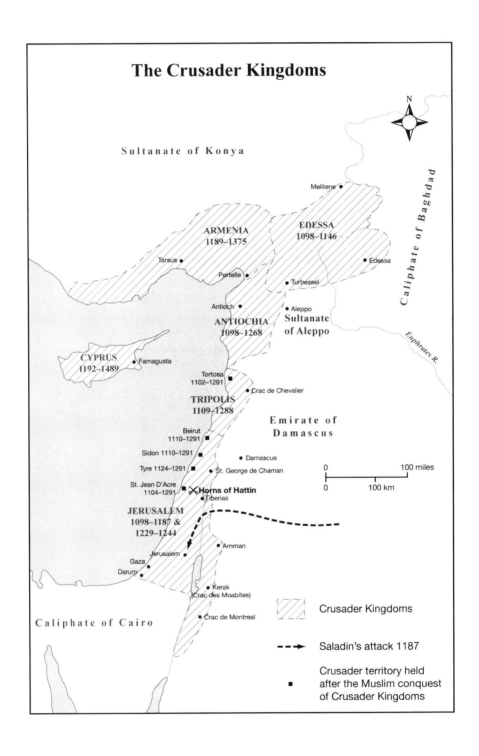

The Crusader Kingdoms

Sultanate of Konya

Caliphate of Baghdad

Melitene

ARMENIA
1189–1375

EDESSA
1098–1146

Tarsus

Edessa

Portelle

Turbessel

Antioch

Aleppo

ANTIOCHIA
1098–1268

Sultanate
of Aleppo

CYPRUS
1192–1489

Famagusta

Euphrates R.

Tortosa
1102–1291

Crac de Chevalier

TRIPOLIS
1109–1288

Emirate of
Damascus

Beirut
1110–1291

Sidon 1110–1291

Damascus

Tyre 1124–1291

St. George de Chaman

0   100 miles

St. Jean D'Acre
1104–1291

Horns of Hattin

0   100 km

Tiberias

JERUSALEM
1098–1187 &
1229–1244

Amman

Gaza

Jerusalem

Darum

Kerak
(Crac des Moabites)

Caliphate of Cairo

Crac de Montreal

Crusader Kingdoms

Saladin's attack 1187

Crusader territory held
after the Muslim conquest
of Crusader Kingdoms

CHAPTER 8

IMPALED AT THE
HORNS OF HATTIN

TWILIGHT FOR THE CRUSADER KINGDOM
OF JERUSALEM, 1187

When the Crusader host stopped for the night far from both the springs where they had last watered on a scorching hot summer's day, and from their destination of Tiberias, Lord of Galilee Raymond knew it did not bode well. Galloping back from the army's vanguard, Raymond exclaimed:

> *"Alas, Lord God, the battle is over! We are dead men.*
> *The kingdom is finished!"*

M ore than 450 years passed after the fall of the Holy Land to the Muslims before Christian Europe took decisive action to wrest back control of the Christian holy places. Europe's masses were riled up with fabricated accounts of persecution of Christian citizens and religious pilgrims by Muslims. Joining the holy expedition, known as a crusade, would fulfill religious duties and absolve the participant from sins, along with bringing the mundane benefit of spoils. For those who fell, a glorious death with heavenly rewards was promised.

After the first wave, known as the People's Crusade, was easily defeated at the hands of the Turks in 1096, the professional knights and soldiers that followed successfully reached the walls of holy Jerusalem in 1099, three years after setting off from Europe. On July 15, 1099, after a five-week siege, Jerusalem—the city in which Jesus had died—fell to the Crusaders.

The victory was celebrated with a murderous rampage. Hell-bent on destruction, the Crusaders attacked Jerusalem's residents with a vengeance. "Thousands of non-combatant Jews, Muslims, and even native Christians were beheaded, shot with arrows, thrown from towers, tortured, or burned at the stake. Human blood flowed knee-deep in the streets of Jerusalem."[1]

The Crusaders set about transforming Jerusalem from a Muslim into a Christian city. They restored the Church of the Holy Sepulcher, believed to be the site of Jesus' crucifixion and burial, and built or rebuilt churches, hospitals and hospices. The Temple Mount—Islam's third holiest site, celebrated by Muslims as the spot from which the Prophet Mohammed embarked on his night-time visit to heaven—was declared Christian, and a great golden cross erected above the Dome of the Rock.

Word of such indignities reached Arab capitals, leading to outrage. An Egyptian force challenged the Crusaders the following month but was firmly defeated near Ascalon (Ashkelon), securing the Crusaders' place as the new masters of Jerusalem.

Groups of Crusader knights seized control of interior regions, expanding and reinforcing their rule. With more towns and cities captured, the Franks, as the Crusaders were known to the Muslims, consolidated their power and secured their borders, establishing the feudal Kingdom of Jerusalem, with the holy city as its capital. While many of the knights returned home, a stream of immigrants arrived in the new Christian kingdom. City walls and defenses were beefed up, and massive stone fortresses were built to safeguard highways, frontiers and interior regions. Despite a Muslim call for *jihad* against the foreign invaders in *Dar al-Islam,* divisions and rivalries among Muslim leaders prevented them from destroying the fledgling Crusader kingdom, whose borders would ultimately encompass modern Israel, Lebanon, Sinai, Jordan, and Syria.

The Crusaders suffered some reverses, most notably the fall of the Crusader principality of Edessa to Zengi, a Turkish emir, in 1144. But the Crusaders would find their nemesis in an ambitious Kurd who rose to power in Egypt. Salah al-Din Yusuf bin Ayub, better known as Saladin, would establish the power base necessary to challenge the Crusaders. Considered Islam's greatest military leader, Saladin understood that Muslims would first need to be unified before they could defeat the Christians. From Egypt, where he had become vizier, Saladin embarked on a unification campaign that extended his rule to Syria and Iraq by 1183, uniting the provinces into one state with the resources to take on the Crusader Kingdom.

In 1185, a time when the Crusaders were plagued by internecine feuding over succession following the death of the leper King Baldwin IV and threatened by famine, Lord of Galilee Raymond III of Tripoli suggested a four-year truce with Saladin, until new arrivals from Europe would invigorate the kingdom. Raymond's pragmatic approach, approved by the barons, was hindered by the notorious Reynaud de Châtillon, Lord of Oultrejordain, the Crusader territories east of the Jordan River. From the vantage of Kerak fortress in modern-day Jordan, presiding over a trade route between Egypt and Syria, Reynaud raided and pillaged caravans and attacked Muslim religious pilgrims on their way to Mecca. Reynaud's audacity was such that he had led a campaign along the Red Sea that threatened Mecca, the holiest of Muslim cities. Saladin was so outraged by these actions that he vowed never to forgive them. Saladin twice besieged Reynaud's fortress at Kerak but was forced to withdraw both times in face of Crusader relief forces.

Paying no heed to the truce, Reynaud hijacked a massive caravan passing by Kerak in 1186, killing its military escorts, taking the merchants prisoner and confiscating the cargo. Saladin sought to resolve this matter diplomatically but Crusader King Guy, who owed his throne in part to support from Reynaud, had little influence over the unwieldy baron. Reynaud's provocations could not go unanswered, and now Saladin wielded the necessary muscle.

Responding to Saladin's call to arms, troops began pouring in from territories he controlled, growing into the largest army he had ever commanded, numbering 30,000 soldiers, including 12,000 cavalry. Saladin boasted that the "dust it raised on the move would darken the eye of the sun."[2]

Wanting no part of the troubles brought on by his rivals, Raymond of Galilee made an independent treaty with Saladin. This was an affront to King Guy, who had outmaneuvered Raymond for the Kingdom of Jerusalem's throne. The Crusader king threatened to move militarily against Raymond's city Tiberias, which would have amounted to civil war, adding to the already tense situation.

Under his treaty with Saladin, Raymond allowed a Muslim force passage into his lordship of Galilee. At the same time, a delegation including the grand masters of both the Orders of the Hospital and of the Temple (known commonly as the Knights Hospitaller and Knights Templar) were en route to Raymond to arrange a reconciliation between him and the king. Hospitallers, as their name suggests, had originally cared for sick pilgrims before taking on the military role of providing armed escort. Templars, whose name came from their headquarters in the expropriated Al-Aqsa Mosque on Jerusalem's Temple Mount, ensured the safety of Christian pilgrims. These military orders, which combined military and religious life, were a key element in Crusader power.

Having ignored the instructions that they had received from Raymond telling them to wait for the Muslim force to leave Galilee before traveling in the area, the Templars and Hospitallers encountered the large Muslim force at Cresson springs near Nazareth and recklessly attacked, resulting in a complete Crusader rout. One historian described it as a massacre rather than a battle.[3] Holding himself responsible for the deaths of his compatriots, Raymond abrogated his treaty with Saladin and paid homage to the king, which he had previously vowed never to do. The Crusader kingdom was now unified.

Crusader unity was in itself an accomplishment given that Reynaud did not consider himself subject to the king's authority, and the military orders were exempt from all authority save that of the pope. All responded to the royal decree for a general mobilization. Eager for vengeance for the massacre at Cresson, the Hospitallers and Templars contributed all their available knights, leaving only small garrisons to defend their castles. In this critical time, the Christians were feeling the pinch of a manpower shortage brought on by a drop in immigration to the kingdom, so literally all able-bodied men were called to arms. "Not a man fit for war remained in the cities, towns or castles without being urged to leave by the King's order."[4]

Saladin sent reconnaissance units to collect information on the Crusader mobilization and, according to Christian sources, the scouts "laid waste and set fire to vast areas from Tiberias to Bethany . . . up to Nazareth and around Mount Tabor."[5] Saladin's full force crossed the Jordan River south of the Sea of Galilee and established camp. Though he could not sustain a prolonged military mobilization lest his disparate army dissolve, Saladin knew better than to risk attacking the Crusaders where they held the advantage; he would need to draw them out where he could press his advantages. Knowing that a Christian army would undoubtedly come to the city's rescue, Saladin moved against Tiberias, capital of Galilee, on Thursday July 2, 1187. Tiberias held out for only one hour before its garrison, led by the Countess Eschiva, Raymond's wife, yielded the ramparts and city and withdrew to its citadel. Messengers were sent to Raymond and to the king entreating them to "send help at once or we shall be taken and made captive."[6] Leaving a small force to maintain the siege, Saladin moved the bulk of his army to Kfar Sabt in the hills above Tiberias.

In response to Saladin's move on Tiberias, Crusader King Guy held a war counsel, where Christian unity proved short-lived. Given the Muslims' unprecedented cohesiveness and power, and—no less important—the intense summer heat, Raymond called for restraint, suggesting Saladin's army be allowed the prize of Tiberias as a way of buying time. Christian reinforcements were promised from Antioch and he also figured that the Muslim army would soon tire of campaigning, disperse and return home.

"Tiberias is my city and my wife is there," Raymond began. "None of you is so fiercely attached, save to Christianity, as I am to the city. None of you is so desirous as I am to succor or aid Tiberias. We and the King, however, should not move away from water, food, and other necessities to lead such a multitude of men to death from solitude, hunger, thirst and scorching heat . . . "[7] King Guy was convinced by this sincere, sound advice.

Reynaud de Châtillon and the influential military orders wanted to fight. Led by Grand Master of the Knights Templar, Gerard de

Ridefort, this camp rejected a non-militant approach as shameful and suggested that King Guy and Raymond were cowards. Guy had been criticized four years earlier in 1183 when, despite the encouragement of Reynaud and the military orders, he opted not to attack a numerically superior Muslim army at the Pools of Goliath (Ein Harod/Ayn Jalut). His restraint had earned him a reputation for weakness and caused him to be deposed as Crusader King Baldwin's regent. Not to face off against Saladin at this time would go counter to the momentum for war. The entire kingdom had been mobilized, and mercenaries hired and paid with a special treasury deposited by King Henry II of England. There was no backing down. Seeing an opportunity to restore his image, the fickle king decided to commit the Crusader army.

Hattin

The Crusader force of 1,200 knights and 20,000 infantrymen and light cavalry assembled at Sepphoris (Zippori), where they had the advantage of springs and pasture for their horses. It was the finest army of Christendom's kingdom in the Holy Land, with the cross emblazoned on each fighting man's tunic, shirt or shield. The Bishop of Acre carried the kingdom's holiest relic: a fragment of the True Cross on which Jesus had been crucified, brought to provide inspiration and providence.

The next morning the Crusaders set out in the repressive heat via the northern route towards besieged Tiberias, some 18 miles (30 km) away, down in the Sea of Galilee basin. Despite his opposition to confronting Saladin, Raymond led the army's way as the enemy was being engaged in his lordship and the custom was for the baron of the lordship to lead the first division. The deployment for the march called for the royal battalion (commanded by the king) and the battalion of the Holy Cross to come next, with Reynaud and the military orders forming the army's rear guard. With each knight requiring several horses to carry himself and his equipment, and assistants who prepared him for battle and helped him mount his sturdy horse, the Crusader army and its accompanying train was huge.

Closely following Crusader movements, Saladin moved his force towards the hills of Hattin, where the road begins its descent towards the lake, and dispatched mounted archers to harass the Crusaders. In swift attacks, Muslim archers descended on the Christians, unleashing volleys of arrows before quickly retreating, vanishing as rapidly as they had appeared. Each attack brought death to more men and horses, sowing fear in the Crusading army, slowing their advance and harming morale. With the heat, their thirst, and continual harassment wearing down the Crusaders, progress was slow.

By afternoon, the Christians were close to the Horns of Hattin, where two peaks (the Horns) rise above a barren plain in the hills above the Sea of Galilee, behind Tiberias. Harried by Muslim archers throughout the day, the Templars could go no further; King Guy gave orders to stop and establish camp where they were, halfway to Tiberias.

Raymond knew their precarious location would not bode well. He galloped back from the front crying: "Alas, Lord God, the battle is over! We are dead men. The kingdom is finished!"[8]

Saladin's forces took the springs where the Crusaders had last watered en route, cutting off the possibility of returning to them. The Muslim army closed in and surrounded the Christians during the night, blocking their option of retreat. Parched with thirst after a day of marching in the intense summer heat, Crusader morale was not good. Hearing the Muslims all around them made it worse. Saladin remained awake all night seeing to logistical matters; he was leaving nothing to chance. Saladin had fought battles and led campaigns against the Crusaders over the previous decade, yet victory had eluded him. This time victory was within reach. Not only did Saladin have the Crusader army surrounded, but they were on hilly terrain that limited the effectiveness of their heavy cavalry. Furthermore, while the Crusaders were parched with thirst, Saladin's forces had access to ample fresh water.

Saladin's presence inspired his men, who were strengthened by the sight of him. The Muslim leader personally commanded his army's center, with his nephew Taqi al-Din commanding the right wing and Muzaffar al-Din commanding the left. Tightening their chokehold on the Christians, Saladin's forces set fire to the dry grass and thistle. The cordon around the Franks was said to be so complete that not even a

cat could get through. Hot, thirsty, stressed from the incessant fire
from Saladin's archers, and now with smoke and heat from the brush
fires adding to their misery, some Christian soldiers wandered off in a
desperate search for water, only to be killed or captured.

After their miserable night, the sun rose over the heights across the
Sea of Galilee, its sweltering heat beating down on the battlefield,
prolonging the hell the Crusaders had been enduring since leaving
Sepphoris the previous day. Saladin's archers unleashed an intense barrage of arrows into the Crusader camp. The Muslims were armed with
400 loads of arrows, plus a further 70 camel-loads. One calculation
put the total at more than one and a quarter million arrows in the
Muslim arsenal.[9] The Christian foot soldiers, with only light armor,
suffered the brunt of the Muslim attacks. The knights were well-
protected in their long-sleeved chain-mail coats, mail hoods topped
with iron helmets, mail gloves and leggings, and shields, but their
mounts were not. Muslim chronicler Ibn al-Athir described: "The
Muslim archers sent up clouds of arrows, like thick swarms of locusts,
killing many of the Frankish horses."[10] Killing these specially bred
horses in battle effectively neutralized the knight, who could not easily
remount a replacement while weighed down by his 70–90lb (30–40kg)
suit of armor. While providing much-needed protection, the complement of armor and protective under- and outer-garments was unbear-
able in the summer heat.

The king's brother Amalric, the Constable, began marshaling the
forces. Lingering flames from the still-burning brush and scrub bore
down on the demoralized Crusaders, their heat accentuating the
soldiers' thirst. Saladin's secretary chronicling the battle described the
Crusaders as panting dogs.[11]

Daylight revealed how precarious the Crusaders' situation had
become. Surrounded, under constant barrage, hot, thirsty, afraid,
with their eyes burning from smoke and sweat, a breakdown in discipline was almost inevitable. At some point, the bulk of the infantry,
desperate for water, broke ranks and fled in an ill-fated attempt to
break through Muslim lines and reach the lake below them. The
Muslims contained them, corralling them up a hill. The knights and
infantry had a symbiotic relationship, reliant on one another. The
king and the bishops pleaded with them to return, to no avail. With-

out the knights' protection, the Muslim cavalry was free to ride the infantry down, killing and capturing large numbers of men. A Christian source recounts: "Thousands and thousands of Syrians were charging at the Christians, shooting arrows and killing them."[12] Crusader foot soldiers dropped their weapons and willingly surrendered themselves.

So pitiful was the Christian predicament that five of Raymond's knights purportedly went to Muslim lines begging them to attack, preferring death in battle to the torture of dying from thirst. They may have had ulterior motives given what would transpire.

Though the Muslims were a more agile force, with mobility that limited the effectiveness of the Crusader knights' charge, the king ordered Raymond and the vanguard to attack. A knights' charge was a potent weapon. Just the sight of him mounted on his horse with his armor, shield, sword, and lance was fearsome and intimidating. The weight of his armor and the momentum of his heavy steed made blows from his lance, broadsword, mace or battle axe all the more lethal. A close-formation charge would smash through enemy formations. Crusader infantry would follow on the knights' heels, finishing off those knocked from their horses, trampled or pushed aside in the knights' wake.

When the king gave the order to attack, Raymond and the knights charged. With the Christian knights rapidly approaching their lines at a gallop, the Muslims responded by simply opening their ranks, allowing the Franks to pass through, and then closed their lines behind them.

Some Christian sources claim Raymond's charge was a tactical break-out from encirclement, others describe it as an escape from impending defeat. Whatever the motive, Raymond and his knights were cut off from their compatriots, and in grave danger. Besieged Tiberias was too dangerous a destination, so they fled north to safety in Tyre, Raymond abandoning his wife and Tiberias to their fates. However, Raymond had previously established a trust with Saladin; he and the sultan had exchanged gifts, so his escape may have been pre-arranged. Raymond's wife, the Countess, was later given free passage by Saladin to join her husband, who would take ill and die a few months later.

Cut off as they were from their ground troops, the mounted

Christian knights were denied the benefit of the infantry's protective screen against enemy cavalry, and foot archers, who kept Muslim archers at enough of a distance that they couldn't attack the cavalry. "Enemies sprang up on every side," one of the sources describes, "shooting arrows and killing them."[13]

Capitalizing on the flight of the Crusader infantry, Saladin became more aggressive, sending his cavalry on repeated charges against the Christian knights, wearing them down. The Christians pulled back to the Horns of Hattin, where some ruins offered protective cover. The king's red tent was pitched towards the summit, and more tents set up as obstacles to thwart Muslim attacks. Saladin moved in for the kill, unleashing his cavalry in an uphill attack towards the Crusaders' royal tent.

The remaining knights closed ranks around the tent to defend King Guy and the relic of the True Cross. Despite their difficult circumstances, the Crusader knights mustered a cavalry charge whose power was augmented by the momentum of attacking downhill. Focusing on the inviting target posed by the concentration around Saladin's tent, the Crusader charge threatened the Muslim center where Saladin commanded the action, nearly overrunning them. Nervously tugging at his beard, Saladin encouraged his troops to rally for an uphill counterattack that forced the Crusaders back. The Crusaders charged again. Saladin rallied his men; the Muslims again fought their way uphill.

The dwindling numbers of knights fought on foot in a steadily shrinking ring until they were simply overwhelmed. The king's tent and standard collapsed, and the relic captured, perhaps more of a blow to the fighting men than the capture of their king. Christians surrendered by the thousands; dead and wounded lay on the battlefield. Arab chronicler Ibn al-Athir wrote: "When one saw how many were dead, one could not believe there were any prisoners, and when one saw the prisoners, one could not believe there were any dead."[14]

As Saladin's men began rounding up survivors, they found many of them too exhausted to surrender. Grasping the extent of his victory, Saladin raised his eyes to heaven and thanked Allah.

A tent was set up for Saladin, who sat drinking water cooled by ice brought from Mount Hermon while the surviving Christian leaders were rounded up and brought before him. Weary from battle, parched from thirst, and fearful of what would become of them, King

Guy, Reynaud de Châtillon, Gerard de Ridefort and other lesser barons stood before Saladin. The Muslim leader greeted them graciously, offering King Guy a drink from his goblet, a gesture that according to Muslim hospitality meant that his life would be spared.

After quenching his thirst, the king handed the goblet to Reynaud—Saladin's sworn enemy, who stood beside him. Saladin knocked the cup to the ground. Some accounts purport that Reynaud, in a final act of bravado, defiantly slandered the Prophet Mohammed. Saladin drew his sword and beheaded the arrogant knight on the spot, and then rubbed some of Reynaud's blood on his own face as a sign of vengeance done. Saladin then reassured the startled Crusader king and his other captives and gave orders for them to be treated well. Saladin's mercy toward defeated enemies was intimidating as it demonstrated that he had nothing to fear from them.[15] Those who could afford to pay were ransomed, leaving the surviving common soldiers to be force-marched to the Damascus slave markets and sold off. King Guy was later released under oath.

Saladin's mercy did not apply to the 230 captured knights of the military orders, whose belligerency and reputation among the Muslims for being untrustworthy warranted that each Templar and Hospitaller be executed. All were summarily beheaded, save for Templar Grand Master Gerard de Ridefort, who later gained his freedom by collaborating with Saladin to secure the surrender of the Templar fortress at Gaza.

Soldiers wishing death rather than a life of slavery in the service of infidels claimed they were Templars. Denied by Christian sources, a handful of surviving Christians apparently were spared by accepting an offer to convert to Islam. Their supposed descendants survive to this day as the Salibiyya (Crusader) tribe in north Arabia.[16]

Aftermath

Saladin moved his army away from Hattin, leaving the battlefield full of rotting corpses. A Christian chronicler wrote: "throughout the three following nights, while the bodies of the holy martyrs still lay unburied, rays of divine light shone clearly above them."[17] Despite the holy spin put on the battle, the reality was that the greatest army the Crusaders had ever fielded had been decimated, its leaders killed or captured, and the relic of the True Cross lost. Arab chronicler Ibn al-Athir wrote: "Never since their invasion of Palestine had the Franks suffered such a defeat."[18] Saladin ordered a Dome of Victory erected at the battle site to commemorate the event.

Tiberias' garrison surrendered to Saladin, the first of a series of Crusader cities and towns to surrender or fall over the next few weeks. Having thrown all their forces into the showdown, the Christians had no reserves to call upon; nearly the entire Crusader kingdom fell to Saladin in short order, culminating in the capture of Jerusalem on October 1, 1187. Only Tyre and a handful of Crusader fortresses held out.

Saladin's army entered the holy city and immediately began restoring Jerusalem's Muslim face, epitomized perhaps by the dismantling of the gold cross from the Dome of the Rock.

The defeat of the Kingdom of Jerusalem came as a shock to Europe. Pope Urban III was said to have died of grief upon hearing the news. Guilt over allowing the kingdom to fall provided the impetus for a new crusade, led by three of Europe's kings. In the spring of 1191, Richard I, King of England, known as Richard the Lionheart, arrived in the Holy Land at the head of the Third Crusade.

Richard's forces would defeat Saladin in battles at Arsuf and Jaffa in 1191 and 1192, recovering coastal territories previously in Crusader hands. However, he understood that without an accommodation with Saladin, there would be no quiet, and he might have to remain in the Holy Land indefinitely. Richard never even attempted to take Jerusalem; he sought a treaty. In 1192 the Peace of Ramla was concluded, acceding Palestine's coast to the Crusaders while Jerusalem remained Muslim, although Christian access to its holy places was guaranteed. Having previously sworn to see Jerusalem only as its conqueror, Richard refused to visit the holy city. Five subsequent crusades followed, but none was remarkable, as the Crusader period by and large had come to an end with Richard's treaty with Saladin, although the Christian kingdom managed to maintain its holdings along the Mediterranean coast for another hundred years.

Saladin died in 1193 having achieved the goal of liberating Jerusalem. The dynasty he founded, known as the Ayyubids, named after his father Ayyub, ruled for nearly 60 years, with lands stretching from North Africa to the mountains of Armenia. It is a tribute to his character that he is held in high regard in both western and oriental sources.

The final end for the Crusaders came with the fall of Acre in 1291 to the Mamluks, former slave warriors who ruled Egypt at the time, whereupon the remaining Crusader holdouts abandoned their positions in favor of Cyprus, bringing an end to the Latin Kingdom's two-century reign in the Holy Land.

Notes

1. Arthur Goldschmidt Jr. *A Concise History of the Middle East* (Boulder: Westview Press, 1979), p.87.

2. "The Horns of Hattin," www.website.co.uk/knights_templar/templar4_7.html

3. Runciman, p.453.

4. Joseph Stevenson (ed.). *De Expugatione Terrae Sanctae per Saladinum*, [*The Capture of the Holy Land by Saladin*], Rolls Series, (London: Longmans, 1875), translated by James Brundage, *The Crusades: A Documentary History*, (Milwaukee, WI: Marquette University Press, 1962), pp.153–159, at www.fordham.edu/halsall/source/1187hattin.html (accessed March 14, 2011).

5. Stevenson. *De Expugatione.*

6. Stevenson. *De Expugatione.*

7. Stevenson. *De Expugatione.*

8. Stevenson. *De Expugatione.* French accounts and Ernoul the Frank blame Raymond for advising the king to halt the advance and to establish camp where they were.

9. Smith, John Masson, Jr. "Ayn Jalut: Mamluk Success or Mongol Failure?" *Harvard Journal of Asiatic Studies* (Vol. 44:2, December 1984), p.322.

10. Silvia Rozenberg (ed.). *Knights of the Holy Land. The Crusader Kingdom of Jerusalem* (Jerusalem: The Israel Museum, 1999), p.153.

11. Elizabeth Hallam (ed.). *Chronicles of the Crusades* (London: Weidenfeld & Nicolson, 1989), p.158.

12. Stevenson. *De Expugatione*

13. Stevenson. *De Expugatione*

14. Kenneth Czech, "City Taken and Retaken." *Military History* (February 1984).

15. William Hamblin. "Saladin and Muslim Military Theory" in B. Z. Kedar (ed.). *The Horns of Hattin: Proceedings of the Second Conference of the Society of the Crusades and the Latin East* (London, UK: Variorum, 1992), pp.228–38: p.237.

16. John J. Robinson. *Born in Blood: The Lost Secrets of Freemasonry, Vol. I.* (M. Evans, 1989).

17. Hallam, *Chronicles.*

18. Czech, "City Taken and Retaken."

CHAPTER 9

WA ISLAMAH! WA ISLAMAH!

MAMLUKS STOP THE MONGOL HORDE, 1260

As the Egyptian Mamluk army arrived and deployed at Ayn Jalut in northern Palestine on September 3, 1260, the Mongols were undaunted. The Mongols had already met and defeated many a formidable army, from Asian warriors to heavily armored European knights. To throw the Mamluks off balance before they could take any initiative, the Mongols, who were already deployed at Ayn Jalut, immediately went on the offensive. Seeing the command flag signaling the attack, mounted archers charged the Mamluk forces and unleashed an initial barrage from their deadly recurved composite bone and wood bows, said to be superior to all other contemporary bows in accuracy, force and range. Unit after unit galloped at the Mamluks, firing arrows from short range. As each wave galloped away to prepare another charge, a subsequent wave immediately came forward and unleashed a salvo in a blitz that threw the Mamluks off-balance. This was precisely the Mongol plan, with the mounted archers softening up enemy formations with their opening onslaught until their armored comrades in tough boiled leather armor charged in on their mounts for the kill.

Recoiling from the ferocity of this initial onslaught, the Mamluk lines wavered. Confusion broke out in the Mamluk ranks as the Mongols pounded them with this well-orchestrated lightning attack. The Mamluks were getting their first taste of the Mongols' character-istic organization, speed and ferocity, justifying the anxieties many Mamluks had going into this.

The Mongols had never been defeated, and they were heading towards Egypt, leaving destruction in their wake. With the Mongols' hatred for Islam, the future did not bode well for the Mamluks. Looking to Baghdad, the Mamluks could see their likely fate if they submitted to the Mongol advance. Much of Baghdad lay in ruins following its defeat. The city had suffered heavily in its resistance against the Mongol siege and assault, then after its fall in February 1258, Baghdad was sacked and pillaged. This cultural and intellectu-al center's schools, libraries, mosques and palaces were destroyed. The Mongols moved in and occupied Baghdad, where they committed horrible atrocities. Nearly the entire Muslim population—numbering in the hundreds of thousands—was killed. The ruling caliph and the entire Abbasid family were executed, bringing an end to the once-glorious Abbasid Empire. Such was the Mongol treatment of those who refused to submit.

Nomads from the Eurasian steppe, the Mongols had emerged as a new force on the horizon in the thirteenth century. It was Genghis Khan (1167–1227) who united the scattered Mongols into a strong tribal confederation that he called the "Great Mongol Empire." And great it was, as it became the largest empire ever in history, stretching across China, Russia, Central Asia and into Europe. Though referred to as "barbarians" or a "horde," Mongol conquests could not have been achieved without brilliant organization and military skill.

With hardy horses and basic yet superb quality weapons of bows, arrows, and axes that each warrior fashioned with his own hands, the Mongols perfected tactics of harassment, attack, evasion against coun-terattack, pursuit, and encirclement. Successful execution required a high degree of organization and cooperation, aspects in which the disciplined, orderly, and efficient Mongols excelled.

However, their reputation was scarred by their brutality in laying waste to areas they conquered. Tens of millions of deaths are attributed to them, even though the intention may have been to frighten future targets of their aggression into easy submission. Travelers in Mongol-captured territory reported destroyed towns and mounds of human bones as a common sight.

The Mongol invasion into what is today known as the Middle East was led by Hulegu, a grandson of Genghis Khan. Departing Mongolia in 1253, Hulegu's forces took Persia (Iran) in 1256 and Iraq in 1258 before moving against Syria. In January 1260, Aleppo was captured and sacked after a siege; its rulers and commanders either fled to Egypt or joined the Mongols. The Syrian cities of Homs, Hama and Damascus all subsequently fell to the Mongols.

With Syria secured, the Mongols set their sights on Egypt, and it seemed they would easily steamroll over Palestine and into Egypt. Mongol forward elements moved into Palestine—some reaching as far south as Gaza, and Hulegu sent envoys carrying a threatening letter to the Mamluk sultan of Egypt demanding submission. "You should think of what happened to other countries and submit to us," he wrote. "You have heard how we have conquered a vast empire and have purified the earth of the disorders that tainted it. We have conquered vast areas, massacring all the people. You cannot escape from the terror of our armies. . . ."[1]

The Mamluks saw the Mongol advance not only as an existential military threat to Egypt, but an assault on Islam. It was cause for consternation in a country still in disarray following the Mamluk overthrow of their masters, the Ayyubids, whose dynasty had been established by legendary Muslim leader Saladin.

Since the 9th century, young boys chosen for their physical excellence had been brought from Central Asia by the Ayyubid sultans of Egypt and Syria, to be trained, educated, converted to and steeped in Islam, becoming life-long elite Mamluk (meaning "owned") slave-soldiers in service to sultans and senior officers. When Ayyubid Sultan al-Salih died in 1249, the Mamluks, who had become extremely powerful, murdered his son and successor al-Muazzam Turan-Shah and seized power. Internal conflicts marred the new Mamluk sultanate, and there followed a turbulent decade of civil strife and intrigue in Egypt, ending with the murder of the new Mamluk ruler, Aybek. After more unrest, the murdered sultan's most senior Mamluk,

Sayf al-Din Qutuz, emerged as sultan in 1259.

With all this instability, the Mongols had little reason to believe Egypt could withstand invasion. However, despite the disarray, the Mamluks understood the gravity of the situation and were defiant. When the Mongol envoys delivered their threat to the Mamluks, Sultan Qutuz had them killed and their heads hung in the capital—a morale booster for his people. Knowing his actions would likely unleash the fury of the Mongols, the sultan set about uniting the people. Using the banner of holy war as a rallying call, Qutuz was able to enlist the support of influential Islamic scholars. Qutuz raised funds and prepared for a military campaign, all the while consolidating his own hold on power.

Though professional soldiers, many Mamluk *amirs*, or officers, were wary of Sultan Qutuz's combativeness. Unexpected support for the aggressive approach towards the Mongols came from Baybars al-Bunduqdari, previously one of Qutuz's rivals. Due to their combined efforts, the military elite was convinced and the die cast for confrontation with the Mongols. The Mamluk army, its ranks supplemented with Syrian troops who had fled the Mongol onslaught, and auxiliaries, was equipped with the latest weapons and gear including helmets, body armor, an arsenal of bows and arrows, lances, javelins, swords, axes, maces and daggers. Though well-armed and trained, the Mamluks had heard of the Mongols' seeming invincibility, and even as they prepared to embark on this expedition, they were scared.[2]

Mongol plans to invade Egypt in force were derailed when Mongol leader Hulegu received word of the death of his brother, the supreme khan. Hulegu was obligated by Genghis Khan's laws of succession to return to Mongolia to the *Khuriltai*, the congress of nobles, to elect the new *khakan,* or great khan. Hulegu withdrew eastward, taking with him the bulk of his forces, leaving his lieutenant Kitbuqa Noyon in charge with only a small part of the original Mongol expeditionary force. The timing for the departure worked out well, for with the hot summer just around the corner, grass and water would not have been plentiful enough to sustain the large Mongol force, whose horses—several per warrior—relied on grazing for sustenance. But the small force that remained was not adequate to take on the Mamluks in Egypt. Augmented by Georgian, Armenian, and locally recruited auxiliaries, possibly including some Franks, Kitbuqa's force could consolidate Mongol control of Syria and hold the line. Whether Hulegu was truly comfortable with the situation due to the continued disarray in Egypt; was unaware of Mamluk military prowess; trusted Kitbuqa's force could hold its own; or simply had no choice, he withdrew.

News of Hulegu's departure certainly helped impel the Mamluks to action against the vastly reduced Mongol force rather than waiting and possibly facing the full strength of the Mongol war machine. Even so, there were many among the Mamluks who still feared what they were getting themselves into. Sensing this undercurrent of fear, Qutuz had to lecture his reluctant army repeatedly on how crucial their mission was to the survival of Egypt and Islam, not to mention all they risked losing if Egypt were to submit.

Perhaps to reward him for his support (or alternatively, to put him in the line of danger—he was a rival after all), Sultan Qutuz gave Baybars command of the Mamluk vanguard. This force engaged forward elements of the Mongol army that had reached as far south as Gaza during the summer of 1260, and the Mongols pulled back. The main Mamluk force, commanded by Qutuz, caught up with the vanguard and moved northward up Palestine's coast. With Crusaders still entrenched in cities stretching up the Mediterranean coast as well as some inland fortresses which could pose a threat to the Mamluk army, especially if they were to ally themselves with the Mongols, Qutuz made it clear to them that they would regret their actions should they make hostile moves. Still smarting from past defeats at the hands of the Muslims, the Crusaders were wise enough to watch from the sidelines, and even allowed the Mamluk army to camp by Crusader Acre (Akko) for several days. Upon learning the location of the Mamluk encampment by Acre and anticipating its route inland through the Jezreel Valley, Mongol commander Kitbuqa moved his forces southward from their positions in what is today Lebanon's Bekaa Valley. Though the Mongols traveled light, carrying little equipment and making do with few provisions, they moved slowly. Their trademark rapid movement in combat required a large number of horses. Stalwart like their masters, the horses survived by the process of grazing in the wild, which made for slow progress.

The Battle

The two armies met in the Jezreel Valley at Ayn Jalut (Goliath's Spring, or Ein Harod)[3] during the early morning hours of Friday, September 3, 1260. The open ground at Ayn Jalut at the foot of Mount Gilboa, where there was room to maneuver and a plentiful water supply, was an ideal battleground for both the cavalry-based forces. Accounts of the size of the opposing forces and details on the course of battle differ considerably. It is believed the Mamluks had a slight numerical superiority over the Mongols, who were thought to field a 10,000-man unit known as a *tuman*.[4]

Differing, sometimes contradictory accounts make a precise econstruction of the battle impossible. The following account is pieced together working with sources and common Mamluk and Mongol tactics.[5]

Though skilled mounted archers themselves, the Mamluks were hard-hit by the opening attack of the "devil's horsemen," as the Mongols were known. When the Mamluks stabilized the situation and counterattacked, the highly mobile Mongols retreated to the safety of their rear ranks, where men on fresh horses were ready to attack again. Though riding larger mounts and better equipped, the Mamluks quickly tired out their horses in their attempt to close ranks with the Mongols in order to bring their heavy weaponry to bear. Lacking pastureland, Egypt's geography dictated that the Mamluks could not support a large cavalry, and each man had only a single warhorse.[6] This meant that the Mamluks could not hope to catch their attackers, with their abundance of spare mounts. Without the luxury of spare horses, Sultan Qutuz saw they would be doomed if they allowed the Mongols to dictate the terms of battle. They would need to conserve their horses' energy and rely on their expertise in archery. Qutuz ordered his Mamluks to hold steady and calmly fire at the successive waves of Mongol attackers, taking advantage of their training and archery skills rather than futile counter charging.

Reading the Mamluks' failure to pursue them as a sign of weakness, the Mongols again went on the attack. Charging forward in another lightning assault, a rapid succession of Mongol horsemen unleashed their arrows. The Mongol army's right flank began overpowering the Mamluks' left flank. When his forces on this flank began retreating,

Qutuz is said to have climbed on a large boulder and begun shouting "*Wa Islamah! Wa Islamah!* [Oh, Islam! Oh, Islam!]" Seeing their commander so courageously invoking their faith evidently inspired his forces to hold steady and keep fighting. Rallying his troops, Qutuz repeated his orders. The Mamluks held their ground and began firing steadily at the attacking Mongols. Unlike the nomadic Mongols, Mamluks had time for regular individual and large-unit training. Shooting faster and straighter, unleashing deadly long-range fire from atop their stationary horses, Mamluk prowess with the bow began taking a heavy toll on the Mongols, neutralizing their short-range hit-and-run horse archery.[7] When the Mongols halted, the Mamluks went on the offensive with their larger, stronger horses. Qutuz led the charge into the enemy ranks, where he is credited with killing a number of Mongols. In the course of the battle, Qutuz's horse was hit, but the sultan was unscathed.

As the Mamluks were gaining the upper hand, the Mongol force was hit by the desertion of Homs ruler al-Ashraf Musa, a Syrian Ayyub who had gone over to the Mongols (whose practice was to incorporate into their ranks those that had submitted to them). Al-Ashraf Musa's intention to desert with his troops during the battle had been conveyed in advance to the Mamluks. In the heat of battle, when these front-line forces abandoned the Mongols' left flank, the Mamluk right flank plowed through the void and moved on the Mongols' center.

Some modern historians claim the bulk of the Mamluk army laid in wait while Qutuz, leading a small detachment, engaged the Mongols before feigning retreat—drawing them into an ambush.[8] However, the false retreat routine was a known Mongol tactic, casting doubt on claims that the Mongols would fall for their own trick. It was also Mongol practice to send large scouting parties in advance, so they were very likely to have known the true size of the Mamluk force they were facing.

However, whichever version of events is accurate, the results are not in dispute. By day's end, the Mongol army was devastated, with 1500 dead, plus casualties and prisoners. Dead and dying men and horses were strewn about the broad Ayn Jalut valley. Despite the deteriorating battlefield situation, Mongol commander Kitbuqa remained in the thick of battle and was killed.[9] Leaderless, the remnants of the Mongol army fled the battlefield, only to be pursued by vengeful Mamluks led by Baybars. Riding hard on their heels, the Mamluks chased the fleeing Mongols, killing any they could find. A group of Mongols attempted a stand on a nearby hill, but they were no match for the force pursuing them. Others tried hiding in some nearby fields of reeds. When the Mamluks spotted them, they set fire to the fields.[10] Some Mongols did succeed in escaping northward, though Baybars' force pursued them into Syria.

Ayn Jalut was the Mongols' first true defeat. This time, the Mongols were not carrying out their custom of cutting off an ear from each enemy corpse to aid them in counting their victims. Instead, those that lived to tell about it only did so because they had fled for their lives. The Mamluks had routed the army that had brought terror to so many, and about which Hulegu had bragged: "Our horses are swift, our arrows sharp, our swords like thunderbolts, our hearts as hard as the mountains, our soldiers as numerous as the sand."[11]

When news of the Mongol defeat reached Damascus, the local Muslim population rose up against its Mongol occupiers. In disarray following the power transition in their capital, the Mongols were unable to stabilize the collapsing situation in Syria, and power struggles would prevent them from avenging their defeat. The Mongols pulled back, creating a power vacuum that left the Mamluks masters of Palestine and Syria. Though defeated, the Mongols continued to pose a very real threat. The Mamluks' chief opponent over the next half century would be the Il Khanate dynasty established by Hulegu in Persia in 1260. This dynasty would grow from its beginnings in Persia to encompass vast areas from Turkey to Pakistan.

Ironically, Hulegu's state—who had laid waste to Baghdad before the elements under Kitbuqa Noyon were defeated at Ayn Jalut by an army rallied to action on religious grounds to fight the infidel— embraced Islam and adopted it as their state religion in 1300 under Hulegu's great-grandson Ghazan. But not even their conversion to Islam could erase their legacy of ruthlessness in the Muslim lands.

During the march back to Egypt in October 1260, Baybars added another chapter to Mamluk Egypt's decade of turbulence by stabbing Sultan Qutuz to death. His motive may have been disappointment at not receiving Aleppo as a reward for his support and exemplary service in the conflict, or pure calculated ambition. Upon returning to Cairo, Baybars declared himself sultan, assuming the title *al-Malik az-Zakir*, The Triumphant King. Though not its first sultan, Baybars is considered the true founder of the Mamluk sultanate by virtue of his extremely capable leadership and ability to govern. An excellent soldier, administrator and politician, Baybars is credited with reversing Egypt's decline.

Baybars invested in his army's strength, building it up to resist and deter further Mongol attempts. In fact, the Il Khanate would attack Syria a further six times, never successfully. In addition to battling the Mongols, Baybars would direct his attention to another enemy: the infidel Crusaders.

Viewed by Muslims as foreign invaders, the Crusaders were an impediment to full Mamluk hegemony, and could serve as a bridge-head should Europe get ideas of renewed crusade. Beginning in 1263, Baybars turned his forces on the Crusaders in a concerted but gradual effort to drive them from Mamluk territory. One by one, the beleaguered Crusader positions fell.

After Baybars' death in 1277 (purportedly from drinking poison he had intended for a rival), the Mamluks continued their campaign against the Crusaders. With the 1291 fall of Acre, the last major Crusader city in Palestine, the remaining Crusader holdouts abandoned their positions for the safety of Cyprus, bringing an end to the Latin Kingdom in the Holy Land.

Left without any true enemies, the Mamluks prospered. Directing their energies to the arts and culture, they set about building civic works and improving infrastructure. In Palestine, the Dome of the Rock was renovated, and the area around the Temple Mount was built up with madrassas, hostels and charitable institutions to aid pilgrims. Palestine also benefited from Mamluk projects linking Egypt with all parts of the sultanate. Roads and way-stations were built, improving movement, communications and security; it took only four days for post to travel between Cairo and Damascus. Jindas bridge in Lod, the "White Mosque" tower in Ramla and parts of Nimrod's fortress in the Golan Heights all give testament to the Mamluks' building spree. Beyond changing the face of Palestine, these former slaves from the European steppe built their state into the center of Muslim power, wealth and learning that dominated the landscape for 250 years.

Notes

1.David W. Tschanz "History's Hinge Ain Jalut" *Saudi Aramco World* (Vol. 58:4), www.saudiaramcoworld.com.

2."In the light of the relative combat power of both armies . . . the Egyptians feared an unavoidable clash with an equally strong and seemingly invincible Mongol army." Thorau, Peter. "The Battle of 'Ayn Jalut: a Re-examination." *Crusade and Settlement*—Papers read at the First Conference of the Society for the Study of the Crusades and the Latin East and presented to R. C. Smail. (University College Cardiff Press, 1985), pp.236–241: p.237. Smith writes: "The soldiers in Egypt knew the Mongols' record and feared meeting them; many surely evaded doing so." John Masson Smith Jr. "Ayn Jalut: Mamluk Success or Mongol Failure?" *Harvard Journal of Asiatic Studies* (Vol. 44:2, December 1984), p.313.

3.Northwest of Beit Shean and east of Afula, near the modern village of Gidona.

4.Thorau, "The Battle of 'Ayn-Jalut," p. 237, writes: "we may certainly take it for granted that in the time of the confusion and upheavals of the decade 1250–1260 the Egyptian regular army would have numbered no more than 10–12,000. It would thus seem probable that the army, including all the auxiliary units, at Qutuz's disposal in 1260 for his war with the Mongols could not have been stronger than 15–20,000 men." As for the Mongols, Professor Reuven Amitai notes "the figures of 10,000–12,000 give it the most credence, although these numbers are not a certainty." Amitai-Preiss, Reuven. "Ayn Jalut Revisited." *Tarih—Papers in Near Eastern Studies* (Vol. 2, 1992), p.124.

5.Amitai writes: "It is difficult to establish an acceptable and realistic account of the battle because none of the sources gives the complete picture and they often contradict each other; at the same time some events are unclear or completely unreported." "Ayn Jalut Revisited," p.129.

6.Smith "Ayn Jalut: Mamluk Success or Mongol Failure?" p.321.

7.Smith, "Ayn Jalut: Mamluk Success or Mongol Failure?" pp.324–5. With a different view, Professor Amitai wrote: "You overrate the Mamluks. They had just gone through 10 years of political confusion—certainly not conditions for building a regular army." (Personal correspondence)

8.Thorau. "The Battle of 'Ayn Jalut: a Re-examination," p.237.

9.One source (Rashid al-Din) claims he was captured and executed.

10.Amitai-Preiss. "Ayn Jalut Revisited," p.142.

11.Goldschmidt. *A Concise History of the Middle East*, p.91.

CHAPTER 10

OUTGUNNED

Mamluk Cavalry Scorn
Ottoman Firearms, 1516

In a traditional ceremony affirming allegiance, soldiers passed through an arch made of two swords, and Egypt's Mamluk sultan Kansuh al-Ghawri swore his officers to loyalty on the Koran. Not far away, the mighty Ottoman army was deployed with its modern weapons ready for battle. The Mamluks, maintaining their contempt for firearms to the very end, still believed their traditional ways of battle would lead them to victory.

Late in the thirteenth century, groups of Turkish-speaking Muslims in Anatolia were united into a confederation by a minor chieftain named Osman. The Ottomans, as his descendants are known, were militant and expansionist. Legend has it that Osman's sword was passed down to each successive Ottoman sultan with the understanding that they keep up the way of the sword, and most lived up to expectations. Spreading rapidly east and west, over time the Ottoman Empire came to fill the power vacuum created by the decline of the Byzantine Empire. From humble origins, the Ottoman Empire became the predominant power in Asia Minor.

Ottoman strength centered around the elite Janissaries. These imported slave soldiers, carefully selected on the basis of physique and intelligence, were educated, trained and imbued with the tenets of Islam. Well-equipped with modern firearms, the highly disciplined Janissaries were a formidable fighting force. Confined to barracks except during campaigns, the Janissaries' sole purpose and focus was military, ever loyal to the sultan and the state.

The Safavids

The emergence of a new state in Persia under Shah Ismail as-Safawi at the beginning of the sixteenth century challenged Ottoman power. Though both states were Muslim, the Safavids adhered to the Shiite sect whereas the Ottomans were Sunni.[1]

Ottoman eastern Anatolia was populated by a large number of Shiites—an inviting audience to the Safavids. Shah Ismail, an ethnic Turcoman, like much of the population of these Ottoman provinces, reached out to the Shiites with a message of revolt. Difficult to rule on the best of days, the nomadic Turcoman tribes idolized Shah Ismail, undermining Ottoman authority over entire areas of Anatolia. Encouraged by Shah Ismail, insubordination grew into an uprising in 1511.

Ottoman sultan Bayezid was not particularly aggressive in countering this threat. With his sons quarreling over succession to the throne, and with civil war a very real possibility, Bayezid had not been free to focus on the rebellious Shiites. Claiming that stronger leadership was needed to deal with the Safavid threat, Bayezid's son Selim, whose warlike nature was admired by the Janissaries, forced his father's abdication in 1512. By killing his four brothers, their sons, and four of his own five sons, Selim eliminated threats to his power and secured his position. Selim quickly adopted a far more bellicose nature towards the Safavids.

In 1513, the new Ottoman sultan launched a vicious campaign against Safavid supporters in eastern Anatolia, killing thousands of tribesmen. His determination and ferocity were notorious. Mere mention of Selim's name invoked terror, and the sultan became known as "Yavuz"—the Grim. The Safavids could not sit by idly as their supporters were massacred, and ultimately the conflict escalated to war, with the Ottoman and Safavid armies meeting at Chaldiran in

Azerbaijan on August 23, 1514. No match for the artillery and firearm-equipped Ottoman forces, the Safavids were soundly defeated and retreated into the Persian interior.

In the lead-up to Chaldiran, Egyptian Mamluk client Ala al-Dawla of Albistan had refused Sultan Selim's request for assistance as the Ottomans crossed his territory. The Mamluks quietly applauded him for this, fearing Ottoman moves and hoping for an Ottoman defeat to bolster their own position in the Taurus frontier region between the two empires. Consequently, Ala al-Dawla was killed by Selim and his land annexed to the Ottoman Empire in 1515, in clear violation of Cairo's rights. Adding insult to injury, Selim sent al-Dawla's head to Mamluk Sultan Kansuh al-Ghawri along with an announcement of the conquest. With the Ottomans also extending their control over Kurdistan, the balance of power in the region between the Ottomans and Mamluks was shifting in favor of the Ottomans. Kansuh saw that he must react to the Ottoman provocation.

For two and a half centuries, the Mamluks had ruled the Middle East, but by the start of the 16th century their grip had weakened. A deterioration of Mamluk government and other factors had led to internal dissent, exacerbated by external threats, posing serious challenges for the Mamluk sultanate.

Domestically, the Mamluk sultanate had been in a process of steady economic decline since the beginning of the fifteenth century. Egypt had been hit by plague, drought, famine, and war, all of which had taken their toll on the economy. Falling revenues for the government meant less money to distribute, and this led to insubordination among the Mamluk recruits, who had become quite greedy. By imposing high taxes, debasing the currency and carrying out mass confiscations, Sultan al-Ghawri was able to supplement the state's coffers enough to appease his soldiers, for the sultan knew his survival depended on keeping the men in arms happy. But his actions depressed the economy and angered and alienated the populace.

Once the bulwark of stability in the central Muslim world, the Mamluk sultanate now found itself threatened by both Portuguese maritime encroachment and aggressive Ottoman expansion. After rounding the Cape of Good Hope in 1497, the Portuguese established themselves in the Red Sea. The discovery of an all-water route around southern Africa replaced the taxable land route that passed through Egypt—a serious blow to the Mamluk economy that aggravated their financial troubles. Mamluk excesses have been blamed for the Portuguese search for a way of bypassing Egypt.

In the face of the Portuguese threat, the Mamluks strengthened coastal fortifications and built a naval fleet, which the Portuguese sank in 1509. The Mamluk sultan turned to the Ottomans for assistance. Angered by Portuguese support for their Safavid enemy, the Ottomans sent munitions, naval supplies and advisors to the Mamluks—support that would serve the Ottomans well. Not only did it give the Ottoman advisors their first taste of Portuguese naval power (which they would later face), it also gave them a glimpse of the poor state of the Mamluk army.

A tradition-bound military society, the Mamluks stubbornly resisted the introduction of the modern firearms such as artillery and arquebuses into their ranks. These new weapons threatened their traditional ways, which centered on horsemanship. Cavalrymen through and through, the Mamluks remained loyal to outdated equestrian battle methods employing sword, lance, and bow, from which they derived their pride and feeling of superiority. "Since the arquebus could not be operated from horseback, its adoption would end a very long and deep-rooted tradition and cause a profound transformation of the structure of the army, and hence of the ruling elite."[2]

Shortly after he became sultan, al-Ghawri revived traditional cavalry training exercises and military displays. These exercises strengthened Mamluk reliance on horsemanship as the foundation of their military might. Visually impressive performances meant to showcase Mamluk military power, these exercises and displays proved an intelligence bonanza for the Ottoman envoy in Cairo, who could clearly see that the Mamluks remained loyal to outdated weapons and tactics rather than adopting firearms, which were already used so effectively by the Ottomans.

Renewal of these exercises intensified Mamluk contempt for both artillery and guns. Mamluks regarded equipping a unit with firearms insulting and dishonorable. That the Ottomans had adopted and mastered such weapons only added to the enmity Mamluks already held towards the Ottomans. Mamluks looked down on the Ottomans, denigrating them for having no knowledge of what they considered honorable traditional warfare. The Mamluks thought that their ways could prevail over forces equipped with firearms—a belief which would cost them heavily.

It wasn't that the Mamluks had no guns. Egypt was casting cannon, destined mostly for coastal defenses. Others went to the citadel in Cairo, yet none was directed to any of the provinces bordering the Ottomans. This had nothing to do with Egypt's poor financial situation—it was solely due to the Mamluks' reluctance to adopt firearms. In 1511, al-Ghawri even created a rifle corps known as the "Fifth Corps." To circumvent opposition, members of the Fifth Corps were recruited from outside the mainstream. The arquebusier, or rifleman, was socially inferior to traditional fighting men. Men of the Fifth Corps were paid less than a standard soldier's salary, and their pay came on a special fifth pay session—separate from all other units, from which came their name.[3] Extra expenses incurred in creating, equipping and maintaining this corps were blamed for the chronic shortages in the treasury. Despite the difficult economic situation, al-Ghawri realized their importance and always found funds to pay his new unit. So upset were the Mamluks by the mere existence of the Fifth Corps that relations with the sultan became strained, and rumors of revolt were ripe. The Fifth Corps was deployed on two occasions: guarding Suez against the Portuguese in 1513, and on a voyage to India in 1515.[4] Since those involvements were outside the traditional realm of the Mamluk cavalrymen, use of the firearms-equipped Fifth Corps was condoned.

That the Ottomans had assisted the Mamluks against the Portuguese a few years earlier had been long since forgotten. The Mamluks were seething from Ottoman aggression along their common frontier, and so Egypt began preparations for war during the early months of 1516. Resolved to confronting the Ottomans, "al-Ghawri now assumed the demeanor of a commander in chief who would personally lead his troops to battle against this aggressor."[5] Aleppo's governor, fearful of an Ottoman move against his city, sent a message urging al-Ghawri to hasten his departure from Cairo. Al-Ghawri busied himself with preparations for the campaign, mustering troops and reviewing weapon inventories.

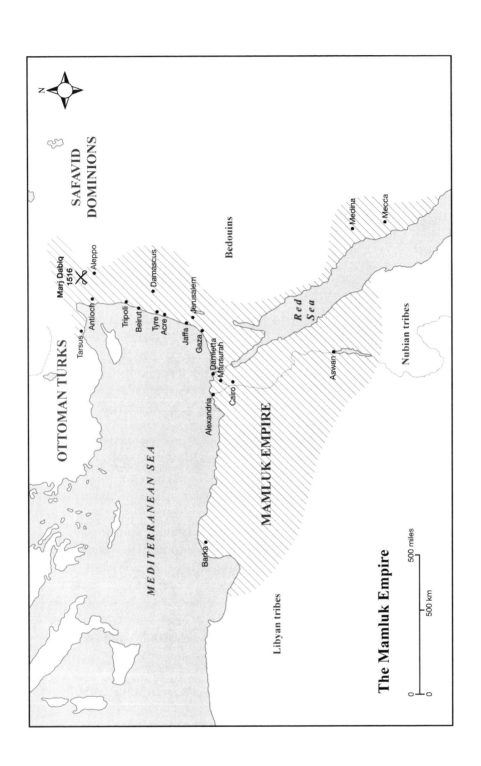

The Mamluk Empire

On April 21, 1516, al-Ghawri issued official orders for the campaign. Less than three weeks later, detachments were on the move. The sultan's battalion set out from Cairo on May 13 to the nearby camp at Ridaniyya on Cairo's outskirts. Al-Ghawri himself set out from Cairo a few days later, joining the forces at Ridaniyya. There he stayed for eight days arranging riding orders and attending to matters in preparation for his absence. The sultan ordered the caliph al-Mutawakkil III, the four chief *qadis* (judges) and other religious figures to join the army on its march to offer prayers for victory. Physicians, clerks and artisans were also ordered to join the campaign. Distinctly absent from the Mamluk host was the Fifth Corps with its guns. Given the poor state of relations between the sultan and the Mamluks because of the Fifth Corps, this decision is understandable.[6] If the expedition resulted in battle, the sultan would have to rely on his Mamluks, and he could not risk divisiveness.

Al-Ghawri appointed his nephew Tumanbay to rule as his deputy. Trusting no-one with his wealth—not even his nephew, al-Ghawri emptied Cairo's citadel of all the gold and silver treasures he had accumulated during his rule beginning in 1501 (all the while claiming financial hardship) and took with him all the funds from the national treasury.[7]

The Mamluk vanguard set out for Syria. Along the way, they were joined by Bedouins conscripted by local sheikhs. On May 24, as al-Ghawri was finalizing his preparations, a courier arrived at Ridaniyya camp with a message from Ottoman sultan Selim calling for peace and offering an explanation about the al-Dawla affair.

After quickly recovering from the blow dealt them by the Ottomans at Chaldiran, the Safavids had raised a new army and had even defeated an Ottoman force. Though Selim had provoked the Mamluks, his main enemy remained the Safavids, whom he passionately hated. Dismissing Selim's overture as a manipulative ruse designed to free the Ottomans to deal with the resurgent Safavids without Mamluk interference, al-Ghawri continued as planned, setting off for Syria with the main Mamluk force the very next day to follow events from that vantage.

Chronicler Ibn Iyas observed that the Mamluk army was smaller and less impressive than it had been in the past. "There were only 944 royal Mamluks and the whole army numbered approximately 5,000 soldiers, or according to another estimate, some 7,000 men."[8] Ibn Iyas described the army's opulent outfittings, but none was modern. And so it was an outdated, ill-equipped army that set off in the spring of 1516 to face the battle-hardened troops of the modern Ottoman army.

The Mamluks' route took them through Gaza, Damascus and Aleppo. Throughout the journey, al-Ghawri had to contend with conflicting information. False reports were being provided by Khayrbak min Yilbay, governor of Aleppo province, about an incursion of Shah Ismail's forces into Mamluk territories and their occupation of other areas.[9] Damascus' Governor Sibay reported no enemy in sight, but warned that economic conditions in his area were not conducive to sustaining a large army. In Damascus, al-Ghawri successfully pressured Sibay to join the campaign.

Al-Ghawri believed that a confrontation between the Ottomans and Safavids was imminent. Adding credence to his belief were assurances brought to him in Aleppo on July 11 by two Ottoman emissaries that the Ottoman dispute was with the Safavids, not with the Mamluks. The Ottoman message requested the Mamluks not to interfere. Still angry at Selim's patronizing attitude towards him in diplomatic correspondence, and certain the Ottomans would next turn on him, al-Ghawri detained the Ottoman emissaries and treated them poorly.

The Ottoman host set off from Istanbul on June 5, its supply train stretching as far as the eye could see, with animal-drawn wheeled carts, carriages, wagons and camels carrying copper cannon, gunpowder, lead, iron and other war materiel. Selim moved his forces to the plain of Malatia, from which he could easily travel eastward towards the Safavids or south towards Syria, according to circumstances.

Along the way, Ottoman spies brought news of the Mamluk army advancing towards Aleppo. Regarding the Safavids as the more dangerous foe, Selim planned to resume the offensive against them. But the Safavids had pulled back, and memories of their successful scorched-earth tactics during their previous confrontation were still fresh in Selim's mind. In mid-July 1516, it was still not clear which enemy would be the Ottomans' priority, but he could not ignore the Mamluk force now poised in Syria. Al-Ghawri's plans of facing an Ottoman army weary and weakened from battle with the Safavids were starting to backfire.

Perhaps sensing the change in Ottoman intent, al-Ghawri now scurried to avoid the prospect of war by releasing Selim's emissaries and dispatching an emissary of his own to the Ottoman sultan carrying a message of neutrality. At this point, Ottoman sources claim that they intercepted a message from al-Ghawri to the Safavids pledging mutual support.[10] It is likely that the Ottomans fabricated the story of the Mamluk message of mutual support to the Safavids as a way of justifying combat against fellow Muslims. It made no sense for al-Ghawri to have entangled himself when he had no interest in fighting at that time.

Outraged by al-Ghawri's alleged duplicity, short-tempered Selim decided on war with the Mamluks. When the Mamluk emissary arrived at Selim's camp carrying al-Ghawri's neutrality offer, his entourage was killed, and the emissary sent back to al-Ghawri with the message: "Meet me at Marj Dabiq!"[11]

The Ottoman army marched towards Aleppo, Syria, and stopped at Marj Dabiq, the plain north of the city. Leaving its treasury and baggage at Aleppo, the Mamluk army marched from the city. Chronicler Ibn Iyas' writings illustrate the glorious manner in which the Mamluks described themselves: "The Sultan called on the army to march out of Aleppo, and the whole army went forth, and they were like shining stars with their arms and prancing? [sic] horses: and every horseman was a match to a thousand infantrymen of the army of the Ottoman Sultan."[12] They went towards Marj Dabiq and set up camp at the adjacent town of Haylan. Al-Ghawri personally inspected the area's layout and deployed his units in preparation for battle.

Marj Dabiq

The Ottoman–Mamluk clash took place at Marj Dabiq on August 24, 1516. Mamluk Sultan al-Ghawri deployed at the head of his army, with the caliph, the four *qadis* and all the religious functionaries at his side, and the Mamluks. On the right flank was the Damascus regiment commanded by its governor Sibay; on the left was Aleppo's Governor Khayrbak and his men. Auxiliary infantry composed of Bedouin, Turcomen, and Kurds supplemented the force. Ottoman sources estimated the Mamluk force at 20,000 to 30,000 men.[13] Against them, Selim fielded a well-trained, well-organized, and experienced body of infantry and cavalry, supported by long-range muskets and artillery. Though awed by the size of the Ottoman army, said to number anywhere from 60,000 to an exaggerated 100,000, the Mamluks were not deterred.[14] They remained confident in the superiority of their traditional ways of war.

At the forefront of al-Ghawri's own contingent were the seasoned veterans—Mamluks purchased and trained by previous sultans. Al-Ghawri's own Mamluk recruits were not battle-tested, so it was not certain how well they would stand firm in combat. With these doubts, the sultan ordered the veterans into battle first. The veterans were clearly more experienced, but he was accused of favoritism, sparing his own Mamluks at the veterans' expense. There is probably some truth to these charges—with intrigue and conspiracy commonplace in the Mamluk political process, it was common for Mamluk sultans, out of paranoia, to purge their predecessors' Mamluks to avoid the prospect of revolt while favoring their own and thus maintaining their support through favoritism and largesse.[15]

The backbone of Mamluk tactics was the cavalry charge followed by rapid withdrawal. Mamluk veterans, followed by the horsemen from Aleppo and Damascus, made the first charge while unleashing a deadly hail of arrows. In this ferocious opening assault, they proved their superior horsemanship by ably maneuvering around the Ottoman artillery, breaking through the Ottoman ranks and driving back the Kurds and Turcomans on the Ottoman flanks. The Mamluks even succeeded in capturing seven Ottoman standards and cutting down some of the arquebusiers. In this close combat, Ottoman firearms could not be brought to bear, and as chronicler Ibn Tulun wrote, "Early in the day the Mamluk army had the upper hand. By noon they were busily engaged in pillage and plunder."[16]

The tide turned when the Ottoman cannon and arquebuses opened fire. The sound of guns firing was deafening, causing panic among the Mamluk men and horses. Artillery projectiles and musket rounds slammed into the Mamluk ranks, causing great numbers of casualties. Experienced after having fought firearm-equipped enemies in Europe, the Ottomans had become quite adept with both artillery and muskets. The Janissaries, formerly the infantry archers of the Ottoman army, had easily taken to firearms in place of traditional weapons. And artillery, though still more of a siege weapon, was proving to be an effective weapon on the battlefield.

"In Marj Dabiq 'every cannon killed some fifty or sixty or a hundred people until that steppe resembled a slaughter-house from the blood,'" wrote Mamluk historian Ibn Zunbul.[17] He noted that most of the dead Mamluks were killed by cannon and arquebus.[18]

Stunned by the heavy losses they had taken in this unfamiliar form of warfare, the Mamluks seemed to realize their predicament. Ibn Zunbul wrote fatalistically, "We cannot resist the Ottoman army and its great numbers and its firearms."[19] "At this critical moment when a resolute advance might yet have won success, Kansuh al-Ghawri and his own Mamluks remained inactive."[20] When he called on his recruits to fall back, the veterans who were bearing the brunt of the fighting felt they were being sacrificed and lost their will. Dissension in the ranks resulted in a loss of cohesion. In the ensuing confusion, Governor Sibay was killed, leaving his Damascus contingent leaderless.

With the situation unraveling, Governor Khayrbak added to the confusion by spreading the rumor that al-Ghawri had fallen in battle. Khayrbak had long been in traitorous contact with the Ottomans, arranging to defect in exchange for a prominent position with them. Keeping his agreement with the Ottomans, Khayrbak broke ranks and withdrew his forces in the midst of battle and fled the field. Khayrbak's treachery was not limited to desertion—he had also been passing valuable intelligence to the Ottomans and misinformation to his own side. In fact, he is said to have played a large role in convincing Selim to move against the Mamluks. Khayrbak's treachery would be well rewarded with his appointment as the first Ottoman governor of Egypt.

With the battlefield situation rapidly deteriorating and groups of his army fleeing, al-Ghawri fell from his horse and died minutes later, apparently from a stroke. His body was whisked away and never found. When the Ottomans learned of al-Ghawri's death, they pressed their attack. After a brief resistance, the Mamluks broke and fled. All the Mamluk standards fell into Ottoman hands, along with baggage belonging to al-Ghawri and the senior Mamluk officers. The plain was littered with mutilated remnants of this confrontation:

> Corpses lay in heaps, many without heads. Faces of the fallen were smeared with blood and grime, disfiguring their features. Slain horses lay scattered about, their saddles thrown from their backs. Gold-embossed swords, steel-mail tunics, tatters of uniforms were strewn all over. . . .[21]

While casualties among officers were high, most of the Mamluk recruits survived and were allowed to flee towards Aleppo. Upon arriving they found themselves locked out. Angry about the treatment they had received from the Mamluk army when it was billeted there, local inhabitants fell on them in revenge. Abandoning their war material and huge treasury in Aleppo, the survivors fled for their lives south toward Damascus.

Among those captured by the Ottomans were the caliph and three of the four *qadis*, one having fled with the retreating forces. Selim received the caliph and treated him well, though he was later deported to the Ottoman capital as a tangible signal that Egypt was no longer the seat of the caliphate—the legitimate religious authority, but merely a province administered from a distant land. Four days after the battle, Selim arrived at Aleppo, where he was hailed as liberator, freeing the populace from the Mamluk yoke. The fleeing Mamluks had left Aleppo's citadel unguarded. Selim had earlier boasted that his weakest man would take Aleppo's citadel, where al-Ghawri had deposited his huge treasury before setting off for Marj Dabiq. Keeping this vow, he sent in an aged clerk to view the treasures. When the clerk reported riches beyond calculation, Selim had to see for himself and was similarly overwhelmed. This windfall for the Ottoman treasury no doubt contributed to continued Ottoman conquests, beginning with the campaign against Mamluk Egypt.

In a matter of weeks, the Ottomans occupied all of Syria and Palestine. Hoping to avoid the grueling march across the Sinai Desert to take Cairo, Selim proposed to al-Ghawri's nephew Tumanbay, who had assumed power in Cairo, that he submit to the Ottomans and govern Egypt as the Ottoman viceroy. Rather than conceding to this common Ottoman practice, Tumanbay was defiant. Left with no alternative, Sultan Selim ordered the Ottoman army across the Sinai, arriving in the Cairo area in late January 1517.

Tumanbay prepared to make a stand at Ridaniyya military camp at the approaches to Cairo. Finally comprehending the necessity of firearms, the Mamluks had hastily assembled what weaponry they could muster to fortify Ridaniyya. All Egypt had however, was siege artillery—unsuited for the type of war it was about to face. When the Battle of Ridaniyya was fought on January 23, 1517, the 20,000-strong Egyptian army was defeated within twenty minutes after the Ottomans swept around the heavy artillery and attacked from the rear. Since the Egyptians could not turn their heavy siege artillery, most of the Egyptian guns did not fire a shot.

Sultan Tumanbay managed to escape and organize some resistance, but it was quickly broken, and he was captured and hanged. The Mamluk sultanate had come to an end; Egypt became a satellite of the Ottoman Empire.

After taking Egypt, the Ottomans continued on to Arabia. Selim doubled the size of his empire, adding all the lands of the Islamic caliphate, save for Persia (Iran), and Mesopotamia. With sovereignty over all the holy places of Islam and possessing vast wealth and power, Selim became the most prestigious ruler in the Muslim world. His reign is considered the prelude to the Ottoman Empire's golden age.

As a way-station on the pilgrim's route to Mecca, Selim wanted to ensure that Palestine had law and order and good services and facilities. When he died in 1520, Selim was succeeded by his son Suleiman. Jerusalem flourished under the new sultan, who became known as Suleiman the Magnificent. Suleiman rebuilt Jerusalem's walls and gates, which had lain in ruins since their destruction in 1219. When Suleiman learned that the architects literally cut corners when they left Mount Zion outside the walls, he had the two men executed, and legend has it they are buried just inside Jaffa Gate. Suleiman's improvements for the city included repairing the city's ancient aqueduct and installing public drinking fountains, building new markets and restoring old ones, refurbishing mosques, and other projects, most notably the Temple Mount's Dome of the Rock, where exterior mosaics were replaced with colored tiles.

After Suleiman's death, Jerusalem lost its prominence in Ottoman eyes. Over time, the Ottoman Empire suffered from a general disintegration of law and order, and Palestine was not immune. Corruption, rebellious governors and simple neglect took their effects, and the Holy Land became a backwater. American writer Mark Twain reported Palestine's poor state in his 1860's travelogue *The Innocents Abroad*, calling Palestine "desolate and unlovely" and saying that it "sits in sackcloth and ashes." Of Jerusalem he wrote: "Renowned Jerusalem itself, the stateliest name in history, has lost all its ancient grandeur and is become a pauper village. . ."[22] Palestine would remain that way until World War I would reshuffle borders, bringing an end to 400 years of Ottoman rule over the Middle East.

Notes

1. When the Prophet Mohammed died in 632, his father-in-law Abu Bakr took over as the first caliph, or successor, leading the *ummah* (community of followers). Abu Bakr was succeeded by Omar, Uthman and then Ali, who was Mohammed's cousin and brother-in-law. The Sunni branch of Islam accepts the legitimacy of the first four caliphs whereas Shiite Muslims believe that Ali, as a relative of Mohammed, was the only rightful successor, and that only his descendants are rightful successors to Mohammed. While both Sunni and Shiite Muslims share the same beliefs, there are differences in religious practices of Sunnis and Shiites, and the split between these two streams remains divisive until today.
2. Michael Winter. "The Ottoman Occupation," in Carl Petry (ed.). *The Cambridge History of Egypt. Volume I: Islamic Egypt, 640–1517* (Cambridge, UK: Cambridge University Press, 1998), p.499.
3. Carl Petry, "The military institution and innovation in the late Mamluk period" in Carl Petry (ed.). *The Cambridge History of Egypt. Volume I: Islamic Egypt, 640–1517* (Cambridge: Cambridge University Press, 1998), p.480.
4. Petry. "The military institution and innovation in the late Mamluk period," p.482.
5. Carl Petry. *Twilight of Majesty. The Reign of the Mamluk Sultans Al-Ashraf Qaytbay and Qansuh Al-Ghawri in Egypt* (Seattle: University of Washington Press, 1993), p.214.

6. "The regulars suspected that al-Ghawri routinely located funds to pay his new corps, while claiming insolvency in the face of their own bonus requests." Petry. "The military institution and innovation in the late Mamluk period," p.482.

7. Petry writes in "The military institution and innovation in the late Mamluk period," p.473, that "Al-Ghawri moved beyond exigency to opportunism as he made mass-scale confiscation a reliable instrument to raise revenue."

8. Winter. "The Ottoman Occupation," p.496.

9. Khayrbak had already concluded a deal with Selim to betray his sultan. Winter. "The Ottoman Occupation," p.496.

10.Winter. "The Ottoman Occupation," p.495.

11.Petry. *Twilight*, p.224.

12.David Ayalon. *Gunpowder and Firearms in the Mamluk Kingdom: A Challenge to Mediaeval Society* (London: 1956), p.77.

13.Winter. "The Ottoman Occupation," p.498.

14.Winter. "The Ottoman Occupation," p.498

15.Petry "The military institution and innovation in the late Mamluk period," p.469.

16.Ayalon. *Gunpowder and Firearms*, p.127.

17.Ayalon, *Gunpowder and Firearms*, p.89.

18.Ayalon, *Gunpowder and Firearms*, p.89.

19.Ayalon, *Gunpowder and Firearms*, p.88.

20.M. A. Cook (ed.). *A History of the Ottoman Empire to 1730* (Cambridge: Cambridge University Press, 1976), p.74.

21.Petry, *Twilight*, p.227.

22.Mark Twain. *The Innocents Abroad* (1869), p.442.

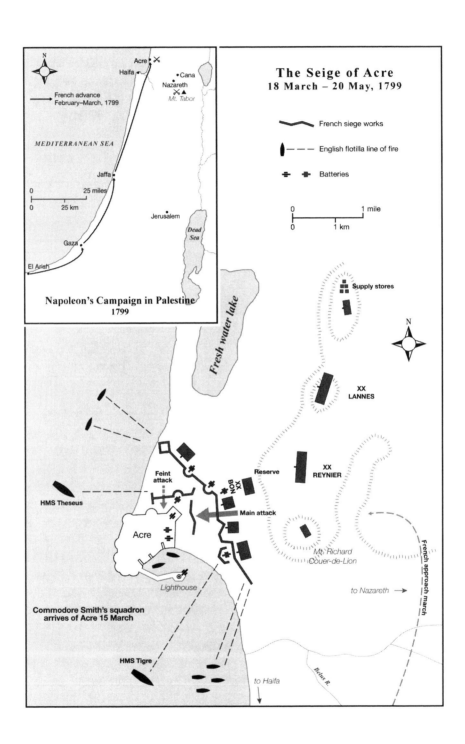

The Seige of Acre
18 March – 20 May, 1799

French siege works

English flotilla line of fire

Batteries

0   1 mile
0   1 km

Napoleon's Campaign in Palestine
1799

N

Acre
Haifa

French advance
February–March, 1799

MEDITERRANEAN SEA

Jaffa

0   25 miles
0   25 km

Cana
Nazareth
Mt. Tabor

Jerusalem

*Dead
Sea*

Gaza

El Arish

Supply stores

Fresh water lake

N

XX
LANNES

XX
REYNIER

Reserve

XX
BON

Feint
attack

HMS Theseus

Main attack

Acre

*Mt. Richard
Couer-de-Lion*

French approach march

to Nazareth

Lighthouse

Commodore Smith's squadron
arrives of Acre 15 March

HMS Tigre

to Haifa

Belus R.

CHAPTER 11

PLAGUED BY DELAYS, AND DELAYED BY PLAGUE

NAPOLEON'S HOLY LAND CAMPAIGN, 1799

When it comes to Napoleon Bonaparte's defeats, the first ones that come to mind are usually the Russian campaign or Waterloo. Yet he was stung by his first defeat years earlier during his Holy Land Campaign, at Acre (Akko). After taking El Arish, Gaza and Jaffa, an overconfident General Bonaparte (as Napoleon was then known) declared: "The army of the Republic is master of the whole of Palestine."[1] This ambitious statement was a bit premature as his army's momentum ran out just two weeks later at the walls of Acre.

Bonaparte's campaign into Palestine was an outgrowth of his conquest of Egypt. When Bonaparte dreamt up the idea of a campaign into Egypt, his intention may have been to threaten rival England's interests in India, although this is unclear. There may also have been more than strategy at play. In proposing such a campaign, Bonaparte, who enjoyed reading military history and perhaps saw himself among the likes of Alexander the Great, may have been acting out his delusions of grandeur.[2] Whatever the reason, in 1798 the French set sail for Egypt in the first European military expedition against the Middle East since the Crusaders.

In July 1798, the 30,000 strong French Armée d'Orient landed and marched on Cairo. Local resistance was no match for the French army; three weeks after the French arrival, Egypt's Mamluks were defeated in a battle within sight of the pyramids. Egypt was theirs. But Bonaparte's jubilation was short-lived as only a few days later, an English fleet under Rear Admiral Horatio Nelson located the French fleet anchored at Aboukir Bay by Alexandria and destroyed it in the misnamed Battle of the Nile. Not only were the French cut off from reinforcement, but the battle left the British masters of the seas.

As Egypt was a suzerain territory of the Ottoman Empire, the French invasion was, in effect, an unprovoked attack on Ottoman hegemony. In response, the Turkish sultan allied with Britain and planned a two-fold assault to oust the French: a ground force sent from Damascus via Palestine, and once the weather improved, a second force being transported by sea from the island of Rhodes.

Rather than waiting for these forces to advance against him, Bonaparte seized the initiative with a preemptive march into Palestine. More than military maneuvering, the move into Palestine may have also been designed to forestall mutiny by his disgruntled army. With its fleet destroyed, the Armée d'Orient was stranded in Egypt. Knowing the dangers of an idle army, yet with desert to the west and south, east towards Palestine was the only option for keeping his forces occupied. Bonaparte planned to advance with his army into Palestine, seize the fortress of Acre (the region's de facto capital), defeat the Damascus army, and then hurry back to Egypt before good weather would allow the Ottoman Army of Rhodes to make its voyage and land in Egypt. Meeting these goals dictated that speed would be the critical element; Bonaparte announced the entire campaign would last one month.

The French army set out from Egypt on what was known as the Holy Land, or Syrian, campaign, with Bonaparte's carriage leading the way for some 13,000 infantry, cavalry, artillerymen and auxiliary, backed by 52 light cannon. On horseback, camel and foot, the Armée d'Orient began crossing the Sinai Desert towards Palestine.

Lead elements advanced from a forward base on February 6, 1799, with the rest of the army following. When they reached El Arish, they were surprised to find their route blocked by a fort defended by 1,500 Ottoman soldiers. This first encounter at El Arish would prove a precursor of the difficulties to come.

After the French took the village of El Arish, the entire Ottoman force sought refuge inside the fort. Having expected a clear route into Palestine, Bonaparte had lightened his army's load for the difficult desert journey by sending its heavy siege artillery by sea. Lacking the artillery necessary to topple the fortress walls, the French had no option but to lay siege—a time-consuming prospect.

While the French were making their preparations to besiege the fort, a 2,000-man force of Ottoman cavalry and infantry sent by Ahmed Jazzar, Syria and Palestine's local ruler, arrived to relieve the Ottoman force. Taking up a position to the rear, this force cut off the French army's option to retreat. But before they managed to move against the French, they were surprised by a French night attack with a deep flanking maneuver that circled behind and attacked their camp. The Turks were completely routed, although most of the men succeeded in escaping.

After the relief force was defeated, additional French forces arrived with field artillery. Once the guns were ready, the battery fired for a whole day until the fort's walls were breached, leading its commandant to surrender. Bonaparte was surprisingly lenient in his surrender terms: paroling the defenders on condition they not take arms against the French for one year. He would not have been so lenient had he known how this unexpected delay, from February 8 to 19, 1799, would impact the outcome of the entire campaign.

Setting off from El Arish, the French force continued its desert journey. By Gaza, their advance was challenged by 3,000–4,000 Ottoman cavalrymen. French cavalry and infantry charged the Turks, who gave way. The French performance was impressive as they had not had a decent meal nor drunk sufficiently for several days after getting lost in the desert.[3] When Gaza was taken, the French supplemented their arsenal with captured cannon and ammunition and replenished themselves with rations and water.

Proceeding up Palestine's coast, on March 3, 1799, the French arrived at the port city of Jaffa, which Bonaparte considered vital for his sea lines of communication with Egypt. Bonaparte deployed his forces around the city, with a blocking force stationed to the north along the Nahr al-Auja (Yarkon River). A French offer of surrender was refused. With its garrison of several thousand men backed by more than fifty cannon, Jaffa's defenders were confident they could withstand the French siege. The French set about preparing their siege works, making up for time lost at El Arish by positioning their artillery under cover of dense groves surrounding the town without wasting time digging trenches. Slowed by effective sallies from the garrison, French preparations took several days.

Before attacking on March 7, 1799, Bonaparte sent an envoy with a final offer for surrender. When the headless corpse of this envoy was thrown from Jaffa's walls, the French were riled up and raring to fight. They opened fire with their artillery and mortars in a bombardment that lasted several hours. The garrison put up a fight, with "lively and sustained fire," as Bonaparte described, but they were no match for the French.[4] By afternoon, Jaffa's southern wall was breached and deemed passable. Grenadiers—the army's assault forces—began storming through but were repulsed several times with heavy losses. Later, forces penetrated through breaches in the wall and through a large undefended passage they discovered next to their breach in the south of the city. Fanning out in the town's narrow lanes, the French overran Jaffa in a quick, violent battle. By nightfall, the French controlled the city.

Although it was common to sack a town that had refused surrender, at Jaffa the French soldiers went on a rampage. They plundered, looted, and killed as they went, leaving Jaffa ravaged. When order was restored, the French were angry to discover among the captured defenders Turkish troops paroled not three weeks earlier at El Arish—in violation of their parole terms. Lacking the resources to guard and feed them, and without ships to carry them back to Egypt, Bonaparte reasoned that he had no choice but to execute the prisoners, and some 2,000 to 3,000 Ottoman prisoners were killed.[5] With so many corpses, bubonic plague broke out in the city, which, with a hint of poetic justice, also affected the French, haunting them throughout the campaign.

Acre

Their advance sustained by the booty of supplies, cannon and ammunition, the French continued north towards Acre. Given his successes until that time, Bonaparte grew complacent and assumed Acre would similarly fall with relative ease. First seeing the city's protective walls and defensive towers from the Carmel Mountains above Haifa, Bonaparte sent a letter to Ahmed Jazzar recommending surrender, tempting Jazzar with promises of commerce and mutually beneficial relations.

Word of the atrocities committed at Jaffa had already made their way to Acre. While Bonaparte hoped this might intimidate the people of Acre into surrendering, Jazzar had no intention of capitulating. With no guarantee that surrendering would prevent a similar massacre, the French actions in Jaffa instead strengthened Acre's resolve.

The French reached the walls of Acre on March 18, 1799 and began their siege. Bonaparte soon discovered that Acre was in a different league to Jaffa. Not only was Acre situated on a peninsula jutting out into the Mediterranean Sea, offering protection on three sides by the British-controlled sea, but its walls, at 25–30 feet (8–9m) high, and an average of 5 feet (1.5m) thick, were of far better material and construction than those at Jaffa. The base of the walls—the primary target for breaching artillery—was even wider, and further protected by a dry moat. Toppling these walls would not be easy. Compounding the challenge, the French would have to make do without heavy guns. In a disastrous setback, the French heavy breaching, or siege, artillery, which Bonaparte had put aboard transport ships sailing to meet the French army at Acre, had been captured at sea by the British and turned over to Acre for use against the French. Left with only field artillery, Bonaparte would need to take the city by direct assault.

Given the circumstances, victory over Acre was far from guaranteed. Not only were the French without the cannon needed to knock down the walls, but Acre had become a proxy battlefield with France's chief rival, Britain. The delays experienced at El Arish and Jaffa had allowed time for the arrival of a British fleet under command of an old adversary of Bonaparte: British Commodore Sir Sidney Smith. Smith had been burned by Bonaparte six years earlier, when the French general, then an artillery officer, had used his guns to drive Smith's ships away from the besieged French port city of Toulon. Arriving at Acre just days before the French, Smith and his

friend Colonel Louis Phelippeaux, a French royalist during the revo-
lution who had been a rival of Bonaparte since their days together in
the French War Academy, assisted Ahmed Jazzar and Acre's 5,000
defenders in hastily preparing defenses.

Were it not for the delays along the way, Bonaparte might have
marched into Acre; but when he arrived on March 18, Acre was being
brought into a condition to resist him. By the time the French were
fully deployed and ready to launch their first attack, Phelippeaux, an
expert in artillery and defenses, had had nearly two weeks to shore up
fortifications. Walls were reinforced, and some 250 artillery pieces—
including the heavy guns the English fleet had taken from the French
ships—had been positioned on the town's fortifications. As a further
defensive measure, underground passageways in the ancient Crusader
city were restored to be used as a means of escape inland in the event
the French penetrated the city walls.

When the first attack came on March 28, the town was in good
order to withstand assault, with nearly every point of approach
covered by at least two directions of fire. Crossing the dry moat under
enemy fire, the French assault forces found their siege ladders too
short to mount the walls and were forced to withdraw with heavy
losses. With this attack, Bonaparte finally understood that taking
Acre was going to take time.

While handicapped by the lack of siege artillery, the French did
have field artillery, supplemented by captured Turkish artillery. This
was one of the campaign's ironies: heavy cannon seized from the
French were defending Acre's walls while the French were firing
Turkish artillery at its former owners. The French light artillery, unable
to knock down Acre's walls, could be used for counter-battery and
harassing fire. To bring both their artillery and soldiers closer to more
efficient ranges, rows of trenches were dug parallel to Acre's walls.
Digging and manning these trenches was dangerous business. Constant
artillery fire from the walls and from the British ships at sea not only
demoralized the French, but also took its toll. The Turks, who excelled
in artillery marksmanship, had ironically been taught artillery tech-
niques by French advisors.

Unable to topple Acre's walls with artillery, the French tried undermining them. Tunnels were dug in an attempt to cave the walls in,

to blow up their foundations or to gain entrance to the town underneath the walls. When the French were tunneling beneath the city's walls, Jazzar's forces dug counter-tunnels to disturb the French efforts. Acre's defenders made courageous sallies against the French trenches and tunnel works. Extra motivation was provided by a bounty Jazzar paid on each French head brought in. When these were displayed on the city's walls, it did little for the rapidly plummeting French morale.

While unable to break the deadlock at Acre, the French won a string of victories in Palestine's Galilee region—the most spectacular at Mount Tabor. The Turkish Army of Damascus, the ground forces dispatched by the Turkish sultan to drive the French away and retake Egypt, was crossing the Jordan River into Galilee. The French engaged the Turks throughout Galilee. At times, so many French troops were in the field that the siege of Acre was left in the hands of relatively few. The bulk of this Ottoman force—a motley mixture of Turks, Arabs (Bedouin), Albanians, Bosnians, Mamluks, Moroccans and Sudanese numbering some 25,000 cavalry and 10,000 infantry—had reached the Plain of Esdraelon (Megiddo, or Jezreel Valley) on April 13 and, joined by 7,000 locals, apparently planned to attack the French forces operating in Galilee and then those besieging Acre.

General Jean-Baptise Kleber—who Bonaparte would soon after entrust with ruling all of Egypt—was sent to Galilee to reinforce a small French force already operating there. When Kleber's combined force of 2,000 men came upon the massive Turkish force, he had no real option but to go on the offensive and attack despite being so vastly outnumbered—better on his terms than waiting for the Turks to decide the battlefield. In prior council with Bonaparte, it was agreed that the best approach would be a surprise night attack on the enemy camp by means of a deep flanking maneuver, like the one successfully executed at El Arish. This was not as preposterous as it sounds, for the professional French soldiers had already proven their mettle successfully fighting off elements of the Army of Damascus many times their number.

At Mount Tabor, poor timing in the night attack found the French forces revealed at daybreak of April 16 while still on the move maneuvering in order to attack the Ottoman camp. Kleber and his force came under attack by nearly the entire enemy host. Hastily preparing a defensive position, the French fought a desperate battle. Throughout the morning, the hopelessly outnumbered French, with only muskets and a few cannon firing grapeshot, withstood wave after wave of enemy cavalry charges and assaults. The disciplined French troops were managing to hold their ground, but surrounded and with ammunition running low, they knew there was no chance for victory against such odds. When all seemed lost, a cannon shot caught everyone's attention. Coming to the rescue in the nick of time—like the proverbial cavalry arriving to save the day—was a French relief force led by General Bonaparte himself. Perhaps after reconsidering the likelihood of Kleber's force single-handedly taking on nearly the entire Army of Damascus, and knowing that this Ottoman force had to be destroyed, Bonaparte opted to take them on in the open field rather than with his back to the sea at Acre.

Having approached undetected, the appearance of this fresh force at their rear—seemingly from nowhere—startled the Turks, who panicked and dispersed. "Terror seized the enemy ranks," Bonaparte wrote. "In an instant, this host of horsemen melted into disorder and headed for the Jordan. The infantry headed for the heights and the night saved them."[6] Lacking the necessary reinforcements to press their advantage, the French pursued the enemy as best they could. The battlefield was strewn with thousands of Turkish dead, and several villages were burned to punish the locals for joining the Turkish ranks. What had been a desperate situation was turned into a great victory.

Despite successes in the field, victory continued to elude the French at Acre. Each time Bonaparte sent his forces to breach the walls, Acre's defenders held their ground. Not one attempt created a true bridgehead into Acre. In one attack, the French succeeded in penetrating into the city. In the face of the French breakthrough, Jazzar's forces seemingly withdrew and the French thought they were finally gaining their foothold. But they had entered a carefully prepared ambush and were cut down with a hail of fire. As in all the attacks, there was heavy loss of life on both sides. Among the casualties were the French expatriate Phelippeaux on one side, and a number of Bonaparte's generals.

Bonaparte remained optimistic of victory, writing: "I shall rain down a great number of bombs and these, in such a confined space, should cause no small amount of damage. And when I have reduced Acre to rubble I shall go back across the desert and be ready to receive any European or Turkish army which . . . wishes to disembark in Egypt."[7]

Despite Bonaparte's sanguine outlook, Acre held the advantage of reinforcement and supply by sea. Late in the siege, the arrival of some 24-pounder heavy siege cannon brought overland allowed the French to renew attempts to knock through Acre's walls. Their arrival, however, was too late. A Turkish fleet with a relief force for the besieged city was due any day. Lacking reserves, and with ammunition for his heavy guns in short supply, Bonaparte understood he would not be able to overcome this additional challenge should the Turkish forces land. Preempting their arrival, Bonaparte ordered an eighth and final attack on Acre in hopes of taking the city on the eve of its relief. In this attack, the newly arrived artillery successfully breached the outer wall. When the grenadier assault forces penetrated, they were surprised to find themselves blocked by an internal wall secretly built under Phelippeaux's direction, and this attempt—like all the others— failed.

With this latest failure to take Acre, Bonaparte took stock of the situation at hand. His army was in a wretched state, with one-third of his men dead, wounded or sick. Morale was at a low ebb, as were supplies. His army simply lacked the wherewithal to take Acre. Adding to his troubles, there was unrest back in Egypt, and Turkish ships were preparing to transport the Army of Rhodes now that the weather was good enough for their voyage and landing. In short, he had run out of time, or—as Bonaparte later explained the defeat— luck. Though victory had many times seemed within his grasp, on May 10, 1799, Bonaparte lifted the siege of Acre.

Despite the military successes against the Turkish field forces, this was Bonaparte's first true failure. Even Bonaparte's tone in one of his dispatches suggests defeat. "I have been perfectly content with the army in circumstances and a type of war very new to Europeans" he wrote. "They have shown how real courage and military talent fears nothing and bears every sort of hardship. The result will be, we hope, an advantageous peace and greater glory and prosperity for the Republic."[8] On May 20, 1799—after 63 days outside Acre—the French forces began withdrawing.

There was jubilation in Acre. Ahmed Jazzar's steadfast determination had prevailed, saving Acre. Leaving nothing to chance, Jazzar took the precautionary measure of building up the city's defenses even though the French had withdrawn.

The vanquished Bonaparte last viewed the city that had proved his nemesis from atop the mountains above Haifa. Then, in an act of vengeance, the French set fire to everything in their wake, burning villages and crops—using a scorched-earth tactic that the Russians would use against them 13 years later.

To facilitate evacuation of the sick and wounded, all able-bodied men traveled on foot as far as Jaffa. Even Bonaparte gave up his own mount to a wounded man. Still not enough mounts were available for all the casualties, so the sick and wounded dragged themselves behind the retreating French columns. Bonaparte's secretary De Bourrienne described the scene: "The entire countryside was on fire. . . . We were surrounded by nothing but dying men. . . . To our right was the sea; to our left and behind us, the desert we were creating . . ."[9] Their pace slowed by both heavy cannon and the many invalids, at Tantoura (south of Haifa) it was decided to throw the artillery into the sea, freeing up more horses and mules to carry the injured and sick.

When the sick and straggling army arrived at Jaffa, Bonaparte saw what a burden the sick were imposing on his battered army. Even though he had earlier risked his well-being by visiting soldiers inflicted with plague in hospital, Bonaparte now ordered the poisoning of plague-infected soldiers and prisoners. When his chief medical officer refused, the general was forced to find someone less scrupulous to carry out this macabre task.

While claiming in his dispatches that only 500 of his men had been killed and twice that number wounded (versus 15,000 enemy casualties), his army was down some 4,000 to 5,000 men when it returned from its tortuous journey back to Egypt in mid-June. To mask the defeat, the return was given an air of victory and triumph; losses were downplayed by spacing out the arrival in Cairo of wounded generals and senior officers, and wounded soldiers carried captured Turkish flags. Three full days of celebration and festivities marked their return.

Bonaparte's army, though having taken a beating, joined with the forces left in Egypt and proved it was still in fighting form when it took on the Turkish Army of Rhodes. Arriving at Aboukir on July 12, the 15,000-man Army of Rhodes landed and quickly established a beachhead. Mustering all available men to fight, Bonaparte's force of 10,000 infantrymen and 1,000 cavalry met the Army of Rhodes and defeated it on July 25, 1799 at the Battle of Aboukir.

That threat defeated, Bonaparte returned to Cairo. His position in Egypt now more secure, Bonaparte turned his attention back to Europe. With forces arraying themselves for another major assault on France, Bonaparte saw it would be best if he were to return to France. Late that summer, he secretly departed, leaving General Kleber in charge. Not long after, Kleber was assassinated while Napoleon's stellar rise is well known.

The French Armée d'Orient was ultimately surrendered after a subsequent joint Ottoman/British attack. As part of the treaty arrangements, the French troops were transported back home on British vessels in March 1801—a humiliating end to Napoleon's grand dreams of conquest in the East.

Notes

1. Bonaparte's Despatches from Egypt, part IV.
2. David Chandler, *Campaigns of Napoleon* (Weidenfeld & Nicolson, 1966), pp.209–211.
3. Bonaparte's Despatches from Egypt, part IV.
4. Bonaparte's Despatches from Egypt, part IV.
5. Bonaparte reports 4,000 prisoners killed in his Despatches (Part IV). Gichon suggests 2,000, but cites other references to numbers ranging from 800–900 to 4,000. "Jaffa 1799," p.30.
6. Bonaparte's Despatches from Egypt, part V.
7. Bonaparte's Despatches from Egypt, part V.
8. Bonaparte's Despatches from Egypt, part V.
9. Shelly Wachsmann and Kurt Raveh. *An Encounter at Tantura with Napoleon.*

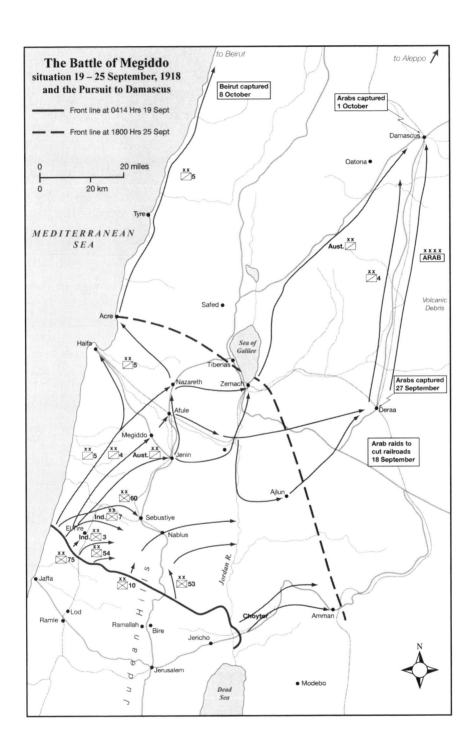

The Battle of Megiddo
situation 19 – 25 September, 1918
and the Pursuit to Damascus

Front line at 0414 Hrs 19 Sept

Front line at 1800 Hrs 25 Sept

0   20 miles

0   20 km

to Beirut

to Aleppo

Beirut captured
8 October

Arabs captured
1 October

Damascus

Oatona

MEDITERRANEAN
SEA

Tyre

XX
5

Aust. XX

XXXX
ARAB

XX
4

Volcanic
Debris

Safed

Acre

Haifa

XX
5

Sea of
Galilee

Tiberias

Zemach

Nazareth

Afule

Deraa

Megiddo

XX
5

XX
4

Aust. XX

Jenin

Arabs captured
27 September

Arab raids to
cut railroads
18 September

Ajlun

XX
60

Ind. XX
7

Sebustiye

El hire

Ind. XX
3

Nablus

XX
75

XX
54

Jaffa

XX
10

XX
53

Jordan R.

Lod

Ramle

Ramallah

Bire

Jericho

Choyter

Amman

Jerusalem

Dead
Sea

Modebo

N

CHAPTER 12

BY WAY OF DECEPTION

World War I in Palestine, 1917–18

British Commonwealth troops were finally in control of the heights commanding Gaza's approaches, and the city's defenses were on the verge of collapse. Some mounted forces had even penetrated into Gaza and were watering their horses. The battle seemed won; Gaza—gateway to Palestine—was almost theirs. Then orders came down to withdraw. Reactions ranged from shock to disbelief. One commander exclaimed: "But we have Gaza!" Tala Bey, Turkish commander of Gaza, was said to have laughed at the spectacle of seeing the victors pulling back.[1]

Unlike their colleagues bogged down in static trench warfare on the Western Front in Europe, the British Commonwealth forces in the oft-overlooked Palestine theater fought a mobile campaign involving some of the best strategizing of the war.

With the Allies' failure at Gallipoli in 1915–16, it became clear that the only way of forcing Turkey out of the war was through breaking its control of Palestine and Syria. As the Turks had been entrenched in these areas for some 400 years, prying open the Ottoman's hold on this territory would be no simple task.

When World War I began in August 1914, Turkey joined Germany and Austria-Hungary against the British Empire and other members of the Western alliance, which was known as the Triple Entente. Germany had taken an interest in the Ottoman Empire at the very end of the previous century and Kaiser Wilhelm II had established economic and military ties with the Turks. The relationship had grown to the point where the Germans effectively controlled the Turkish army. It was said Turks provided its army's brawn while the brains were supplied by Germany, which provided core services such as communications, transport, and air support.

Encouraged by its victory at Gallipoli, the Turks entertained notions of taking Egypt, especially the strategically important Suez Canal. Lifeline of the British Empire, the Suez Canal allowed British Commonwealth countries to supply Britain with men and resources for the war without exposing them to the dangers of attack by German warships and submarines in the Atlantic Ocean. The Germans supported the Turkish moves, as an assault on the canal would tie down a large number of British troops, siphoning off men and supplies from the main war effort in Europe.

Though vital to the defense of its Egyptian base of operations, the British considered the canal as an obstacle that protected Egypt. After the Turks moved across the Sinai Desert and made their first attempt to attack the canal in February 1915, the British view changed. After repulsing Turkish attacks, it was seen that rather than being a defensive barrier, the Suez Canal was an asset that needed to be protected. This was accomplished by moving the British Commonwealth Egyptian Expeditionary Force, or EEF, into the Sinai Peninsula. Their mission ultimately grew to include the capture of Palestine and beyond.

A success against the Turks would be a much-needed morale-booster for the British, whose forces were stalemated on the Western Front. But there would be no quick victory on the Palestine front, as the EEF's advance across the barren desert was contingent upon a supply of clean water.

Supplying an army in the desert—especially an army with horses—requires a well-developed supply network. Camels heavily laden with supplies followed on the heels of the fighting men, but this was not adequate to meet supply needs. Water was often in short supply, and only drinkable after boiling. The British set about building a railway and water pipeline as they proceeded eastward across the desert, with the construction setting the pace of the army's advance. As the front advanced, the pipeline of water was extended. After steadily advancing across the Sinai Desert, pushing the Turkish army back, the EEF reached Palestine's borders at the end of 1916.

"But we have Gaza!"

While some serious clashes had taken place between the two sides while the EEF advanced across the Sinai, particularly in a battle at Romani, the relative ease with which Sinai was taken from the Turks led General Sir Archibald Murray, commander of British forces in the Middle East, to believe his forces would also take Palestine with little difficulty. There was no clear dividing line between the opposing armies along the Gaza–Beersheba line; vast desert stretches—into which each army probed—separated them. Over-confident after recent successes, EEF commanders believed that if pressured, the Turks might pull out of Gaza, opening what was called the "gateway to Palestine." But the Turks had other ideas. Deployed in strength in the coastal fortress of Gaza, Turkish forces under German General Friedrich Kress von Kressenstein had no intention of relinquishing their positions.

General Murray determined to surprise Gaza and capture its garrison, estimated at 4,000–5,000-strong. Ringed with Turkish positions commanding the approaches, chief among them the formidable defenses at Ali Muntar Hill, and further protected by loose sand dunes and huge cactus hedges, Gaza would be no easy take.

Logistics limitations, allowing the forces to operate only one day ahead of its supplies, dictated that Gaza be taken in one day. Lieutenant General Sir Charles Dobell's Eastern Force, the name for the EEF forces operating east of the Canal, would have to quickly take Gaza in order to water its horses in the town's wells. The attack plan called for infantry to take Ali Muntar Hill early in the day as a springboard to a push from the south and southwest. Mounted forces were to circumvent Gaza to block a Turkish withdrawal or efforts to reinforce the position.

Through a series of night marches, with two infantry divisions numbering some 20,000 troops concealed from enemy air patrols by sand dunes and palm trees, the EEF avoided detection while advancing eastward. Major General A. G. Dallas commanded the infantry assaulting the positions at Ali Muntar. In the early hours of March 26, 1917 Dallas' force set out from their staging area southwest of Gaza. Their first challenge was crossing Wadi Ghuzzee, a dry watercourse, which cut across the terrain, with steep banks that could only be crossed at certain places. It was a black night, so traversing the wadi was no easy task. A dense fog rolled in from the sea in the pre-dawn hours, making navigation extremely difficult. While the fog protected the EEF's advance from detection by Turkish observers, it also caused disastrous delays in the attack plan.

When the fog lifted after six in the morning, there were further inexplicable delays in the infantry's progress. Mounted forces successfully penetrated deep into Turkish territory undetected, sealing off Gaza. Yet despite the time constraints so crucial to the operation's success, there was no sign of the infantry division tasked with taking prominent Ali Muntar Hill. It turned out they were still deploying south of Gaza preparing for the attack, and its commander could not be reached for some time. Poor communications and slow execution of orders down the chain of command plagued the operation, and would continue to do so throughout the day. When Lieutenant General Sir Philip W. Chetwode, commander of Eastern Force's advance troops, finally established communications with Dallas, he exhorted Dallas to get moving.

The attack on the Ali Muntar Hill area only got underway at noon under heavy Turkish artillery and machine-gun fire. The Turks had been alerted to the advance when one of their patrols encountered the attackers, resulting in a brief skirmish. Hearing shots, two German aircraft stationed nearby took off, spotted and strafed the host before flying back to raise the alarm. When the attack finally came, the well-concealed Turks manning positions on the high ground had an easy time cutting down the infantry advancing over the open country towards them. The EEF lacked adequate artillery support due to a shortage of ammunition, and what little they did have was missing its mark. Considered of secondary importance compared to the

Western Front, the Palestine front was receiving low priority in resource allocations.

Efforts to adjust the fire support to more relevant targets were slow, again due to communications. Despite these difficulties, the EEF infantry fought courageously and managed to make their way through the maze of cactus fields. By evening they had secured Ali Muntar Hill and driven the Turks from the high ground overlooking Gaza. The EEF's right flank was protected by a thin line of mounted troops.

With the delay in the infantry attack, it was decided shortly after noon to put the mounted forces to work exerting pressure on the Turks in an effort to accelerate Gaza's collapse. Originally slotted a secondary flank security role, the mounted forces were ordered to assault Gaza from the east. Again, orders took an excessive amount of time working through the chain of command, and it was not until day's end when all was ready for the attack to begin. The mounted forces fought their way through the Turks' rear lines and reached Gaza's streets by nightfall. "Every indication pointed to a rout and general surrender at any moment."[2] The battle seemed won; Gaza was almost theirs.

Then orders came down from General Dobell: Withdraw. There was shock and astonishment. One commander demanded to see the order in writing. Lieutenant General Harry Chauvel, commander of the Australia and New Zealand Mounted Division, epitomized the reaction with his exultation: "But we *have* Gaza!"

The troops in action did not have the benefit of reconnaissance reports from British airmen and cavalry patrols reporting Turkish reinforcements en route. While in retrospect the order for general withdrawal appears folly, at the time EEF command was seriously concerned about the Turkish relief force, unconvinced that they would be able to protect all their exposed flanks. Moreover, mounted forces deep behind Turkish lines desperately needed to water their horses. "Many horses had been 36 hours without water. It was, therefore, necessary to bring in the mounted divisions; and, it was then considered unsafe to leave the infantry on the captured ground with their flank exposed. . . . Thus we gave up the commanding position gained."[3]

With the cumbersome communications, EEF commanders were evidently not fully aware of actual developments in the field, with their infantry securely on Ali Muntar Hill and some of the mounted forces already watering their horses. Given the information available to them, the mounted divisions were ordered to withdraw and the infantry to quit Ali Muntar Hill—the position for which they had fought so hard, and for which they had paid the price of some 400 dead and 2,900 wounded—and establish defensive positions in the adjacent high ground for the night. It was with great consternation that they pulled back after what, for all intents and purposes, was a victory. The defeated Turks were amazed to see the EEF force withdraw.

Turkish reinforcements entered Gaza during the night. When EEF infantry tried to retake Ali Muntar the following day, they met stiff resistance and abandoned the effort, withdrawing during the early hours of March 28, 1917 and ending what would become known as the First Battle of Gaza.

"A Second Gallipoli"

Based on overly positive accounts of the attack in inaccurate dispatches to the War Office in London, such as General Murray's report of "a most successful operation. . ."[4] and exaggerated assessments of the relative ease with which Gaza could be taken in a second attempt, another attack on Gaza was authorized.

The mission again went to General Dobell. The attack plan he came up with built largely on "First Gaza": a frontal attack by infantry against the full strength of the Turkish position, with the mounted forces assaulting the flank. Learning from his first attempt, the general added a third infantry division to assist in dislodging the Turks from their positions. It was said that all soldiers involved, from commanders down to the troops, were convinced the plan would fail.

Beginning early in the morning of April 17, the EEF unleashed a punishing artillery bombardment on Turkish positions by field guns and naval vessels anchored offshore. Following the barrage, the infantry attacked Turkish lines, supported by six "landships," as the new battlefield innovation that came to be known as tanks were then known. But the Turks were ready. From German aircraft observations, the Turks were well aware of EEF preparations. They had reinforced their 20,000-strong garrison with ample machine guns and artillery, which were ranged to cover every immediate approach to their lines. Additional trenches had been dug and protected by barbed-wire obstacles.

When the attack came, the EEF was dealt a punishing blow. Nearly every attempt by infantry and mounted troops to reach Turkish lines failed. Tanks, used as portable machine-gun nests scattered along the front in advance of the infantry, proved magnets for Turkish fire, which knocked them out of action. The Turks held their ground and then counterattacked against the EEF's exposed flanks. German aircraft ruled the skies, strafing and bombing the attackers. There were some EEF successes, but none significant enough to affect the course of battle. When headquarters took stock of the failures after three days of fighting with no significant gains while suffering upwards of 6,000 casualties, the offensive was called off. British military command in London began referring to Gaza as "a second Gallipoli."

After twice resisting assaults on Gaza, the Turks began to doubt British military capabilities. Colonel T. E. Lawrence, better known as "Lawrence of Arabia," wrote: "The Turks . . . had been puffed up by successive victories to imagine that all British generals were incompetent to keep what their troops had won for them by dint of sheer hard fighting."[5]

The Turks reinforced their lines, ushering in a frustrating six months of static warfare. While the Turks dug in, changes were taking place on the British side. In a command shake-up, General Murray was removed from his post and replaced by General Sir Edmund Allenby, who arrived in theater in June 1917. His assumption of overall command of the Egyptian Expeditionary Force would teach the Turks that they had been wrong about British generals. Full of energy and purpose, Allenby drove and inspired his forces. "The Bull," as Allenby was known, reorganized the troops into a new force structure, inspected the entire front, personally reconnoitered the no-man's land separating the two armies and regularly visited his men along the front. In both a symbolic and practical move, he moved headquarters from Cairo to Sinai. His forces trained hard and drilled, regaining their morale. A few months after his arrival, Allenby was ready to attack along the entire front.

Allenby's arrival coincided with a greater commitment by the British War Office to the Palestine theater of operations, epitomized by Prime Minister Lloyd George's instructions to Allenby to take Jerusalem as a Christmas present for the British people. With the war in Europe bogged down in static trench warfare, Lloyd George knew the people needed a morale-booster. To accomplish this task, Allenby's arrival was accompanied by additional troops, munitions, heavy guns, equipment and supplies, including Bristol fighters, which would clear the skies of German aircraft.

While the EEF was busy training, the Turks continued to dig in. Gaza had become a fortified camp protected by lines of trenches reminiscent of the European front. Secure behind their defenses, the Turks were confident.

Even though Gaza was the Turks' strongest point, the EEF had twice attacked it head-on. Unable to break the Turkish grip on Gaza via conventional means, a clever plan relying on deception, surprise and speed was devised. A feint would be made at Gaza, quickly followed by a powerful thrust against the Turkish left flank deep in the desert at Beersheba—some 35 miles (60km) to the southeast— which the Turks thought unapproachable by a powerful force due to the distances involved and the lack of available water. Once Beersheba and its precious water supplies were secured, the EEF would then roll up the Turkish line towards Gaza. Though its lines were less developed around Beersheba, Turkish defenses had every advantage of observation. Situated in a shallow depression, Beersheba is surrounded by high ground that commands its approaches, especially Tel Sheva on Beersheba's eastern side—site of an ancient Canaanite city, which the Turks had fortified and entrenched with machine gunners. Strong Turkish defenses lay to the west and southwest of the town.

The plan posed a number of challenges. In order to be within striking distance of Beersheba, situated in the heart of the desert, great distances would have to be crossed over open country. This was overcome with a series of night marches, bringing forward overwhelming numbers of men and guns, backed by transport, all undetected by German aircraft. By night, the barren dry plains came alive with columns of men and horses. Water continued to pose the most serious hindrance. Allenby's plan hinged on one crucial point: capturing Beersheba's wells intact. The assault would need to be quick—lasting no more than one day—completed before the attackers' water supplies were exhausted.

An elaborate ruse was devised to convince the Turks that the main attack was on Gaza and the attack on Beersheba a mere feint. False army papers indicating "wrong positions for Allenby's main formation, a wrong direction of the coming attack, and a date some days too late" were allowed to fall into enemy hands."[6] The ruse was said to have been read by General Kressenstein himself, who believed it unquestioningly. That the Turks took the bait was evident from their work on Gaza's defenses to the detriment of preparations along the Beersheba line.

EEF infantry divisions were concentrated opposite Gaza's defenses. All began with a massive bombardment of Gaza on October 27, days before the actual assault. Joined by French and British naval vessels anchored offshore, EEF land- and ship-based artillery—aided by balloon observers—pounded Turkish trenches and artillery batteries. After serving earlier in the war on the Western front, Allenby "was full of Western ideas of gun powder and weight."[7] The attention on Gaza reaffirmed the belief that this is where the EEF would again strike.

After the last of their series of night marches towards Beersheba on the night of October 30, 1917, over 40,000 EEF troops were in position for the attack on Beersheba, which would begin the next morning. The plan called for the infantry to smash the town's defenses to the south and west while the mounted forces were to envelop the town and attack from the east, adding further pressure to the Turkish defenses as well as preventing Turkish reinforcement or escape, and being prepared to quickly secure the town upon capture.

In the early hours of October 31, Turkish trenches to the west and southwest of Beersheba were hit by a cruel artillery bombardment by more than one hundred guns. The first phase of the assault on Beersheba came after the artillery barrage, with two infantry divisions attacking Beersheba's western fortifications. As the EEF infantry advanced, Turkish machine guns raked the plain with heavy, accurate fire while German aircraft bombed and strafed the attackers. Infantry made their way forward and charged through the Turkish defenses, fighting with bayonets in savage hand-to-hand fighting until the Turks were driven from their positions at around 13:00.

After crossing difficult ground en route, the Desert Mounted Corps, recently created as part of Allenby's force reorganization, attacked strongly fortified Tel Sheva. Concealed Turkish machine guns and German aircraft dropping bombs and diving with machine guns blazing slowed the advance. The heavier than expected fighting delayed the plan for a combined infantry and mounted assault. Tel Sheva's defenses broke and fell by 15:00—far later than intended, threatening the entire operation, which hinged on capturing Beersheba's wells. Only one and a half hours of daylight remained, yet the wells—the pivotal element of the attack— remained in Turkish hands. More Turkish positions stood between the precious water and EEF forces. The mounted forces had ridden through the night and needed watering. It had been anywhere from 26–48 hours since their horses had last drunk water. When word got back to Allenby's headquarters that the force had been held up and was considering alternate watering options in the event that Beersheba's wells were not taken, Allenby reportedly said "water your horses in Beersheba tonight—no more than that, no less . . ."[8] With the next nearest available water twelve hours away, there really was no alternative. The horses' speed was the only hope of overcoming the last Turkish positions between the EEF and the wells. English Yeomanry cavalry had been detached for a covering role and were not readily available; the only option was the Australian Light Horse. A mounted force whose mobility and speed allowed them to cover great range, the Light Horse were infantry who rode horses for transportation but dismounted to attack; they were not cavalrymen. This did not stop Brigadier General William Grant of the 4th Light Horse Brigade from offering to take on the assignment of a mounted cavalry charge.

Despite the urgency, it was some time before the units were formed up for attack, for the men and horses had been dispersed as a protective measure against German air attacks. At 16:30, Grant led two mounted regiments against Beersheba's eastern defenses, advancing in the face of Turkish machine-gun fire. Brandishing their bayonets like cavalry swords, the Australian Light Horsemen—in what has been called one of the last great cavalry charges in history—charged the Turkish lines at full gallop. As the Turks discerned the horsemen through the clouds of reddish dust, they became very uneasy in the face of this surprise mounted advance, for they feared the cavalry. Turkish fire was largely ineffective. "Habitually, rifles and machine guns fire high at rapidly incoming targets and the less steady the soldiers the more is forgotten in sight correction."[9]

The light horsemen reached the Turkish lines, some leaping over the trenches on their way into town to secure the wells while others dismounted to engage the Turks in savage hand-to-hand combat. "You can't imagine Light Horsemen with bayonets . . . charging across the trenches and that sort of business to clean out the fort . . . it was just a matter of winding the whole show up then. We did finish up by watering in Beersheba that night."[10] The wells, so vital to the EEF, were captured intact, despite having being prepared for demolition.

The fall of Beersheba—which the Turks had considered an impenetrable position—made them uneasy about their ability to hold the entire sector. Germany's official observer, Gaston Bodart, noted in his report that "the position at Gaza, in consequence of this victory, now became untenable."[11] When a 70-strong EEF camel-borne raiding force sent to harass Turkish troops retreating from Beersheba cut the road south of Hebron, the Turks mistakenly thought Allenby's force was moving on Jerusalem via Hebron. They countered this perceived threat by pulling troops away from Gaza. With the EEF controlling Beersheba, they now threatened to outflank Gaza and choke its supply routes. However, water shortages north of Beersheba slowed the EEF's next moves. Attacks on Turkish positions continued against Gaza's left flank; the pressure on Gaza was mounting.

On the morning of November 2, 1917 EEF infantry captured Gaza's first line defenses. While they paused to consolidate their lines around Gaza, pressure was maintained by other units chipping away at the Turks' defenses until the Turks caved in and withdrew their forces, which pulled back and redeployed around Jerusalem.

With Gaza's left flank broken, the attack on the city was renewed at midnight on November 6, 1917. The EEF attack met little opposition, and the mostly abandoned city was taken the next day. This time, Gaza was unquestionably theirs.

By Way of Deception—Part II

It had taken three attempts—the last one involving an elaborate ruse—to finally break the Turks' hold on the Gaza–Beersheba line, unlocking the so-called gateway to Palestine. Now the Turks were on the run. After months suffering from heat and boredom while slowly pushing the Turks out of the Sinai desert in 1917, the British-led EEF troops were now in motion. With both Beersheba and Gaza captured and the Turks in disarray, it looked to General Sir Edmund Allenby as if he was on his way to quickly accomplishing his mission to "conquer the city of Jerusalem and bring about the downfall of the Ottoman in Palestine."[12]

The early days of November 1917 were characterized by days and nights of ceaseless activity as the EEF advanced rapidly, constantly fighting. The Gaza–Beersheba defensive barrier had been shattered; thousands of Turkish prisoners, heavy guns and supplies had been taken. But water shortages slowed the force, which was being pressed relentlessly by Allenby in an effort to achieve a massive Turkish surrender. Even the legendary Australian Light Horsemen, known at times to forgo their own needs in favor of watering their thirsty horses, had their limits. Despite their best efforts, the lack of water proved as much an enemy to the EEF as the Turks themselves. Turkish forces retreated, saved at times only by brave rear-guard holding actions by German machine gunners and Austrian artillerymen, who slowed Allenby's forces long enough to allow the Turks to retreat and redeploy.

Allenby's forces advanced up Palestine's coast, conquering the coastal plain as far north as Jaffa on November 16, and the following month reached the Nahr al-Auja (Yarkon River) and beyond, but water shortages foiled the British general's hopes of destroying the Turkish army in a *coup de grace*. Delivering British Prime Minister Lloyd George's request to capture Jerusalem as a morale-boosting "Christmas present for the British nation" would now require a slow campaign through Judea's hills.

The rapid advances on the open plains ended with the change in terrain. After withdrawing from Gaza, the Turks had managed to redeploy in the narrow passes and exposed ridges around Jerusalem. Flushing out the well-entrenched defenders would be a slow and tedious process. Geography dictated the assault would essentially be an infantry campaign, with machine guns, rifles and bayonets doing the brunt of the work. The infantry's task was complicated by a supply bottleneck, with only the main highway from Jaffa fit for wheeled transport, supplies and heavy guns.

Just as so much had depended upon it in the desert, water again had an impact on campaigning, this time in the form of rain. When the rains hit on November 19, Palestine, where seasons can change almost overnight, saw a complete shift in weather conditions. Bitter cold weather, for which the EEF was completely unprepared, set in. The combination of exposure and lack of sleep from constant fighting took its toll on the fighting men, and many became sick. Supplying the men on the front lines became even more difficult, with transportation grinding to a halt as all turned to mud.

Between the weather and the defensible mountainous terrain, the EEF's advance slowed to a crawl. When better weather returned, allowing transport to resume, the Turks' luck ran out. Trucks and thousands of camels and donkeys pressed into service moved supplies along the difficult Jaffa–Jerusalem road. With its supply network back in place, the EEF steadily flushed the Turks out of their defensive positions ridge by ridge, suffering heavy losses.

Another EEF force was moving up the southern approach to Jerusalem, from Beersheba towards Hebron. Out of respect for the holy places, EEF forces halted south of Hebron until learning it had been evacuated by the Turks, and then proceeded to the outskirts of Bethlehem, which was taken after it, too, had been abandoned. Jerusalem's southern approaches were now cut.

The final thrust against Jerusalem began on December 8 with a heavy artillery bombardment of Turkish positions west of the city. Allenby recounted: "The troops . . . pressed steadily forward. The mere physical difficulty of climbing the steep and rocky hillsides and crossing the deep valleys would have sufficed to render progress slow, and the opposition encountered was considerable."[13] When the EEF reached the Jerusalem–Nablus road, on which the city was now dependent for supplies, Jerusalem was in danger of being completely cut off. On the night of December 8, 1917, Turkish soldiers fled from the city towards Jericho and Nablus. The following morning, on December 9, Jerusalem's mayor delivered a formal letter of surrender. Jerusalem was surrendered to the EEF without a shot being fired within the city limits. The EEF moved in and established a perimeter around the city, although Turkish resistance sought to confine the EEF victory to just the city itself.

Jerusalem's capture became official with General Allenby's entrance to the city on December 11, 1917, which became famous for its simplicity. Riding a tall white horse, Allenby approached Jaffa Gate of the walled Old City along a route lined by representatives of the Allied forces. Forgoing the ostentatious entrance into the city that was becoming for a conqueror, the large, impressive figure of Allenby, with white hair and mustache, ruddy cheeks and protruding chin, dismounted out of respect, choosing not to ride over the stones on which Jesus had walked, and entered Jerusalem on foot, followed by his staff and guests. The ceremony itself, devoid of bands, flag-raising ceremony or other fanfare, was also a simple affair. Allenby stood on the steps of the historic citadel, or Tower of David, adjacent to Jaffa Gate, and pledged to maintain and protect the status quo in the holy places "according to the existing customs and beliefs of those to whose faiths they are sacred."[14]

Allenby's thoughts were likely on the mission that lay ahead, for Turks remained well entrenched throughout central and northern Palestine. Jerusalem had been taken as ordered, but the battle for Palestine was far from over. The British war cabinet ordered further operations, with the ultimate aim of capturing Damascus and Beirut.

With the ground too wet for movement beyond limited operations to secure his lines, Allenby saw there was no choice but for a break from major offensive operations. Across the Jordan, Colonel T. E. Lawrence was busy harassing the Turks with a band of Arab rebels and fomenting Arab rebellion against Turkish rule in support of the British war effort. Among the few indigenous groups who had not remained loyal to Turkey, Arabs in the Hijaz region (encompassing today's Saudi Arabia and Jordan) commanded by Emir Feisal, son of the Sharif of Mecca, attacked sections of the 800-mile (1,300-km) Turkish-built Damascus to Medina Hijaz railway line—lifeline of the 20,000 Turkish troops stationed south of Amman. Attacks on the railway had contributed to Jerusalem's capture by squeezing the Turks around Jerusalem as the EEF threat to the city had intensified.

More than just carrying out acts of sabotage, the Arab uprising attained some very real gains. Following their capture of Aqaba in July 1917, the Arab rebels began acting as Allenby's right flank. To mark their elevated importance in British eyes, Emir Feisal's army was put under Allenby's command, with the general responsible for their operations and equipment. Lawrence served both as Feisal's advisor and liaison officer to Allenby. The Arab uprising was estimated to have tied down or affected 40,000 Turkish troops and a good amount of their artillery, imposing a very real strain on Turkish fighting strength. "Their active revolt had been of immense advantage to the British in western Palestine. Without their cooperation, spasmodic and uncertain as it was, the force opposed to Allenby would have been substantially stronger, his right flank would have been always exposed to heavy pressure, the local Arabs might have been openly hostile, and the whole course of the campaign must have been seriously affected."[15] Not everyone held the same view. Colonel Richard Meinertzhagen, the intelligence officer who masterminded the ruse used to break the Gaza–Beersheba line, wrote in his war diary that Lawrence's Arabs were "a looting rabble" and "had little more than a nuisance value."[16]

Allenby planned a move on Jericho as a preliminary step towards a thrust across the Jordan River. By mid-February 1918, better weather and an improved supply situation opened the way to a renewed offensive. With EEF lines stretching across western Palestine from the coast to Jerusalem, Allenby could strike anywhere. Faced with such uncertainty, the Turks were forced to spread their forces thinly. As in many places, the force defending the Jericho route was not particularly strong. After a break of more than two months, the EEF renewed its offensive on the morning of February 19, 1918. EEF infantry backed by artillery advanced down the Jerusalem–Jericho road, with the right flank guarded by a force moving over mountain passes from Bethlehem towards the Dead Sea. Turkish defenses were concentrated on the main road, with additional forces deployed in the barren, rocky hills on its flank. The fighting moved quickly down to Jericho and the Dead Sea, the lowest point on earth. The situation on the flank was more difficult, where geography made for tough going over the precipitous hills. The Turks, well entrenched in the ridges, swept the EEF advance with machine-gun and artillery fire. But when the main EEF advance threatened to cut off their lines of communication, the Turks withdrew, evacuating even beyond Jericho, across the Jordan River or northward. Jericho, which the Turks had stripped of supplies and any booty of benefit, was taken on February 21, 1918, only two days after the offensive began, in a spiritual victory emulating that of Joshua and the Israelites. Though its capture offered little in material terms, it did open the door for operations across the Jordan River.

Allenby's focus shifted eastward. The Arab Northern Army, as Lawrence's Arab forces were known, was striking northwards, drawing Turkish forces away from Amman. Allenby sought to move against Amman, relieving pressure from the Arabs and allowing them to strike even further north, perhaps as far as a vital railway junction at Deraa (in modern-day Syria) that could affect the entire Turkish logistics system in the area. But the EEF's forays across the Jordan in the spring months failed. EEF troops crossing the Jordan River took a beating from the Turks, suffering heavy casualties. The plans to take Amman were abandoned—a setback for the EEF and a morale-booster for the Turks, who hadn't had much to be happy about since the early days at Gaza. A second foray across the Jordan similarly ended in withdrawal, with the Turks sending the EEF reeling. In a further setback for Allenby, large numbers of seasoned troops were pulled out of his theater of operations and hastily transferred to the Western Front. While failures, the two thrusts across the Jordan diverted Turkish troop strength eastward, a result that would greatly serve EEF efforts in the upcoming operation to dislodge the Turks from the rest of Palestine.

After the unsuccessful attempts on Amman, the EEF hunkered down in the Jordan Valley. Reinvigorated by their recent successes, the Turks became more aggressive—keeping EEF forward positions under regular artillery fire. The Desert Mounted Corps—champions of the earlier campaign in the desert and the capture of Beersheba and Gaza—was stationed in the Jordan Valley. Hot, dusty, and infested with flies by day and malaria-carrying mosquitoes by night, the Jordan Valley was a miserable posting for the mostly Australian and New Zealander mounted corps. Allenby knew the Turks were terrified of the horsemen and that they thought wherever they were, the EEF would next strike. This played into a larger plan Allenby was formulating to defeat the Turks in a *coup de grace* that would bring total enemy defeat in his theater of operations—the victory that had eluded him right after taking Beersheba and Gaza.

Building on the Turks' fear of the mounted forces, Allenby embarked on an ambitious plan to convince the Turks that his attack was to be to the east by means of a fictitious reinforcement of the mounted corps' Jordan Valley positions. In a masterful feat of deception, rumors were spread about plans for a renewed assault across the Jordan River. Troops marched down into the Jordan Valley by day and were trucked out at night. Dust was deliberately generated both to create the appearance of heavy activity and to make life difficult for Turkish observers. They went as far as to construct dummy horses of wooden frames covered with blankets. In actuality, the mounted divisions left the Jordan Valley, though leaving their camp intact to add to the deception. With all the "evidence" of reinforcement, Turkish observers could not discern the camp was empty. Aggressive air activity kept the EEF lines and rear largely free of enemy aerial observation. Air service overflights and Turkish deserters added to the intelligence information on Turkish dispositions, all of which confirmed the Turks had taken the bait. Convinced that the threat lay across the Jordan River, Turkish heavy artillery, dumps, stores and camps were all positioned and reinforced accordingly. Meanwhile, during the first weeks of September 1918, Allenby was massing artillery, infantry and mounted troops on Palestine's central Sharon plains, all without Turkish knowledge.

A confident Allenby visited his men, camouflaged among the Sharon region's orange and olive groves, his presence inspiring them. By midnight of September 18, 1918, with all the necessary elements in place, Allenby gave the green light. The operation began at 01:00 on September 19 with a bombing run by the single Handley-Page bomber in the theater. Targeting the Afula railway and communications junction, the aerodrome at Jenin and Turkish army commands at Nablus and Tulkarm, the attack wreaked havoc on Turkish communications just as the battle was to begin.

Before dawn, some 300 artillery pieces in the Sharon sector (running from coastal Arsuf inland) opened up on the Turkish lines. After the intense barrage softened up Turkish defenses, EEF infantrymen in their dome-shaped steel helmets, with fixed bayonets, crossed the open ground towards the Turkish trenches. The Turks resisted but the EEF infantry quickly punched through the Turkish lines, creating a breach they immediately set about expanding. A massive mounted force of 9,000 horsemen then charged through the gap the infantry had forced in the coastal sector and raced northward across the Sharon plain heading towards Galilee, with the objective of seizing Afula and Turkish headquarters in Nazareth before heading southeast down the Plain of Esdraelon (Megiddo, or Jezreel Valley) to Beisan (Beit Shean) on the Jordan River, some 80 miles (130km) from where they had begun their advance. This would be accomplished in a mere 34 hours. Turkish forces astride the breach were to be of no concern to the horsemen; the infantry would take care of them. The horsemen were instructed to remain focused on their mission of reaching Galilee to encircle the Turks.

Allenby's plan, which built on the superiority in both quality and quantity of his mounted forces, was for the infantry to drive the Turkish forces back and into the horsemen's hands, who would be waiting to collect them in their dragnet. The Turks had actually been correct in their belief that the mounted forces they feared so much would spearhead Allenby's next move, only they believed these forces were still deployed in the Jordan Valley.

The mounted forces raced northward towards their objectives. Time was of the essence as two critical mountain passes through the Carmel Mountain range to the Plain of Esdraelon in Lower Galilee had to be traversed by the horsemen before the Turks could organize resistance which could cause delays that might endanger Allenby's entire plan.

When a Turkish force was spotted en route from Afula to block the pass leading to that town, the horsemen pressed their advance, travelling the long, narrow, winding pass in the dark. In the morning, they attacked the unsuspecting Turkish unit as they were deploying, eliminating that threat. The way to Afula was cleared, and they went on to capture the town.

General Otto Liman von Sanders, who had taken over command of all Turkish and German forces in Palestine in February 1918 following the loss of Jerusalem and other defeats, followed the attack from his headquarters in Nazareth. Sanders was keeping track of the EEF breakthrough on the Sharon plain but, not realizing that Galilee was teeming with EEF mounted forces, he did not fear immediate attack. When EEF cavalry rode into Nazareth at dawn on September 20, they occupied most of the town without event. When some resistance was organized, the horsemen pulled back, allowing Sanders the opportunity to escape in his pajamas.

With such a rapidly moving advance, EEF generals criss-crossed the country in their cars, staying forward to keep abreast of rapidly changing events. Air service flights and new radio communications technology helped in coordinating the multiple forces involved and following events on the ground in this highly mobile environment.

On the Turkish side, the situation was not clear at all. EEF infantry was attacking across the width of the country, up the Sharon plain and in the hills astride Nablus. Without the benefit of telephone and telegraph connections, Turkish commanders had little access to situational reports other than the often-incoherent reports from soldiers fleeing the EEF onslaught.

British observer W. T. Massey wrote: "Our progress during September was rapid, and the extent of our advance, on a very wide front, is so great that it may be the impression at home that we were weakly opposed. That would be wholly wrong."[17] It wasn't that the Turks did not resist; they were simply outclassed. Allenby's plan had so completely fooled the Turks that the attack had come as a complete surprise. When Turkish troops realized their rear lines were swarming with EEF mounted forces, they correctly feared they were being cut off. Panicking, they began fleeing while they still could, which fit nicely into Allenby's plans.

Within only two days, the Turkish retreat deteriorated into a rout, assisted by EEF air service and cavalry attacks on retreating enemy columns. The battered Turks were more than happy to surrender when they fell into Allenby's cavalry cordon. Allenby was said to have been so certain of success that situation updates he received in the midst of the battle of various victories were almost old news to him.

Allenby's report of September 20, 1918 noted: "On the north our cavalry, traversing the Field of Armageddon, had occupied Nazareth, Afule, and Beisan, and were collecting the disorganized masses of enemy troops and transport as they arrived from the south. All avenues of escape open to the enemy, except the fords across the Jordan between Beisan and Jisr-ed-Dameer were thus closed."[18]

The Turks evacuated the coastal cities of Haifa and Acre (Akko), and Allenby's forces moved in and took both without a fight. The Galilee town of Safed, already clear of Turks, was also taken. The next step was to capture Tiberias and Zemach on the Sea of Galilee, opening the way for an advance on Damascus. With these last objectives secured, the so-called Battle of Megiddo came to an overwhelmingly successful end. A line across the width of Palestine, from Haifa–Nazareth–Tiberias had been secured; all Turkish railway and road lines of communication were now in EEF hands; some 70,000 prisoners had been taken; countless guns, transport and other equipment were destroyed. The Turkish 7th and 8th Armies had by and large been destroyed, and few Turkish troops remained between Allenby's new lines and Damascus. "Allenby concluded proudly and with truth: 'Such a complete victory has seldom been known in all the history of war.'"[19] Even Gaston Bodart's official German report concurred, calling the victory "beyond doubt the most complete victory of the Entente in the war . . ."[20]

But the job was not yet complete. Allenby ordered the advance to reach Damascus. Forces were sent across the Jordan River to capture Amman and up the Golan Heights to Kuneitra as a prelude to a move against Damascus. On September 30, 1918, Damascus was taken, although not before the Turks and Germans fled. French forces, recently contributed to the theater so their country could have a say in the post-war settlement, occupied Beirut on October 6, 1918.

The advance pressed a further 200 miles to Aleppo, which was taken on October 26, 1918. The Turks finally sued for an armistice, which was agreed to on October 30, bringing the war in the theater to an end. On November 11, 1918, an armistice was signed with Germany, ending what became known as the war to end all wars. In post-war arrangements, Palestine became a British protectorate under League of Nations Mandate, while Syria came under French control. The British, initially welcomed as liberators in Palestine, soon found themselves at odds with the Jewish population. A slew of contradictory and conflicting British wartime promises to both Jews and Arabs also came to light, planting the seeds for today's Arab–Israeli conflict.

Notes

1. Steven Allan. "Gaza: The Unsurrendered City." *ERETZ Magazine* (Issue 49, November–December 1996), pp.36–41, 63: p.40.
2. H. S. Gullet. *The Australian Imperial Force in Sinai and Palestine—1914–1918.* (Queensland: University of Queensland Press, 1923), p.282.
3. Sir M. G. E. Bowman-Manifold. *An outline of the Egyptian and Palestine campaigns, 1914 to 1918* (Chatham: W. Y. J. Mackay & Co., 1922), p.31.
4. Gullet. *The Australian Imperial Force in Sinai and Palestine*, p.296.
5. T. E. Lawrence. *Seven Pillars of Wisdom* (Penguin Books, 1926), p.392
6. Lawrence. *Seven Pillars of Wisdom*, pp.393–4.
7. Lawrence. *Seven Pillars of Wisdom*, p.330.
8. http://www.jcu.edu.au/aff/history/net_resources/ellwood/ellwood10.htm
9. David L. Bullock. *Allenby's War: The Palestine-Arabian Campaigns 1916–18* (Blandford Press, 1988), p.75.
10.http://www.jcu.edu.au/aff/history/net_resources/ellwood/ellwood10.htm
11.Bodart, Gaston. "Report on the Fall of Jerusalem, 9 December 1917," in Charles F. Horne (ed.). *Source Records of the Great War, Vol. V* (National Alumni, 1923), www.firstworldwar.com/source/jerusalem_bodart.htm (accessed March 14, 2011).
12.Allan. "Gaza: The Unsurrendered City," p.37.
13.Allenby, Sir Edmund. "The Fall of Jerusalem," in Charles F. Horne (ed.). *Source Records of the Great War, Vol. V* (National Alumni, 1923), www.firstworldwar.com/source/jerusalem_allenby1.htm (accessed March 14, 2011).
14.Allenby, Sir Edmund. "The Fall of Jerusalem," in Charles F. Horne (ed.). *Source Records of the Great War, Vol. V* (National Alumni, 1923), www.firstworldwar.com/source/jerusalem_allenby1.htm (accessed March 14, 2011).
15.H. S. Gullet. *The Australian Imperial Force in Sinai and Palestine—1914–1918.* (Queensland: University of Queensland Press, 1923), p.659.
16.Colonel R. Meinertzhagen. *Middle East Diary* (London: The Cresset Press, 1959), p.41.

17.Massey, W. T. "Allenby's Progress," in Charles F. Horne (ed.). *Source Records of the Great War, Vol. VI* (National Alumni, 1923), www.firstworldwar.com/source/allenby_massey.htm (accessed March 14, 2011).

18.Allenby, Sir Edmund. "The Battle of Megiddo," in Charles F. Horne (ed.). *Source Records of the Great War, Vol. V* (National Alumni, 1923), www.firstworldwar.com/source/megiddo_allenby.htm (accessed March 14, 2011).

19.Chauvel, p.173.

20.Bodart, Gaston. "The Fall of Turkey," in Charles F. Horne (ed.). *Source Records of the Great War, Vol. V* (National Alumni, 1923), www.firstworldwar.com/source/turkey_bodart.htm (accessed March 14, 2011).

British General Edmund Allenby, Commander of British forces in Palestine during World War I, rides a horse alongside the walls of the Old City of Jerusalem in December 1917. Jerusalem was surrendered to the British-led Egyptian Expeditionary Force on December 9, 1917 without a shot being fired in the city limits. Allenby had been asked by British Prime Minister Lloyd George to capture the holy city as a Christmas present for war-weary England. (Eric Matson, Israel Government Press Office)

Mounted Australian soldiers leading Turkish prisoners. The legendary Australian Light Horsemen had more than proven their mettle in breaking the Ottoman hold on the Gaza-Beersheba front, and would continue to carry out crucial roles in operations against Ottoman forces. (Eric Matson, Israel Government Press Office)

Yad Mordechai before the onslaught. Named after Mordechai Analevicz, the 22-year-old leader of the 1943 Warsaw Ghetto uprising against the Nazis, the kibbutz stood in the way of the Egyptian thrust toward Tel Aviv in May 1948. A number of the collective farm's members were Holocaust survivors who had made their way to Palestine as illegal immigrants and now stood ready to defend their new home. (Courtesy of Kibbutz Yad Mordechai Archive)

Guardhouse with barbed wire. Kibbutz Yad Mordechai was certainly not prepared to withstand a thrust by the Royal Egyptian Army with infantry brigades, heavy artillery, tanks, and armored units, supported by an air force. Courtesy of Kibbutz Yad Mordechai Archive

Egyptian howitzers in action against Yad Mordechai, footage from Egyptian film.
(Courtesy of Kibbutz Yad Mordechai Archive)

Egyptian infantry advance on Yad Mordechai, footage from Egyptian film. (Courtesy of
Kibbutz Yad Mordechai Archive)

Yad Mordechai defenses. Bren Gun. Yad Mordechai's fortifications consisted mostly of trenches and sandbag-reinforced bunkers. With a small arsenal of light weapons and hand grenades, just over 100 defenders held off a brigade-size Egyptian force. (Courtesy of Kibbutz Yad Mordechai Archive)

Yad Mordechai, completely destroyed. (Courtesy of Kibbutz Yad Mordechai Archive)

Yad Mordechai's damaged water tower, seen after the kibbutz was retaken. Egyptian artillery used the kibbutz's water tower to range their guns. The tower was hit repeatedly, and precious water streamed from holes. The collapsed tower remains to this day, riddled with holes from the 1948 shelling.
(Courtesy of Kibbutz Yad Mordechai Archive)

Yad Mordechai following recapture by Israeli forces.
(Courtesy of Kibbutz Yad Mordechai Archive)

The shore Battery at Ras Nasrani prevented Israeli or Israel-bound shipping from entering the Gulf of Eilat. Notice barrel has been spiked after capture. (Israel Government Press Office)

After being dropped deep into Egyptian territory on October 29, 1956, Israeli paratroopers prepare trenches and clean their weapons at their deployment just outside Mitla Pass. (Avraham Vered, Israel Government Press Office)

Light aircraft helped maintain communications with IDF troops engaged deep in the Sinai. (Israel Air Force History Dept)

Southern Command Chief of Staff Lieutenant Colonel Rehavam "Gandhi" Zeevi flew out in a Piper Cub the morning of October 31, 1956 to meet Paratroops commander Ariel Sharon for an on-site assessment. Zeevi stressed the need to avoid unnecessary operations in order to minimize casualties, but authorized Sharon to dispatch a patrol to reconnoiter Mitla Pass. (Israel Air Force History Dept)

IDF paratroopers on a practice jump from an Israel Air Force C-47 Dakota. (Israel Air Force History Dept)

The Golan Heights are a formidable natural barrier. The Syrians had established a network of heavily fortified positions along the border, with all possible routes of attack mined and covered by pre-ranged firing positions. Dug into the rough volcanic basalt was a Soviet-designed defensive network that was nearly impervious to air and artillery attack. (Moshe Milner, Israel Government Press Office)

The assault on Tel Faher. Making their way up the twisting route to Tel Faher, the Israeli infantrymen had to cross dense layers of barbed wire and a minefield before reaching Tel Faher's trenches and bunkers. (Israel Defense Forces Archive)

The Golani attack on Tel Faher. With the Israeli attack plan in shambles, communications confused, its tanks knocked out of action, and the few remaining halftracks drawing heavy fire, the Israelis decided to dismount and continue their assault on foot. (Israel Defense Forces Archive)

Tel Faher's reinforced bunkers and pillboxes, some cut into the rock, were interconnected via rows of concrete-lined communications trenches. Manning the positions and dugouts was a company from the Syrian 187th Infantry Battalion armed with anti-tank guns, recoilless rifles, heavy machine guns and mortars. (Israel Defense Forces Archive)

Israeli M-3 Halftrack knocked out of action during the advance on the Golan. With the Syrians' advantageous firing positions, antitank fire targeted Israeli armor with great effectiveness. None of the Israeli tanks made it up to Tel Faher, and more than half the halftracks were damaged or stuck on the attack route. (Israel Defense Forces Archive)

Specially improvised bulldozers cleared the way for the armored columns to advance. Combat engineers were at the forefront, removing mines and carving a path for the tanks while under heavy fire. (Israel Defense Forces Archive)

IDF forces in action by Tuwafik. In the southern Golan Heights, Israeli tanks and mounted infantry fought their way up the treacherous, winding mountain road, breaking through the Syrian defenses at Tuwafik. Paratroopers helicoptered ahead behind Syrian lines, but for the most part found only isolated pockets of Syrian resistance. (Israel Defense Forces Archive)

Damaged IDF tank under repair. Technical teams rapidly returned damaged tanks to service. (Israel Defense Forces Archive)

Israeli AMX-13 light tanks during a short stop on the Syrian frontier before going into action on the Golan Heights. (Ram Lahover, Israel Government Press Office)

Memorial to the Golani Brigade soldiers who fell at Tel Faher, which was renamed "Golani Lookout." (Israel Defense Forces Archive)

IDF Centurion tanks moving into positions for a counter-attack on the Golan Heights. The fresh Israeli reserve units halted the near–and, in some cases, actual–retreat of what remained of their front-line forces and set about checking the Syrian advance. By midnight on day two of the war, the reserves had managed to stabilize what had been a disintegrating front. (David Rubinger. Israel Government Press Office)

IDF convoy moving northwards past a destroyed Syrian tank on the Golan Heights. Hundreds of wrecked and burnt Syrian tanks and armored vehicles and other vehicles littered the landscape. (Zeev Spector, Israel Government Press Office)

Syrian T-62 tanks and bridging equipment knocked out by the Israeli anti-tank ditch. Syrian mine-clearing tanks and bridge-layers led the way to overcome the Israeli obstacles, like the 20 mile (30km)-long anti-tank ditch along the border from Mount Hermon to Rafid, an obstacle Syrian armor had to cross under fire from Israeli tanks positioned behind ramparts. (Eitan Haris, Israel Government Press Office)

Syrian T55 and T54 tanks knocked out of action on the Golan Heights. (Menashe Azouri, Israel Government Press Office)

IAF F-15 "Baz" from the Knights of the Twin Tail Squadron credited with downing 4 Syrian aircraft. Between June 7–11, 1982 IAF F-15s downed 34 Syrian aircraft while the F-16s surpassed them with 46, decimating the Syrian Air Force. (Israel Air Force History Dept)

Destroyed Syrian air defense ZSU-23-4 "Shilka" antiaircraft quadruple-barrel 23mm gun vehicle. With its integrated radar, this highly capable weapon system could detect and hit low-flying aircraft in a two-mile range with a wall of fire, making it ideal for protecting Syria's SAM sites. (Israel Air Force History Dept)

IAF C-2 Kfir of the 1st Fighter Squadron taking off from Hazor Air Force Base for a mission over Lebanon. The Kfir is armed with AIM-9D Sidewinder air-to-air missiles, 500-lb Mk.-82 bombs, and jettisonable fuel tanks. (Israel Air Force History Dept)

E-2C Hawkeye airborne early warning (AEW) command and control aircraft gave the Israelis an advantageous aerial battlefield picture. Packed with powerful computers, situational displays and secure communications, the Hawkeye is capable of detecting and assessing threats from approaching enemy aircraft over ranges of about 300 miles—more than enough to peer into Syria. Operators tracked Syrian aircraft as they took off from their airbases and vectored F-15 and F-16 fighters to intercept them. (Moshe Milner, Israel Government Press Office)

CHAPTER 13

ISRAEL'S "MAGINOT LINE"

1948 War of Independence

"Go and rest," Colonel Nahum Sarig, the *Palmach*'s commander of the southern Negev region, told them. "You all deserve it."[1] After six days holding up an Egyptian brigade-size force, the fighters of Kibbutz Yad Mordechai certainly did deserve a break.

In May 1948, Egyptian media trumpeted news from Kibbutz Yad Mordechai as the capture of "one of the fiercest and most powerful strongholds of the Zionist settlements, built according to the most modern defense plans."[2] Dubbed a "Maginot Line," it was described as having two-story-high heavy-gun posts and "surrounded by a trench three feet deep—after ten steps there was another trench five feet deep and still further on one six feet in depth. The final defense line was electrified barbed wire."[3]

The description was far-fetched. Yad Mordechai's fortifications were far more humble, consisting mostly of trenches and sandbag-reinforced bunkers. With those simple defenses and a small arsenal of light weapons and hand grenades, just over 100 defenders held off a brigade-size military force from May 18 to 23, 1948, buying vital time that the fledgling state of Israel needed in the desperate first days of Israel's War of Independence (also known as the 1948 Arab–Israeli War). For that, the battle has been called one of the most decisive of the war.

The conflict officially began with Israel's declaration of statehood on May 14, 1948. Half a year before, on November 29, 1947, the United Nations passed a resolution calling for the partition of the British Mandate of Palestine into separate Jewish and Arab states. The so-called Partition Plan was accepted by the Jews and rejected by the Arabs. Determined to prevent the establishment of a Jewish state in Palestine, the armies of Egypt, Syria, Transjordan, Iraq and Lebanon attacked the day after Israel declared independence.

Kibbutz Yad Mordechai, a collective farm situated just over a kilometer from the Gaza Strip on the main road leading north, stood in the way of the Egyptian thrust toward Tel Aviv. The settlements—especially those on the frontiers—were being counted on by the *Haganah*— the pre-state underground army that, upon statehood, became the Israel Defense Forces (IDF)—to be centers of resistance, holding out against the expected onslaught. All able-bodied Jewish men and women in Palestine belonged to the *Haganah*. Originally a loose structure of local defense groups, the *Haganah* had grown into a large organization charged with the defense of Palestine's Jewish settlements. With its limited forces and equipment, the *Haganah* relied on every Jew to stand and fight.

Kibbutz Yad Mordechai

Kibbutz Yad Mordechai was named after Mordechai Analevicz, the 22-year-old leader of the 1943 Warsaw Ghetto uprising against the Nazis. A number of its members were Holocaust survivors who had made their way to Palestine as illegal immigrants after World War II, and now stood ready to defend their new home. Defensive preparations for the kibbutz were organized by Grisha Zilberstein, who was in charge of headquarters and disposition of manpower and arms, and Munio Brandvein commanded the defensive positions. A command post was built with communication links to 10 sandbag-reinforced outposts on the kibbutz 1.8 mile-long (3km) perimeter, each to be manned by a force of three. The kibbutz strongpoint was a pillbox built to the south, some 1,000 feet (300m) outside the perimeter fence.

Yad Mordechai's defensive force consisted of fewer than one hundred men: a mix of kibbutz members and newly arrived refugees from Europe being housed at the kibbutz. Its arsenal included antipersonnel "Shoe Mines" planted in front of the defensive posts, one PIAT antitank weapon with three rounds, a pair of 2-inch mortars with 50 shells, one Browning .30-caliber machine gun, one German-made light machine gun, four submachine guns, 37 rifles and about 400 hand grenades, supplemented by Molotov cocktails. With that, the defenders were expected to hold off several months of sporadic attacks by lightly armed Arab irregulars. That was nothing new, as the kibbutz had already faced such assaults. Yad Mordechai had been isolated and, at times, cut off completely during the spring 1948 "battle of the roads," when local Arabs blocked the routes connecting Jewish settlements, effectively putting them under siege.

Yad Mordechai was certainly not prepared to withstand a thrust by the Royal Egyptian Army with infantry brigades, heavy artillery, tanks, and armored units, supported by an air force. The new Israeli state's defensive strategy was built on the premise that Egypt would largely sit out the war. Initially intending not to intervene in the conflict, Egypt was almost forced to enter it due to competing interests and rivalries. Fearing that Transjordan's British-trained and -led Arab Legion—the best force in the region—would seize the lion's share of liberated Palestine and gain prestige, Egyptian King Farouk committed some 10,000 men against Israel in a two-pronged attack. One column moved towards Beersheba, planning to continue on to Jerusalem, while the second headed north up the coastal route, expecting to reach Tel Aviv within days. With friendly Arab villages along the way, the road to Tel Aviv would be virtually clear once the border settlements were passed.

The Israeli Palmach (an abbreviation for *"Plugot Machatz"* or Strike Companies of the *Haganah*) left a force of 16 men at Yad Mordechai, supplementing the kibbutz's strength and arsenal with its rifles and two British Bren .303-inch light machine guns. Field commander Brandvein spoke of the kibbutz's important strategic location: "Here we sit on the main road between Cairo and Tel Aviv. We are a barrier. You see how we have been able to cut off Arab traffic. If this place is captured, the Egyptian army can go straight north to the center of the country."[4] Palmach commander Nahum Sarig echoed those sentiments, writing that "the fighters knew that the battle wasn't only for Yad Mordechai but also for Tel Aviv and the entire country."[5]

Planning on penetrating deep into Israel, the Egyptian forces required secure lines of communication, to which Yad Mordechai, sitting alongside the main road, posed a potential threat. After unsuccessfully attacking two Jewish settlements further south, the Egyptians saw that it would be a mistake to attack every one along the way. Yad Mordechai's location, however, dictated that it could neither be bypassed nor merely contained—the Egyptian command ordered it to be taken. Soldiers of the Egyptian army's Seventh Brigade moved in, and the 1st Battalion was charged with taking the kibbutz.

While the kibbutz was implementing its defense plan on the evening of May 18, 1948, a pair of Royal Egyptian Air Force (REAF) Supermarine Spitfires strafed and bombed it. Faced with the reality of imminent attack, the Palmach evacuated 70 children and 42 others from the kibbutz, including children's caretakers, pregnant women, mothers with babies, and the sick. One hundred and thirty people remained: the kibbutz members (including 30 women) and the small Palmach contingent. The women prepared refreshments for the men in the positions and helped care for the wounded. Three women also served as runners after communications were knocked out by Egyptian artillery, and one held a command position in the trenches.

The Egyptians' first serious assault began on the morning of May 19. Egyptian aircraft dropped incendiary bombs, setting off fires throughout the kibbutz. Then their artillery, situated a few kilometers back, opened fire, using the kibbutz's water tower to range their guns. The tower was hit, and precious water streamed from holes caused by shell fragments (The collapsed tower remains to this day, riddled with holes from the 1948 shelling). Directed by a spotter plane, Egyptian 25-pounder field guns, 6-pounders and mortars bombarded the entire kibbutz in a methodical pattern for four hours. The only lull came after the Egyptians dropped leaflets announcing an hour-long truce for the kibbutz to surrender. When the hour passed, the bombardment resumed.

The Egyptians directed particularly heavy fire at the pillbox, making their intentions quite clear. Blocking their advance from the south, the pillbox would need to be taken if the Egyptians were to make an infantry assault on the kibbutz. The seven men manning the pillbox followed the Egyptians' progress through binoculars. With armored cars providing cover fire, Egyptian soldiers began traversing a deep ravine known as a wadi, and then advanced toward the pillbox. After patiently waiting for them to come within effective range, the men in the pillbox opened fire. Riflemen picked off the Egyptian officers while a Bren gun fired into the ranks. The attack dissolved into confusion and the Egyptians retreated, seeking cover. After regrouping, the Egyptians came at the pillbox a second and third time. Both times, they broke and fled in the face of carefully directed fire from their objective.

With three infantry thrusts defeated, the Egyptians renewed their artillery barrage on the pillbox, as if to exact revenge. Fires broke out in the fields between the pillbox and the kibbutz, leaving the men inside feeling their isolation. When Egyptian infantry came at them a fourth time, the defenders prepared grenades and allowed the attackers to approach, nervously waiting as the Egyptians came closer and closer. When the order came, each man threw his grenade and opened fire. Some soldiers took cover behind fallen comrades, while others fled. A few Egyptians, however, managed to probe around the pillbox and approached from behind, cutting through its wire defenses. The situation in the pillbox had become grave. Surrounded, with only a few grenades remaining, their Thompson submachine gun out of ammunition and the Bren firing only single shots, the pillbox commander ordered a retreat to the kibbutz, which was successfully accomplished after the Egyptians inexplicably pulled back.

With the pillbox neutralized, the Egyptians could now reach the kibbutz. Protecting its southern approach were posts 1 and 2, which would bear the brunt of the Egyptian attack. Built on top of small hills, those positions had clear views of the approach and good fields of fire. Emerging from behind White Hill, a low mound about 300 feet (100m) in front of the posts, some 60 Egyptian soldiers came at the kibbutz under heavy covering fire. Brandvein had ordered the defenders to "shoot only when the Egyptians get to the fence."[6] With great discipline, the Israelis held their fire. As they approached, the

Egyptians tripped antipersonnel mines, resulting in casualties. More fell when the defenders fired mortars, threw grenades and opened small-arms fire. In another wave, the Egyptians made it to the barbed wire entanglements just 30 feet (10m) below the positions, and many were killed while cutting the wire. Seeing their comrades fall, a number of Egyptians turned and fled. Brandvein told how he helped stop one thrust when he "hit them with enfilading fire with the machine gun and saw them drop."[7]

In all, three or four Egyptian assaults were repulsed. This did not come without cost to the kibbutz—six men had been killed and about 20 wounded. Egyptian casualties were much heavier, estimated at between 100 and 200.

With ammunition already running low and some weapons out of action, the Israelis scavenged a dozen British rifles, ammunition, a PIAT antitank rocket launcher with 12 rounds and two Bren guns from dead and wounded Egyptians on the battlefield during the night. They also laid additional antipersonnel mines and burrowed protective cavities into the trench walls.

With morning, the Egyptians renewed their attack. This time the mortar and artillery barrage was more precise, seeking out the trenches while machine-gun fire continually raked the kibbutz. Then smoke shells were fired, which the defenders knew was meant to mask an infantry advance. When the wind shifted, the smoke cleared, revealing Egyptian troops working at the entanglements with wire-cutters. The attack was stopped with rifle fire and hand grenades. Armored cars led the second Egyptian assault with machine guns blazing, but mortar fire from the kibbutz kept them at bay. That and the third attack were also repulsed, each with heavy losses to the Egyptians. With its own casualties mounting, the kibbutz pleaded with Israeli command for reinforcements, but Israel was under attack on all fronts. In addition to the Egyptian thrusts, Transjordan's Arab Legion was threatening Jerusalem while Syrian, Lebanese, Iraqi and irregular guerilla forces kept the pressure on Israel's north. Resources had to be dedicated to defensible positions and not to isolated settlements.

Israeli Command was able to dispatch one platoon of 30 Palmach men, with their standard equipment plus some additional weapons and ammunition, as replacements for Yad Mordechai's dead and wounded. When they succeeded in reaching the kibbutz at 02:00, the Palmach men helped repair trenches damaged by Egyptian artillery and relieved some of the posts. Their arrival brought welcome additional manpower, as well as the morale-building knowledge that Yad Mordechai was not completely cut off.

Yad Mordechai was not alone in calling for reinforcements that night. The new Palmach arrivals told of an Egyptian radio communication reporting 300 to 400 Egyptian casualties, with 1st Battalion no longer in fighting form. The 2nd Battalion was ordered in to finish the job.

During World War II, the British had recognized that their Egyptian allies "had neither the will nor the capability to undertake a serious military role."[8] The 1948 campaign proved that little had changed, in spite of the infusion of weapons and equipment the Egyptians had inherited from the British. Faced with unexpected resistance and heavy losses at Yad Mordechai, the Egyptian offensive lost momentum. The shelling continued day and night for two days. An Egyptian convoy bypassed the kibbutz while soldiers deployed in the surrounding hills, tightening the stranglehold on Yad Mordechai. Wishful thinkers among the defenders hoped that the Egyptians had decided to leave the kibbutz alone, but they were using the lull to organize newly arriving reinforcements and additional assets.

On May 23, Egyptian artillery opened a ferocious barrage. Believing this to be another diversionary bombardment while the Egyptians bypassed the kibbutz, Yad Mordechai's defenders crouched in their trenches. When they lifted their heads, they were surprised to see tanks—being deployed against the kibbutz for the first time—and Bren carriers (light, tracked armored vehicles mounting machine guns) advancing, trailed by infantry. While tanks fired into the kibbutz's defensive posts, the Bren carriers pressed forward.

An Egyptian tank and some troops managed to penetrate the kibbutz and stopped behind Post 1, which the Israelis abandoned. A runner confirmed the position's loss: "Position 1 retreated. Armored vehicles broke through the fence."[9] Converging on the area where the tank stood, the kibbutz defenders threw hand grenades and fired PIAT rounds, all to no effect. The tank remained stationary, firing its machine gun. It was not clear whether it had been damaged. Perhaps the crew was disoriented—all alone, lost in a built-up area of the kibbutz and not really sure what to do next. The Israelis fired more PIAT rounds, again without success. Improvised fortified grenades— two grenades combined with a quantity of TNT—also failed to penetrate the tank's armor or dislodge its treads. After some time, the tank began to move again. Finally, one of Yad Mordechai's fighters charged the tank and threw a pair of fortified grenades that exploded next to the machine-gun slit. As he rushed the tank, he was cut down with machine-gun fire, but the tank had finally been disabled and had to be towed out by a second Egyptian tank during the fighting. Men were pulled from other posts to help fend off the Egyptians. Post 1 was reoccupied, and the Egyptians were driven from the kibbutz. More Egyptian soldiers tried to enter the kibbutz through the torn fence but were stopped by machine-gun fire while mortar fire held off their armor. As dusk settled, the Egyptians broke off their attack and pulled back.

The price of the day's fighting had been high. When they took stock of their losses the Israelis found that seven men had been killed, bringing total casualties up to 23 dead and 35 wounded. The kibbutz had also suffered equipment losses. In the course of fighting, the mortar and Browning machine gun had been destroyed. Many guns were out of commission, and those that remained were low on ammunition. The kibbutz fences had been destroyed, defensive positions were in poor shape from the constant artillery barrage, and some positions were without hand grenades. Worst of all, the defenders were exhausted.

"By this time our position was completely finished," Commander Zilberstein recalled. "We had run completely out of ammunition and we had nothing with which to fight. After this I returned to the central command and there we began to discuss what we should do. We immediately decided that unless we got help to relieve all the fighters at their posts, who had reached the end of their strength, we could not stay here any longer."[10]

Responding to the kibbutz's status report, the Israelis tried to send relief forces. A Palmach unit set out with 10 armored trucks from nearby Kibbutz Gvar Am late that night. Attacked by Egyptian forces along the way, only three of the convoy's trucks managed to get through, reaching a point 1,000 feet (300m) from Yad Mordechai. The trucks carrying weapons and most of the reinforcements did not get through. Two Palmach company commanders slipped into the kibbutz to assess the situation. Appalled by the level of destruction and nearly overcome by the dizzying stench of corpses and the suffocating heat of the crowded shelters, one of the officers noted, "We felt the people had reached the end of their strength."[11]

"We can hold out," one of Yad Mordechai's commanders persisted, "but we must rebuild our fortifications, and that can only be done at night. But the people here simply don't have the strength for this type of work, and without fortifications we can't hold out."[12] The kibbutz pleaded for more weapons and reinforcements, with which they vowed to continue holding off the Egyptians. With its convoy blocked, all the Palmach could offer was to evacuate the wounded and leave a small force to supplement the kibbutz's defenders. Fourteen of Yad Mordechai's wounded were evacuated in the armored trucks, along with a number of the women.

Knowing there would be no additional relief, Zilberstein noted, "We decided that we would retreat from here that same night." After checking that nobody was left behind, the men and women gathered at a staging area, took a final look at their destroyed home, and headed off into the darkness through Egyptian lines towards Kibbutz Gvar Am.

Palmach forces attacked the Egyptian position that had blocked the convoy's route, providing a diversion that helped the trucks carrying the wounded to get through. Off in the distance, the Israeli troops could see the people of Yad Mordechai making their way to safety. When the Egyptians discovered the evacuees' movement, they opened fire. In the confusion of the nighttime evacuation under Egyptian fire, two stretcher-bearers and the wounded man they carried became separated from the group and were captured. Nothing was ever heard of the three again and they were added to the list of dead, increasing the number of deaths in the stand at Yad Mordechai to 26 (18 from the kibbutz and eight Palmach men). Such heavy losses were representative of the War of Independence, in which 6,000 citizens—one percent of the entire Jewish population of Israel—lost their lives, and 15,000 were wounded.

"We really managed to get out under their noses and by dawn we managed to reach Gvar Am," Zilberstein recalled. In the morning, the Egyptians resumed their bombardment of Yad Mordechai. Only after several hours of shelling did they realize that the kibbutz had been abandoned. In the afternoon, 2nd Battalion finally entered the kibbutz.

The Egyptian newspaper *Al-Musara* reported, "After conquering Yad Mordechai, the route to Tel Aviv is open before the Egyptian forces."[13] But that was not the case. After occupying the kibbutz, an Egyptian column of some 500 vehicles began its delayed drive north up the coastal road towards Tel Aviv. But the combat at Yad Mordechai had sapped the offensive of strength and broken its momentum—it took the Egyptian column four days to reach what is today the port city of Ashdod, just 15 miles (24km) north of Yad Mordechai, where it was halted by a bombed-out bridge, now known as *Gesher Ad Halom* or "Up to Here Bridge." Palmach southern commander Nahum Sarig called each day gained at Yad Mordechai "more precious than gold in that it gave sufficient time . . . to concentrate a blocking force, to organize a line of defense, which was what stopped the enemy advance at Ashdod."[14]

Truce and Counteroffensives

Now an officially recognized state, Israel was busy purchasing artillery, military matériel and aircraft. The country had been in the gravest danger during those early days when all it had was the meager supply of arms illegally imported or otherwise acquired during the Mandate period. Among the weapons to arrive that month were Israel's first fighter aircraft, Avia S-199s (re-engined Czechoslovakian-made Messerschmitt Me-109Gs). The first four hastily assembled aircraft were pressed into service on May 29, when the Israel Air Force 1st Fighter Squadron set off on its debut mission against the Egyptian column halted at Ashdod. Each aircraft swooped down, dropping bombs and strafing the column. Their untested 20mm cannons and machine guns quickly jammed, and overall the air attack resulted in little actual damage, but the Egyptians scattered in face of the unexpected air attack, and lost the initiative. Bogged down some

23 miles (37km) from Tel Aviv, the Egyptian threat to Israel's center was over.

A truce came into effect on June 11, allowing each side to retain its territorial gains. Yad Mordechai was in the area controlled by Egypt. When the Egyptians refused to honor a truce provision allowing for the resupply of surrounded Jewish settlements, fighting erupted again. The newly reinforced Israeli army launched Operation *Yoav*, which drove the Egyptians from most of the territory they had seized.

Israeli forces would go on to take the entire Negev Desert, as far south as Um Rashrash, known today as Eilat. In the north, Syrian and Lebanese gains were reversed, and Arab volunteer forces known as the Arab Liberation Army were pushed out of Israeli territory. Only Transjordan's Arab Legion held its ground, remaining entrenched in the salient at Latrun commanding the main road to Jerusalem, and maintained its hold on Jerusalem's walled Old City.

On November 5, 1948, the Israelis retook Kibbutz Yad Mordechai. Zilberstein described the Egyptian retreat as "made with such haste that Yad Mordechai fell into our hands like fallen fruit. On that very day we returned and since then we started to rebuild the place with energy."[15]

Having fought so hard for their home, the people of Yad Mordechai gladly returned to their border location rather than opt for a safer place in the center of the country. Haganah Commander in Chief Israel Galili told the residents upon their return: "Your battle gave the whole south six precious days for fortification, for organization, for the securing of additional arms. The Egyptians learned here the valor and the obstinacy of the Jewish fighter. They recognized how much they would have to pay in lives and material if they were to go forward. The nation owes much to Yad Mordechai."[16]

Notes

1. Margaret Larkin. *The Six Days of Yad Mordechai* (Yad Mordechai Museum, Israel, 1965), p.238.
2. Larkin. *The Six Days of Yad Mordechai*, p.246
3.Larkin. *The Six Days of Yad Mordechai*, p.246.
4.Larkin. *The Six Days of Yad Mordechai*, p.79.

5.Brandvein, Munio (editor and compiler). *B'Mabat M'haHutz [A Look from the Outside. Listings of the Yad Mordechai Battles from May 19–23, 1948]* (Yad Mordechai: 1984). Nahum Sarig in *Sefer haPalmach*, p.6.

6.Brandvein, Munio. Interview with author.

7.Brandvein, Munio. Interview with author.

8.Steve Rothwell. "Military Ally or Liability, The Egyptian Army 1936–1942" *Army Quarterly & Defence Journal* (Vol. 128: 2, April 1998).

9.Brandvein. *B'Mabat M'haHutz*. Pinchas Shaish in *"B'ikvot haLochemim": Sufot baNegev*, p.10.

10.Zilberstein, Grisha. Transcript of undated interview.

11.Brandvein. *B'Mabat M'haHutz*. Simcha Shiloni in *Sefer haPalmach*, p.12.

12.Shiloni. *Sefer haPalmach*.

13.Brandvein. *B'Mabat M'haHutz*. Egyptian materials reprinted in *"B'ikvot haLochemim": Sufot baNegev*, p.16.

14.Brandvein. *B'Mabat M'haHutz*. Nahum Sarig in *Sefer haPalmach*, p.6.

15.Zilberstein, Grisha. Transcript of undated interview.

16.Larkin. *The Six Days of Yad Mordechai*, p.252.

CHAPTER 14

ATTACKED, CAPTURED AND ABANDONED

1956 SINAI CAMPAIGN

The aggressive brigade commander got what he wanted: authoriza-tion to send a patrol to reconnoiter Mitla Pass. Colonel Ariel Sharon's 202nd Paratroop Brigade was 125 miles (200km) behind Egyptian lines, deployed just east of this crucial mountain pass con-necting central Sinai with the Suez Canal and the city of Suez in Egypt proper. His brigade's 890th Battalion, under Major Rafael "Raful" Eitan, had parachuted in the previous day. The Israel Air Force's entire fleet of 16 Douglas C-47 Dakota transports, under the protec-tive cover of ten IAF Gloster Meteor jet fighters, dropped the 395 paratroopers deep into Egyptian territory at 16:59 on October 29, 1956. After landing several miles off mark, Eitan (a future Chief of Staff of the IDF) organized his men and marched two hours to their deployment by a crossroads known as the "Fork," near the Parker Memorial landmark east of Mitla Pass. The Israeli paratroopers dug in and awaited the eight jeeps, four 106mm recoilless antitank guns, two 120mm mortars, ammunition, equipment and supplies that were dropped to them later that evening.

What became known in Israel as Operation *Kadesh*, or the Sinai

Campaign, was underway. The paratroop drop at Mitla was actually a pretext for a larger Israeli-French-British tripartite action against Egypt. Israel would focus on Sinai, the triangular-shaped desert peninsula to its southwest, while France and Britain would launch their own offensive, Operation *Musketeer*, aimed at taking control of the Suez Canal, nationalized by Egypt just three months earlier. France was at odds with Egypt over its military support for anti-French forces in its colony Algeria, and Britain—with economic and commercial interests at stake—had much to lose from Egypt's nationalization of the canal. A joint Franco-British attack plan was born even before Israel was approached to join in September 1956. At the time, Israel was deeply concerned about a massive influx of modern weapons to Egypt from Czechoslovakia that would give Egypt the means with which to carry out its threats to destroy Israel. Egypt had already flexed its muscles three years earlier when it closed the Straits of Tiran to Israeli or Israel-bound shipping, effectively blockading Israel's southern port of Eilat. Egypt was also actively supporting terror attacks against Israel by Arab infiltrators known as *fedayin*. The frequent fedayin attacks against Israel and the Israeli reprisals were resulting in heavy casualties. Israel was ready to strike at Egypt's growing military might, re-open the Gulf of Aqaba and destroy the fedayin terrorist infrastructure.

In an agreement concluded at Sèvres, France, just five days before the Paratroop drop, a plan was created whereby Israel would initiate hostilities against Egypt, creating an alleged threat to the Suez Canal. France and Britain would then issue an appeal-cum-ultimatum they knew Egypt would reject, thereby justifying Franco-British military intervention. The Israeli *casus belli* was an airborne incursion deep behind enemy lines. The Paratroops were selected for the mission because the Israeli military leadership knew, based on previous performance, that they could hold their own. "Naturally," said IDF Paratroop Brigade reconnaissance company commander Lieutenant Micha Ben-Ari (Kapusta), "the IDF put the whole fight on the paratroopers' shoulders."[1]

Taking into account the possibility that the French and British could fail to keep their commitment to launch airstrikes against Egypt twelve hours after the ultimatum was issued, Israel's opening move was limited in scope so the troops could be withdrawn, conveying that the Israeli airdrop at Mitla was no more than a retaliatory raid for Egyptian-sponsored terror activity. Initially Israeli Chief of Staff Lieutenant General Moshe Dayan envisaged the war plan as an infantry campaign, with the armored forces relegated to a support role. Israeli Prime Minister and Minister of Defense David Ben-Gurion was concerned Egypt would react to anything more than an infantry incursion by sending its Ilyushin IL-28 bombers against Israeli cities. To defend against this eventuality—and to reassure Israel—the French agreed to provide Israel with air cover. French Air Force, or *Armée de l'Air*, Dassault Mystere IVA fighters and Republic F-84F Thunderstreak fighter-bombers were based at Israeli airfields to defend Israel's skies.

While Eitan's paratroopers were digging in at Mitla in the early evening of October 29, 1956, a convoy of airborne troops led by Paratroop Brigade commander Ariel Sharon was making its way across 180 miles (300km) from the Jordanian border, across Israel and through the Sinai desert to link up with them. Prior to the campaign, Sharon and the rest of his 202nd Brigade had been positioned on the Jordanian border to give the impression that the Israel Defense Forces were poised to strike eastward. Tensions with Jordan were running high given that country's support for terrorists acting against Israel, and Israeli reprisals seemed likely. It certainly explained Israel's military mobilization. A large reprisal attack against Jordan earlier that month at Kalkilia by Sharon's paratroopers had caused Jordanian King Hussein to invoke its defense treaty with the United Kingdom, ironically at the same time that the UK was discussing military co-operation *with* Israel. Carrying on the tradition of Sharon's legendary Unit 101 commando force, which was merged into the Paratroops, the 202nd Brigade executed Israel's policy of aggressive retaliation against its neighbors that supported terror. There was talk of Iraqi forces intervening to bolster Jordan, which Ben-Gurion had made clear would trigger an Israeli military response. Jordan reinforced defenses along its border with Israel.[2]

Sharon's column included two mechanized battalions in M-3 halftrack armored vehicles, field artillery and mortars, and thirteen French-built AMX-13 light tanks. The convoy—hundreds of vehicles in all—cut across southern Israel and crossed into Egypt. The difficult desert terrain took its toll on the vehicles, but Sharon pressed his column forward. The paratroops fought and took the Egyptian position at Kuntilla northwest of Eilat. At dawn they defeated Themed after a short battle and by late afternoon captured Nakhle. Many Egyptian soldiers were killed in the battles, and allegations emerged that the Israeli troops killed Egyptian soldiers and non-combatants surrendering to them rather than taking them prisoner. At 22:30 on October 30—after some 30 hours on the move since crossing into Sinai, Sharon's convoy linked up with Eitan's force dug in east of Mitla. A line of communication had been established; Eitan's battalion was no longer isolated.

Sharon found the deployment at Mitla vulnerable and in need of improvement. They were now a full brigade—some 1,200 men— exposed on low, open ground, providing an inviting target to both air and ground attack. Before Sharon's force had arrived, a number of Eitan's men had been wounded in a strafing run by a formation of Egyptian Air Force Mikoyan-Gurevich MiG-15 fighters. The Israelis had also been hit by mortar fire from the pass. Sharon was up in arms that the elite paratroops were under orders to remain at the rendezvous—vulnerable and idle in the midst of a war, even though the fact that they were the IDF's most experienced troops was precisely the reason they were in that position.

Mitla Pass

The restless 28-year-old Sharon began pressing his superiors for a thrust through Mitla Pass. A force was organized and ready to move into Mitla Pass by 04:00. A winding 15-mile (25-km) long pass, Mitla is enclosed by high ground to the north and south. At both the western and eastern extremes, the pass narrows to easily defended chokepoints, the eastern-most being known as Heitan defile. Control over these two narrow straits controls Mitla Pass, blocking access either to the Suez Canal or into central Sinai. From the intelligence in hand, it was believed there were no significant Egyptian forces deployed in the pass. The original war plan called for the Paratroops to jump west of the pass—some 20 miles (30km) east of the Suez Canal, but aerial reconnaissance photos revealed what was believed to be Egyptian military activity, so the jump destination had been moved to the eastern terminus.

Sharon's request to enter Mitla was denied by General Officer Commanding (GOC) Southern Command, Major General Assaf Simhoni. By this time, the Franco-British appeal had been issued calling on Egypt and Israel to accept a cease-fire, withdraw their forces to a distance of ten miles from the Suez Canal and accept temporary occupation of key positions along the canal to ensure free passage through the waterway, or else the British and French would force compliance. The combatants were given twelve hours to respond. Israel accepted the terms of this precoordinated ultimatum on condition that Egypt also accepted. The Israeli leadership knew their French and British allies were to begin airstrikes on Egypt the following morning. Israeli Chief of Staff Moshe Dayan's orders were clear: 202nd Brigade was "to reorganize in its present location and not to advance westwards to capture the Mitla Pass."[3]

Sharon held the view that staff officers could not fully appreciate the situation on the ground, and therefore "the upper echelon should intervene only if they are actually on the battlefield, if they know everything intimately, if they are forward where they can see and understand all the elements that affect the conduct of the battle."[4] Sharon undoubtedly expressed his opinion accordingly, reasoning that Israel Air Force over-flights reported no enemy between the Suez Canal and Mitla, while they *did* indicate an Egyptian armored brigade about 40 miles (65km) to the north at Bir Gafgafa, moving towards Mitla. Entering Mitla Pass would provide adequate positions for his brigade to defend itself. In the morning, when the French and British were supposed to launch airstrikes on Egyptian airfields, they instead extended their ultimatum by another twelve hours, casting doubts on whether they would come through as promised. Sharon and others— apparently including GOC Southern Command Simhoni—were already weary of this reliance on outsiders, especially the British, who until recently had been so hostile to Israel. When informed the night before that the French and British would not launch their air attacks in the morning, David Ben-Gurion—whose recollection of the paratrooper blocking force cut off in enemy territory during the recent Kalkilia operation was still fresh in his mind—considered recalling the paratroopers from Mitla.

Southern Command Chief of Staff Lieutenant Colonel Rehavam "Gandhi" Zeevi flew out in a Piper Cub the morning of October 31 to meet Sharon for an on-site assessment. Evidently Sharon was convincing, at least partially; he received permission to send in a patrol to reconnoiter the pass. Zeevi stressed the need to avoid unnecessary operations in order to minimize casualties, stating, "We must not pay a price in Jewish blood."[5]

Sharon took the liberty of sending in a much larger contingent than authorized: he organized a battalion-sized force comprised of two infantry companies mounted on halftracks, three AMX-13 tanks, the brigade reconnaissance company and 120mm mortar batteries, followed by an ambulance and trucks carrying fuel, supplies and ammunition. While the IDF battled Egyptian forces across Sinai, the Paratroops' commanders felt all they had done was drive across the desert, so they were itching to fight and be the first to reach the Suez Canal. Perhaps they were too eager, as there was a cavalier attitude; advancing to Mitla was approached like an excursion rather than a wartime mission. Sightings of men moving about the hills flanking the pass were dismissed as likely being fellow paratroopers, or perhaps Egyptian stragglers, with no need for concern, and no force was sent to secure the flanks in the heights above.

"I gave specific instructions not to enter into battle with the enemy," Sharon would later say. "The patrol, we hoped, would reach the other end of the Pass, 25 kilometers away, unheeded. It was a daring action, and therefore the force had to be well protected."[6]

Just before the paratroopers made their jump to Mitla, specially equipped IAF North American Aviation propeller-driven P-51 Mustangs had severed Egyptian communication lines in Sinai. While causing disruptions, this effort did not prevent word of the Israeli airborne and ground attack from reaching Egyptian command. Though Egyptian Chief of Staff General Abd el Hakim Amer was out of the country attending a conference of chiefs of staff of Egypt, Syria and Jordan in Amman, Egypt's defenses sprang into action. Even Moshe Dayan was complimentary of the Egyptian response, noting that "it must be said that they lost no time in reacting to [Israeli moves]."[7] All Egyptian forces were put on alert, and the Egyptian 2nd

Infantry Brigade dispatched its 5th Battalion, reinforced by a company from the 6th, to Mitla on October 30 to counter the Israelis. Deploying to prepared defensive positions on both sides of the Heitan defile with an arsenal that included 40 recoilless guns, 14 medium machine guns and twelve antitank guns, the Egyptians established themselves in caves, natural obstacles and other well-concealed defensive positions. Though the mountain pass was honeycombed with Egyptian positions, they were not visible from the air. The Israel Air Force attacked convoys of vehicles and artillery moving from the Canal Zone towards Mitla, including a convoy in the defile that turned out to be the empty vehicles belonging to the Egyptian troops entrenched in the heights. The latest IDF intelligence assessment was that the pass was free of Egyptians.

The paratrooper "patrol" set off for Mitla Pass at 12:30 on October 31, with force commander Major Mordechai "Motta" Gur, commander of the 88th Battalion (and a future IDF chief of staff) riding in a halftrack with his battalion's reconnaissance company in the vanguard. Sharon's deputy brigade commander, Lieutenant Colonel Yitzhak "Hake" Hoffe, followed with the tanks. Eitan's men complained that they made the jump to Mitla yet the other guys were getting the action.

The convoy had barely entered Mitla when it was greeted by Egyptian fire from the ridges commanding the pass. Assuming the fire was from a small defensive force, the paratroopers pressed ahead. When the lead halftrack entered the Egyptian killing zone, the Egyptians unleashed a barrage from bazookas, recoilless guns and machine guns. The halftrack was hit and disabled; both its driver and commander killed and men in the exposed back of the vehicle were hit. The vehicles following raced ahead through the Egyptian barrage, bypassing the damaged lead vehicle. With destroyed Egyptian vehicles cluttering the way, turning around or reversing out of the pass under heavy fire did not seem viable; they had no choice but to press ahead. The halftrack in which Motta Gur rode made it only another 500 feet (150m) past the lead halftrack before it was hit and stopped, with Egyptian fire pinning its soldiers down in the middle of the pass. Smoke from smoldering vehicles and the intense Egyptian fire obscured visibility as vehicles rushed through. Deputy brigade commander Hoffe, with a number of halftracks and two of the tanks, made it through to safety about two kilometers past the firestorm, believing Motta Gur was ahead of him. More halftracks and an ambulance were knocked out of action further back by the lead halftrack, with dead and wounded. The mortars and the brigade reconnaissance unit were instructed not to enter the pass. The convoy was now divided into four groups, spread out and intermingled. To further complicate matters, not all the groups had communications with one another.

Preoccupied with the potential threat posed by the Egyptian tank force to the north, brigade commander Sharon delegated to *Daled* (akin to Delta) battalion commander Lieutenant Colonel Aharon Davidi the mission of destroying the Egyptian resistance. Motta Gur would later accuse Sharon of cowardice for remaining behind while a battle raged to save the trapped force. The armored force about which Sharon was so concerned pulled back that night, eliminating the threat.

Motta Gur, in contact with Davidi, called for the reconnaissance unit to be sent into the heights flanking the pass to relieve pressure on the forces trapped within. The paratroops' supporting heavy-mortar batteries were deployed to open counterfire on the northern ridges while the brigade reconnaissance unit under Lieutenant Micha Ben-Ari was sent up the steep northern slopes to outflank the Egyptians and descend on them from higher ground. Ben-Ari described seeing the Egyptians firing down onto his fellow paratroopers. "Groups of them were sitting, filling magazines and running them to the soldiers sitting and firing down towards Motta's force trapped in the pass."[8] Once the reconnaissance unit was spotted, the Egyptians opened fire on them from all directions. The paratroopers charged and killed a number of Egyptians, but under intense fire, they had no choice but to pull back. They would attack two more times in an attempt to relieve pressure on their comrades trapped in the pass below, suffering heavy casualties as they went. Ben-Ari recalled charging the Egyptians under a hail of murderous fire. "Segev, the radioman who was on my right was hit by a bullet and died right there. Yaakobi, my good friend, charging a meter to my left, was killed by a burst of gunfire."[9] Moments later, Ben-Ari took a bullet in his chest—

his fifth combat injury—but made his way to safety.

Attempts at attacking the entrenched Egyptians were hampered by Egyptian fire from the opposing ridge and by the difficulty of discerning their precise firing positions.

Davidi thought of sending a jeep into the pass to draw Egyptian fire, thus revealing their source. Davidi's driver, 21-year-old Yehuda Kahn-Dror, volunteered for what amounted to a suicide mission. His face pale, Kahn-Dror drove off to near-certain death. He was badly wounded in the effort, yet managed to crawl out of the pass. Later succumbing to his wounds, Kahn-Dror was posthumously awarded the *Itur haGvura*, or Medal of Valor. This was but one example of selfless bravery demonstrated in this battle. With sketchy communications due to heavy screening in the confined pass, Motta Gur's radioman, Dan Shalit, repeatedly risked himself by climbing to exposed ground to maintain communications, for which he received a commendation, and in the ensuing battle to weed out the Egyptians, Lieutenant Oved Ladijinsky, commander of one of the companies battling the entrenched Egyptians, threw a grenade at an Egyptian bunker, only to have the grenade roll back towards him. To save the life of a soldier beside him, Oved shielded the soldier with his body and was killed, for which he was posthumously awarded the *Ot haOz*, or Medal of Courage. Ten soldiers were decorated for their exemplary bravery, gallantry, and for risking their lives in the battle at Mitla.

A halftrack was now sent into the pass to draw fire—again to identify the hidden Egyptian firing positions, and to attempt to evacuate some of the wounded. Despite heavy Egyptian fire, the halftrack succeeded in reaching the trapped force, evacuating six wounded men and reporting back on the sources of Egyptian fire. Its commander, Second Lieutenant Dan Ziv, was awarded the *Itur haGvura*. Around this time, a formation of four Egyptian Air Force Meteors bombed the paratroops' deployment outside the pass, knocking its mortar battery out of action and setting off their ammunition truck in a massive explosion.

The Israelis gained the upper hand when they used darkness to their advantage. Not only would the Egyptians' weapons be less effective, but the paratroopers were highly experienced in night training and operations, when darkness offered cover and protection. Venturing into Mitla in the light of day was not an ordinary operation for them.

Armed with a better sense of the Egyptian deployment, Davidi formulated a plan for a nighttime two-pronged attack. The men with deputy brigade commander Hoffe at the western side of the confined defile took to the hills and attacked the Egyptians from the west. Once they had secured their objectives, a large force went into action from the eastern side. Fighting the Egyptians at close range—at times hand to hand—the paratroopers overcame the Egyptians' hidden firing positions. Paratrooper Avshalom Adam stayed close to the cliffs to remain hidden in the shadows. He came so close to enemy positions that he could not respond to fellow soldiers calling to him lest the Egyptians hear. With one unit providing cover fire, he closed in on Egyptian machine-gun positions, waiting to hear ammunition belts run out, when he "would jump up and throw a grenade inside."[10]

After taking out a fortified Egyptian bunker with a grenade and then finishing off survivors with his Uzi submachine gun, paratrooper Muni Maroz came across a makeshift Egyptian position of rocks and boulders shielding soldiers firing away. Preparing a grenade as he moved in, protected by the darkness, Maroz took out the position with his grenade but spotted one enemy soldier getting away in time and lying down nearby. "With my weapon cocked," he recounted, "I moved towards the Egyptian soldier lying on his stomach pretending to be dead. When I pulled the trigger, I heard the blood-curdling click of a bolt finding an empty magazine. When I bent over to take the Egyptian's rifle with fixed bayonet, he came to his senses, got up on his knees and grabbed a hold of my leg, trying to pull me down to the ground." Maroz called out for help from another paratrooper he knew was in the area, who arrived "like a guardian angel." The second paratrooper—apparently also out of ammunition—smashed the Egyptian soldier in the head with the stock of his Uzi. The Egyptian's rifle bayonet was used to complete the job.[11]

The Israeli paratroopers neutralized the Egyptian positions in the pass one by one, first on the southern heights, which eased the situation for the paratroopers embroiled in fighting on the northern heights. By midnight it was over, the Egyptians having been flushed out of every bunker, burrow and cave. The Israeli casualties, who had been trapped in the pass all day, were finally evacuated; the rest of the paratroopers regrouped at the positions east of the pass. Summing up the action at Mitla, Chief of Staff Dayan wrote: "The Pass was therefore attacked, captured and abandoned."[12]

French and British forces entered the fray on the night of October 31 with an air attack by Royal Air Force (RAF) English Electric Canberra and Vickers Valiant bombers. "During the first twenty-four hours of their involvement, British and French aircraft flew over five hundred sorties . . . and destroyed more than one hundred Egyptian aircraft."[13] The Egyptian Air Force reacted by dispersing their aircraft or sending them out of the country for safety, relieving pressure on the Israeli forces on the ground in Sinai. Ongoing French and British airstrikes would destroy a further 100 Egyptian aircraft on the ground.

Once the French and British began their attacks, Egyptian President Gamal Abdel Nasser began pulling his Sinai forces back towards the canal, supporting the contention that if Sharon and the paratroopers had held their ground, the costly battle at Mitla would have been avoided. Chief of Staff Moshe Dayan was furious about Sharon's disregard for orders. In his *Diary of the Sinai Campaign*, Dayan wrote: ". . . my complaint, a grave complaint, against the paratroop command is not over the battle itself so much as over their resort to terming their operation a 'patrol' in order to 'satisfy' the General Staff."[14] In the ensuing fallout, actions of the senior commanders at Mitla were scrutinized, and Sharon was ultimately replaced as brigade commander. Years later Sharon would serve as a minister of defense and prime minister of Israel. About the paratroopers' performance the chief of staff was unequivocally positive, noting: "I doubt whether there is another unit in our army which could have managed in these conditions to get the better of the enemy. . . . The valor, daring and fighting spirit of the paratroop commanders are qualities which should be applauded and encouraged, but the battle was not essential."[15] The paratroopers were able to turn the tide at Mitla because of their collective experience gained from dozens of reprisal actions and cross-border missions over the previous three years. It was during this period of reprisals that the Paratroops' *esprit de corps* and fighting spirit of which Dayan wrote had been born.

Dayan bemoaned both that the action at Mitla was taken against his orders and its "murderous consequences": 120 paratroopers were wounded and 38 killed. Egyptian losses were significantly higher, with some 260 dead counted; the rest had slipped away.[16]

After a two-day rest, the paratroopers were called upon for the assault on Sharm el-Sheikh at the Sinai Peninsula's southern tip. The primary political objective of the campaign, capturing Sharm el-Sheikh, would re-open passage through the narrow Straits of Tiran in the Gulf of Aqaba, which, we recall, Egypt had closed to Israeli shipping. With the infantry brigade tasked with capturing Sharm el-Sheikh advancing slowly down Sinai's difficult eastern coast, Eitan's battalion was ordered down the Sinai Peninsula's western route while a reinforced company of paratroopers that had motored across Sinai was now given the opportunity for a combat jump to take the Egyptian airfield at A-Tur. The two groups of paratroopers linked up, and with the infantry brigade captured Sharm el-Sheikh. A pair of the threatening Egyptian coastal guns that had enforced Egypt's blockade is now housed at an IDF museum in Tel Aviv.

The IDF Armored Corps Proves Its Mettle

By the time Sharm el-Sheikh was taken, Israeli armored, mechanized and infantry units, formed into divisional task forces, had already met their objectives of breaking through the line of fortified Egyptian defenses at Abu Agheila, Rafah, and El Arish, the so-called triangle built to block any Israeli attempt on Sinai. Surrounded by minefields and barbed wire and backed by dug-in tanks, artillery, mortars, and antitank guns, these positions blocked the three main routes traversing Sinai: the flat Mediterranean coastal route in the north passing through the Gaza Strip and El Arish through Romani to Kantara, the central axis through Abu Agheila and Bir Gafgafa to Ismailia, and the route through Mitla Pass to Suez, reached by lateral crossroads. Most of the 30,000 Egyptian troops in Sinai and Gaza were concentrated in this sector.

Impatient with the infantry's progress at Kusseima—an important crossroad near the border and one of the IDF's early objectives—on October 30, GOC Southern Command Simhoni ordered the 7th Armored Brigade into action. Chief of Staff Dayan was furious, as the use of armor at that stage contravened his orders and risked an escalated Egyptian response. When his anger subsided, Dayan realized the benefit of their position and ordered the 7th Armored Brigade to capture the central axis. A probe revealed an undefended defile called Daikla Pass that would put the Israelis behind the Egyptian positions by Abu Agheila compound, yet only tracked vehicles could maneuver the pass. In an audacious move, 7th Armored Brigade's tanks left their wheeled fuel, ammunition, and supply vehicles behind and pressed on, putting them in position to attack Abu Agheila from the rear.

Despite stubborn Egyptian resistance, the Israelis broke through the Egyptian line of static defenses. Soon Israeli armored columns were racing across Sinai towards the Suez Canal on both the Mediterranean coast and central axes. The IDF Armored Corps proved its mettle in this war, earning their prominent place in future Israeli war planning. Gaza with its fedayin terror bases and training camps was the last objective secured in this sector.

In little more than 100 hours of fighting, Israel seized the entire Sinai Peninsula at a cost of 181 killed, 800 wounded and 4 captured. Egyptian losses were about 1,000 killed, 4,000 wounded, and 6,000 captured. Israel's victory brought with it a windfall of captured war bounty, including some 100 tanks, 200 artillery pieces, 1,000 vehicles and an Egyptian Navy destroyer, the *Ibrahim el Awal*. While shelling Haifa, the Egyptian vessel was intercepted by French and Israeli navy boats and rocketed by the Israel Air Force, leading to its surrender. Coupled with its heavy loss of aircraft, Egypt had suffered a serious blow. Despite the losses, Egyptian President Nasser, who had taken power in Egypt in 1954, came out a winner. His defiance and heroic stand against colonial powers of France and Britain earned him acclaim in the Arab world, leading to his becoming considered a leader of the Arabs.

British and French forces launched an airborne and amphibious operation on November 5, seizing both Port Said and Port Fuad in the northern extremity of the Suez Canal. The 90,000 men, 130 warships—including aircraft carriers—and more than 500 aircraft committed to the operation by France and Britain, would be reined in after less than two days, the result of intense international diplomatic pressure, including ultimatums from the United States and Soviet Union. In a miscalculation, it was thought the United States would be distracted by its presidential election and the Soviets by revolt in Hungary, but both countries took a firm stance against the invasion. For France and Britain, the war was a political disaster, seen as two fading powers' last attempts at exerting influence. For Israel, their role was critical. Without the French and British, Moshe Dayan wrote, "it is doubtful whether Israel would have launched her campaign."[17] The cooperation only added to the affinity France felt towards Israel and cemented the relationship; France would supply Israel with its armament needs for the next decade.

Israel also consented to the diplomatic pressure being exerted to withdraw its forces from Sinai, but it won the concession of a UN peacekeeping force known as the United Nations Emergency Force (UNEF) positioned at Sharm el-Sheikh and the Gaza Strip. By March 1957 the last Israeli forces pulled out of Sinai.

Only eight years after its precarious establishment, Israel had exhibited military prowess, proving it could fight and win on the battlefield. Beyond achieving its objectives for the campaign, Israel had demonstrated deterrence in a way her neighbors could not ignore, and was no longer diplomatically isolated. Perhaps for the first time Israel could enjoy a sense of security.

Notes

1. Avi Zur. Interview with Micha Ben-Ari.
2. Dayan described: "It is apparent that our deception plan was successful. Up to the last minute, that is, up to our paratroop drop at Mitla, the General Staffs of all the Arab armies believed that it was our intention to march on Jordan. Jordan accordingly reinforced her defense system along her border with Israel . . ." Dayan, *Diary of the Sinai Campaign* (New York: Schocken Books, 1965), p.89.
3. Dayan. *Diary of the Sinai Campaign*, p.95.
4. Ariel Sharon and David Chanoff. *Warrior: The Autobiography of Ariel Sharon* (New York: Simon & Schuster, 1989), pp.137–8. Sharon wrote this about Operation *Shomron*, the paratroopers' raid on Kalkilia earlier that month, when he had held differences of opinion with his superiors. He clearly states: "there should be as little interference as possible with the commander in the field."
5. Oren, Amir. "38 soldiers killed. Who approved the action?" www.haaretz.com. October 29, 2006.
6. Matti Shavitt. *On the Wings of Eagles: The Story of Arik Sharon, Commander of the Israel paratroopers* (Tel Aviv: Olive Books of Israel, 1970), p.137.
7. Dayan. *Diary of the Sinai Campaign*, p.91.
8. Zur. Interview.
9. Zur. Interview.
10.Personal Account. Avshalom Adam. IDF Paratroopers History Site.
11.Personal Account. Muni Maroz. IDF Paratroopers History Site.
12.Dayan. *Diary of the Sinai Campaign*, p.102.
13.Lon Nordeen. *Fighters Over Israel* (London: Greenhill Books, 1990), p.46.
14.Dayan. *Diary of the Sinai Campaign*, p.102. Dayan did not punish Sharon for disobeying orders, and was forgiving in another case where the 7th Armored Brigade was ordered into action prematurely against his orders, about which he wrote: "I could not avoid a sympathetic feeling over the hastening of the brigade into combat even before they were required. Better to be engaged in restraining the noble stallion than in prodding the reluctant mule!" (Dayan. *Diary of the Sinai Campaign*, p.96) As for Sharon, this would not be the only occasion on which he would disregard orders. In the 1973 Yom Kippur War, while commanding an Armored Division operating by the Suez Canal, Sharon flagrantly violated orders by crossing the Canal into Egypt proper—a daring move that cut off the Egyptian Third Army and contributed to Egypt's defeat. A military tribunal later exonerated him on grounds that his actions were militarily effective.
15.Dayan. *Diary of the Sinai Campaign*, pp.101–2.
16.Dayan. *Diary of the Sinai Campaign*, p.102.
17.Nordeen. *Fighters Over Israel*, p.37.

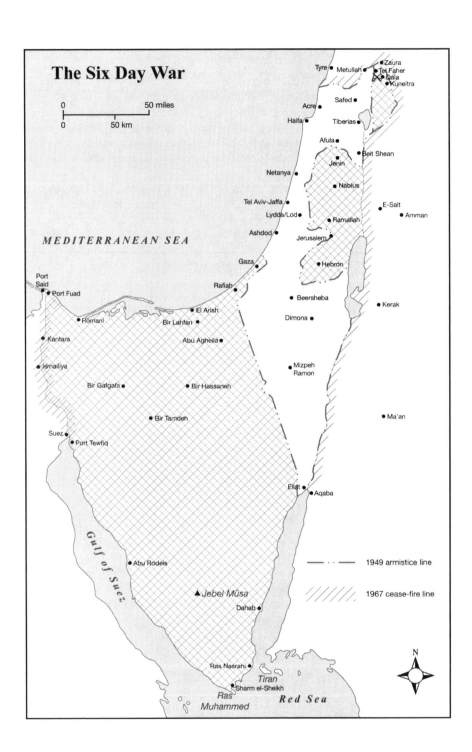

The Six Day War

0   50 miles

0   50 km

Tyre ●   Metullah ●   ● Zaura
           ● Tel Faher
           ● Qala
           ● Kuneitra

Safed ●

Acre ●

Haifa ●   Tiberias ●

Afula ●

     ● Beit Shean

Jenin ●

Netanya ●

   ● Nablus

Tel Aviv-Jaffa ●

Lydda/Lod ●   E-Salt ●

     ● Ramallah   ● Amman

Ashdod ●

   Jerusalem ●

MEDITERRANEAN SEA

Gaza ●

     ● Hebron

Port
Said
   ● Port Fuad

         Rafiah ●

     ● Beersheba

         ● Kerak

        ● El Arish

● Romani   Bir Lahfan ●   Dimona ●

● Kantara

       Abu Agheila ●

● Ismailiya

         ● Mizpeh
           Ramon

Bir Gafgafa ●   ● Bir Hassaneh

     ● Bir Tamdeh   ● Ma'an

Suez ●
   ● Port Tewfiq

         Eilat ●
           ● Aqaba

G u l f   o f   S u e z

● Abu Rodeis

▲ *Jebel Mûsa*

     Dahab ●

—— · ——   1949 armistice line

///////   1967 cease-fire line

Ras Nasrani ●

Tiran

● Sharm el-Sheikh

*Ras
Muhammed*   *Red Sea*

N

CHAPTER 15

HOW THE HELL DID
ANYONE GET UP THERE?

1967 Six Day War

Soldiers hugged and kissed one another. A few shed tears of joy. Some even joined in a festive folk dance. This celebration did not mark the end of a battle, but the beginning of one. It was Friday, June 9, 1967—the fifth day of the war that would become known as the Six Day War—and the IDF's Golani Infantry Brigade had just received orders authorizing operations against Syria.

Based in Israel's northern Galilee, the Golani troops felt a special responsibility for this sector. Yet for years its troops had watched helplessly while Syrian artillery randomly shelled Israeli fishermen on the Sea of Galilee, farmers in the Hula Valley, and the northern villages of Dan, Dafna, Shaar Yishuv, Beit-Hillel and HaGoshrim, destroying houses, setting crops alight and causing civilian casualties. Short of all-out war, there was little they could do. With the outbreak of war on June 5, 1967, Golani's soldiers were eager to settle the score. But as the IDF concentrated on the Egyptian and Jordanian fronts for four days, tension built up among the Golani as they waited to have their go. With international pressure for a cease-fire mounting, it was looking as if they might not get that chance.

Syria's efforts to make life miserable for Israel had even included a major engineering project to divert the Jordan River's headwaters and cut off northern Israel's water supply. Tensions along the border escalated until early April 1967, when Syrian artillery harassment increased in ferocity. In a subsequent dogfight, six Syrian Mikoyan-Gurevich MiG-21 fighters were shot down by Israel Air Force Dassault Mirage III fighters. At that point, Syria pressured Egypt into joining these latest efforts against Israel. Relatively isolated in the Arab world at the time, Egypt's President Gamal Abdel Nasser welcomed the opportunity. Calls for Israel's annihilation and other anti-Israel propaganda began radiating from Egypt. Nasser dispatched the bulk of his army, with hundreds of tanks and artillery pieces, to the Sinai Peninsula.

Israel closely monitored all developments but dismissed them as muscle-flexing on Nasser's part as long as the United Nations maintained its Sinai buffer force, installed following the 1956 Sinai Campaign as protection for Israel. When Syria accused Nasser of hiding behind the UN forces, however, he ordered them out on May 16, 1967. The evacuation of UN posts changed everything—Egypt and Israel were now eye to eye.

Nasser then upped the ante on May 22–23 by blockading the Straits of Tiran, the waterway leading into Israel's southern port of Eilat. That same action had contributed to Israel's Sinai invasion of 1956, and Israel still regarded it as an act of war. While Western powers and the UN scurried to find a diplomatic solution, the Arab world was unifying against Israel. Jordan's King Hussein flew to Cairo and concluded a mutual defense pact. Syria and Iraq reached similar agreements with Egypt. Nasser was on a high as these events catapulted him to center stage. Israel was on her own, with overwhelming forces arrayed against her on all fronts.

The war began on June 5, 1967, with Israel committing nearly its entire air force to a daring pre-emptive airstrike that surprised and virtually annihilated the Egyptian, Jordanian and Syrian air forces. IDF ground forces then swept across the vast expanse of the Egyptian Sinai Desert and Jordanian West Bank. East Jerusalem with the Old City was captured; Israel's capital was now united.

Despite ambitious plans to capture the eastern Galilee before advancing on Haifa, the Syrians—who had lost some 50 aircraft in the opening day's airstrike—largely sat out the war, except for three feeble attacks across the border, which amounted to little more than reconnaissance in force. That served Israel well while the IDF focused on the Egyptian and Jordanian fronts. Late in the week the Syrians stepped up their artillery barrages, as if goading Israel to attack. At that point, having defeated the Egyptian and Jordanian armies, Israel was able to reinforce the Golani force to where three armored brigades and five infantry brigades were poised to take on the Syrians.

Galilee residents implored the Israeli government to push the Syrians back to where their artillery could no longer torment them. However, with the Soviet Union threatening to intervene and the UN arranging a cease-fire, it seemed that the Syrians might retain their presence on the Golan Heights, symbolized by the ominous stone fortress of Tel Aziziat, which locals called "The Monster." But once it became clear the Soviets would stay out of the conflict, Israel's hands were freed. When the Syrians unleashed another round of shelling, violating the cease-fire, the Israeli GOC Northern Command, Major General David "Dado" Elazar, gave the go-ahead to launch the offensive. Given the background to that order, it was no wonder that there was such an outpouring of emotion among the Golani soldiers when told they would go into action against Syria.

Rising from the plains along almost the entire length of Israel's northern border with Syria, the Golan Heights themselves are a formidable natural barrier. The Golan Heights are made up of a 480 square mile (1,250 square km) volcanic (basalt) rock plateau perched above the Hula Valley to the west and Jordan Valley to the south. It rises gently from 600 feet (180m) in the south to 3,000 feet (915m) in the north, with abrupt escarpments dominating the valleys to the west and south. It is transected in some areas by impassable canyons, limiting the number of routes leading up from the valleys to the heights. The Syrians had established a network of heavily fortified positions along the border, and all possible routes of attack were mined, and well-covered by pre-ranged firing positions. Dug into the rough volcanic basalt was a Soviet-designed defensive network comprising level upon level of steel and concrete-reinforced bunkers, emplacements, pillboxes, and tunnels that were nearly impervious to air and artillery attack. One long-time resident of the area told of airstrikes against those positions that, judging by their intensity, seemed sufficient to silence them for good. But a few minutes after the smoke cleared, the Syrians would be back in action, firing at the Israeli communities below.

Manning the formidable defenses on what they called the "Palestine Front" were three Syrian brigades that in June 1967 received infantry, mechanized and armored reinforcements—some 56,000 troops in all. General Ahmed Sweidani's army fielded 300–550 tanks, mostly Soviet T-34s and T-54s, and more than 1,200 artillery pieces, including some of the most up-to-date Soviet mortars, howitzers and field guns, manned by Soviet-trained crews. Mobile and dug-in tanks, antitank guns, rocket launchers and antiaircraft guns added to the defenses.

As it turned its attention to the Golan Heights, the IDF had its work cut out for it—the Syrians seemed to have every military advantage except air superiority, which they made up for with some 200 antiaircraft guns. The Israelis would have to climb the Golan's steep rise in full view of well-entrenched Syrian troops. The IDF was taking on what appeared to be an impossible task.

Backed by artillery and close air support, the IDF attacked at multiple points along the border, with the main thrust directed against the Golan's northern fringe. The plan was to capture fortifications in that sector and to open the Banias–Mas'ada axis, the northernmost route leading to Kuneitra, capital of the Golan. The armored force was expected to overrun the Zaura area while the infantry was tasked with seizing the fortifications by Banias.

Before the assault, Israeli fighter-bombers streaked overhead dropping high-explosive ordnance and napalm onto the Syrian positions. While not that effective against the positions themselves, the airstrikes brought nearly all movement to a standstill. Syrian antiaircraft guns challenged the IAF, posing a threat that had to be eliminated before the IAF could provide effective close air support.

Just before noon, Colonel Abraham "Albert" Mandler's 8th Armored Brigade set out from Givat ha'Em, north of Kfar Szold. The terrain afforded little cover against observation from the Heights, and the Syrians began shelling the Israelis from the time they left their staging areas. The IAF put down a carpet of fire ahead of Mandler's armored columns, which included IDF-upgraded M-4 Sherman tanks known as Super Shermans, and infantry on M-3 halftracks, with specially improvised bulldozers leading the way. Combat engineers were at the forefront, clearing away mines and carving a path for the tanks while under heavy fire.

Syrian artillery took a heavy toll on the bulldozers and vulnerable halftracks, but in little more than an hour the Israelis had taken the Syrian positions at Gur-al-Aksar and Na'amush. The well-camouflaged Syrian bunkers were built deep into the rock and were immune to mortar fire, requiring the Israeli soldiers to take them out one by one with hand grenades.

So far, all was going according to plan, which called for Mandler's force to reach the Trans Arabian Pipeline (TAPline) route traversing the sector and then take the Zaura position at the base of Mount Hermon, securing a foothold on the northern Heights. There, however, the Israelis went astray. After taking their original objectives, an error in navigation left the vanguard Biro Battalion (named for its commander, Lieutenant Colonel Arye Biro) heading due south towards the Qala compound, a very heavily fortified Syrian position in a different sector. The Israelis realized their error when they found themselves attacking Sir-adib, below Qala. They took Sir-adib but were pinned down by heavy fire from Qala. The other armored forces continued according to plan and reached the TAPline route.

The Biro Battalion vainly looked for a way to bypass Qala and cut back towards Zaura, rather than advancing up the narrow, winding route to Qala, which was thought to be mined on the shoulders. Despite their efforts, the Israelis saw no option but to attack Qala head-on. The Israeli high command saw value in this deviation from the plan. A breakthrough at Qala would open the Nafakh–Kuneitra axis, allowing the IDF to advance much faster and deeper into the Golan than originally planned.

Many of Biro Battalion's tanks had already been knocked out by shells, damaged by mines, or hit during the initial breakthrough, and the rest made easy targets for the guns at Qala. Lieutenant Colonel Biro was injured and evacuated. Command of the 21 remaining tanks went to his executive officer—who was killed half an hour later.

Lieutenant Nethaniel "Nati" Hurwitz, a 25-year-old company commander, then took command of the battalion. A shell struck Hurwitz's tank, injuring him and knocking out the tank's radio. Unable to communicate with his force, Hurwitz had to switch tanks, only to have to do so again when his second tank was also hit.

Large concrete antitank barricades known as "dragon's teeth," covered by Syrian antitank guns and machine-gun nests, blocked the approach to Qala. Hurwitz called in artillery support that knocked out the antitank guns, but not before they had disabled 11 Israeli tanks. The damaged tanks provided cover fire while the 10 tanks still in working order maneuvered through the dragon's teeth. Three tanks were hit on the approach to Qala, and then several more were knocked out by a hidden Syrian tank before it was spotted and silenced by an armor-piercing round.

Word came in from Battalion Command that seven Syrian tanks were en route to Qala. For Hurwitz's dwindling force, it was now a race to reach Qala before the Syrian reinforcements arrived. One of the three Israeli tanks that had made it into Qala was knocked out by bazooka fire, and the remaining two hid among the town's houses. Hurwitz called for assistance while crewmen from disabled tanks and lightly injured soldiers secured the captured areas with Uzi submachine guns and grenades.

Meanwhile, most of the 8th Armored Brigade had found its way to Zaura, as planned. Infantry accompanying the tanks crawled up the steep terrain, cut through the barbed wire entanglements and crossed the minefields to approach Zaura's defenses. A tank force succeeded in breaking into the Syrian compound, though not without first losing several tanks. After a brief struggle, Syrian resistance broke. Isolated elements posed some problems, with Syrian soldiers emerging from hidden positions and trying to disable tanks with grenades or kill Israeli commanders. Mechanized infantry followed the tanks and cleared out the Syrian positions. After securing Zaura, the tanks hurriedly made their way 4 miles (6km) south to link up with Hurwitz's force at Qala.

The remnants of the Biro Battalion at Qala waited in desperation for the relief force. In response to their desperate calls for assistance, air support arrived just minutes before nightfall, swooping down on

Syrian tanks as they arrived on scene, buying some time for the tiny force until elements of the 8th Brigade finally arrived from Zaura. Together, the combined Israeli armored forces completed the capture of Qala shortly after nightfall. Of the 21 tanks Hurwitz had when he assumed command earlier in the day, only two remained in working order. Hurwitz himself had gone through four. For his initiative and leadership, Hurwitz was awarded the *Itur haGvura*—Israel's highest military decoration.

Reporting on his ride with armored forces, British war correspondent Michael Bennett wrote: "Bunkers, gun emplacements, communication networks made to withstand any assault, were destroyed in hours. The bravery of the tank crews was beyond description, in the face of what looked like a suicidal frontal assault over a terrain not normally accepted as suitable for tanks. It was an honour to ride with such men."[1]

While the armored forces were fighting their way up the heights, a force from Colonel Yonah Efrat's Golani Brigade set out to take on the formidable company-sized Syrian border positions of Tel Aziziat and Tel Faher, just south of Banias. Tel Aziziat's concrete emplacements dominated the northeast Hula Valley. Tel Faher, situated 1,500 meters to the east on higher ground, commanded the approaches to Tel Aziziat. The Israeli attack plan called for both positions to be outflanked, which meant first overcoming the positions at Tel Faher and the adjacent position of Bourj Babil. Those two critical objectives fell on Golani's fully mechanized Barak Battalion, whose troops were mounted on M-3 halftracks, supported by a company of M-50 Super Shermans and AMX-13 light tanks. Led by Lieutenant Colonel Moshe "Musa" Klein, the Barak Battalion's *Aleph* and *Gimel* (akin to Alpha and Charlie) companies—about 125 officers and men with 19 halftracks and nine tanks—were to attack Tel Faher from the rear by means of a deep flanking maneuver to the TAPline road. Once Tel Faher was secured, *Bet* (Bravo) Company would attack Bourj Babil. After those two positions were in Israeli hands, a second Golani battalion, the "Boka'im HaRishon" would go into action against Tel Aziziat.

Of all the Syrian positions, Tel Faher was the largest and most strongly fortified. Situated on two hills, Tel Faher was commanded by the larger and higher northern position, where its main bunker was located. Secure behind layers of dense barbed wire entanglements and protective minefields, Tel Faher's reinforced bunkers and pillboxes, some cut into the rock, were connected via rows of concrete-lined communications trenches. Manning the positions and dugouts was a company from the Syrian 187th Infantry Battalion, including a unit armed with 57mm antitank guns, recoilless rifles, heavy machine guns and a battery of 82mm mortars.

At 13:00, following airstrikes and an artillery barrage on the Syrian positions and artillery, the Golani infantry crossed the Green Line, as the border was known, near Givat ha'Em. Following in the treads of Colonel Mandler's tanks, the Israeli force was immediately hit by a barrage of antitank and artillery fire from several Syrian positions. Tel Faher and Tel Aziziat were close enough for mutual fire support, and could also rely on the neighboring positions of Zaura and Ein Fit further up the heights, as well as Bourj Babil and Hirbat a-Suda.

Heavy, accurate Syrian fire and difficult terrain slowed the Israeli advance. A smoke screen failed to mask their approach, and as tanks and halftracks were stopped on the boulder-strewn path, the distance between the vehicles increased, and the force began suffering casualties. Communications became confused, and with the intense Syrian barrage contributing to the fog of war, the Israelis could not locate the intended attack route to the TAPline. Two hours had passed, and they were falling behind schedule, so Lieutenant Colonel Klein changed the plan. Instead of flanking Tel Faher and attacking from its more vulnerable eastern side, the men of the Barak Battalion would stage a direct, uphill assault.

From advantageous firing positions, the Syrian antitank fire targeted Israeli armor with great effectiveness. Not one of the Israeli tanks made it up to Tel Faher, and more than half the halftracks were damaged or stuck on the attack route. Klein's command halftrack took a hit, throwing off all on board. With the remaining halftracks drawing heavy fire, the Israelis decided to dismount and continue their assault on foot. Contact had been lost with much of the force, so orders had to be given verbally. Major Alex Krinsky, the battalion artillery officer, passed orders to Lieutenant Aharon Vardi's *Aleph*

Company. Four of *Aleph* Company's seven halftracks had been hit and 35 of Vardi's 60 men had been killed or wounded. Vardi and his men dismounted from their halftracks, and Krinsky divided the company. He would lead 12 men to attack Tel Faher's northern fortifications, while Vardi and the other 13 men would assault the southern positions.

Making their way up the twisting route to Tel Faher, Vardi's men faced a forest of barbed wire, just meters beyond which—across a minefield—lay their objective, Tel Faher's trenches and bunkers. They cut through the wire until heavy fire drove them back. Bangalore mines also failed to blast an opening through the wire, leaving the Israelis stranded and pinned down until infantryman David Shirazi came forward on his own initiative and lay across the barbed wire, becoming a human bridge. After the others had passed over him, Shirazi caught up with them and, as a "MAG'ist," as machine gunners were called after their FN MAG 7.62mm machine guns, he led the way into the outer trenches. Remaining cool under fire, Shirazi laid accurate suppressive fire that silenced several Syrian positions until he was killed by a sniper. Shirazi was posthumously awarded the *Itur haGvura* for his actions, which remain legendary to this day.

Syrian machine-gun nests continued spitting out murderous fire into the Golani infantrymen as they continued to advance uphill through the maze of trenches. When it became evident that the Barak Battalion would not quickly take Tel Faher according to plan, the Boka'im HaRishon battalion was ordered into action against its own assigned objectives. Moving into Syrian territory, the Boka'im reached the patrol road connecting the Syrian positions. Led by the battalion commander, Lieutenant Colonel Benny Inbar, *Bet* Company's seven halftracks and three tanks turned north, taking the fringe position at Bachrayat before assaulting heavily fortified Tel Aziziat from the rear.

The rows of barbed wire entanglements surrounding the position were only the beginning of Tel Aziziat's defenses. Crisscrossed with concrete and basalt stone bunkers, pillboxes, and deep, covered communication trenches, Tel Aziziat was topped by a concrete turret. Manning those formidable defenses was an infantry company of some 70 soldiers reinforced with small arms, machine guns, antitank guns and a World War II German Mark V Panther tank.

When a mine stopped one of *Bet* Company's tanks, combat engineers cleared the way under fire. Seeing the Israelis approaching, Tel Aziziat's defenders quickly mined the entrance to their position. When one of the Israeli halftracks set off a mine, the entrance was blocked. The original Israeli attack plan had called for the troops to ride their halftracks to the top of the position, but now the Golani troops had no choice but to dismount and go in by foot, clearing the trenches in a systematic fashion—working in pairs, one soldier provided suppressive fire while his partner threw grenades into each Syrian position.

The assault was proceeding like a well-rehearsed training exercise until fire from a concealed trench killed one Golani and injured others attempting to approach. Once the source of the fire was located, a rocket grenade silenced the sniper's nest. In the brief operation, the Golanis suffered only one soldier killed and seven wounded, while the Syrians lost 30 men dead and 26 captured; a handful managed to escape. By 17:05, the menacing Syrian position known as "The Monster" was in Israeli hands. The victorious soldiers raised the flags of Israel and of the Golani Brigade from a prominent tree over the newly captured position.

Up at Tel Faher, the battle was not going easily. What had been planned as a coordinated assault had deteriorated into engagements by small, dispersed groups. The Barak Battalion's *Aleph* Company was fighting a pitched battle against Tel Faher's stubborn defenders. Over the course of two hours, Vardi's group of 13 fought from bunker to bunker. In taking the trenches, all but three of the soldiers were killed or wounded, while the survivors ran out of ammunition.

Another force reached the southern positions after flanking Tel Faher, but while they knew that Vardi had gone in, they had no contact with him. After ramming through the gate, the Israelis cleared out trenches until they finally linked up with Vardi and his survivors and secured the southern positions.

In Tel Faher's northern sector, Krinsky and his dozen troops were clearing out the first trenches under deadly sniper fire from the stone fortification atop the position. By the time the Israelis approached the second tier of trenches, Krinsky had been hit and killed, and all but one of his men had been killed or wounded. Concerned about the battle's progress, battalion commander Moshe Klein followed the footsteps of "Force Krinsky," and learnt of its precarious state. To keep the battle's momentum going, Klein ordered the unwounded soldier to follow him as they charged into the trenches. The soldier yelled, "Battalion Commander—snipers!" Klein failed to heed the warning, and moments later he was shot dead.

At that point, Golani Brigade commander Colonel Efrat ordered in his reserve force—Captain Reuven "Ruvka" Eliaz's elite *sayeret* special reconnaissance unit, with its one tank, five halftracks and two jeeps—and sent in his deputy for an on-scene report. More Israeli troops also arrived, as men from Barak's *Gimel* Company—originally tasked as the assault force along with *Aleph* Company, reached the Syrian positions. Back after almost effortlessly taking the small fringe position of Bourj Babil between Tel Faher and Tel Aziziat, *Bet* Company and its four halftracks also joined the battle, arriving at the same time as the sayeret.

These reinforcements helped flush out the resilient defenders from the northern fortifications' trenches. The Golanis had to fight hard for every inch of ground. "We fought hand to hand with whatever we had," recounted one soldier. The Syrian defenders' determination and resolve was commendable, but by nightfall the Israelis finally secured Tel Faher.

Of the 13 positions taken by the Golani brigade on the Golan Heights, Tel Faher was the most difficult and costly to take. The battle site was renamed *Mitzpe Golani*, or Golani Lookout, as a memorial to the 34 Israeli soldiers killed and some 100 wounded there. The casualties included most of the Barak Battalion's command structure, from the battalion commander and his deputy down to company commanders. With so many of the senior officers killed at the outset of the battle, junior officers played a major role in leading the troops to victory.

Television producer Bill Cunningham, surveying a captured Syrian position, described the scene in amazement: "Tier upon tier of trenches and gun emplacements all commanding the plateau below. How the hell did anyone get up there?"[2] Chief of Staff Lieutenant General Yitzhak Rabin echoed those sentiments, saying, "Only when you see the enemy fortifications and bunkers up close can you understand what a difficult mission the Golani had . . ."[3]

Secondary attacks further south in the Heights also made inroads against the Syrian defenses. From Gonen, IDF troops fought their way up the Urfiya–Rawiye axis towards the TAPline route, opening the way for an armored force to advance into Syrian territory. Along the road running north of Bnot Yaakov Bridge, a combined force of tanks and infantry cracked the string of Syrian positions at Jelabina, Dardara, Tel Hilal and Darbashiya. On these and other attack points, IDF successes were straining the Syrians' ability to hold on.

By the end of the day, the entire Zaura–Qala region was in Israeli hands. While there was still a long way to go, the IDF was positioned to push towards Kuneitra from both the northern Banias–Mas'ada axis and the Nafakh–Kuneitra axis further south. Keeping alert for a possible counterattack, the Israelis spent the night fueling up their vehicles, replenishing provisions, bringing up reinforcements and regrouping in preparation for the next day's fighting.

On the morning of June 10, the IDF took Banias, Ein Fit, Mas'ada and Majdal Shams at the foot of Mount Hermon. The whole of the northern area along what until then had been the Syrian–Lebanese border was secured, clearing the northern approach to Kuneitra. From Qala, Israeli tank forces also pressed their attack eastward towards the Golan's capital.

When word reached them of the collapse of the northern Golan's defenses and of Israelis advancing towards Kuneitra from two directions, Syrians elsewhere in Golan knew their path of retreat was being cut off. Many Syrian officers, generally politically appointed Alawite religious sect officers, were quick to abandon their mostly Shiite Muslim soldiers for the safety of the rear.

Another front was opened on the morning of Saturday, June 10 by an Israeli advance southeast of the Sea of Galilee. Tanks and mounted infantry fought their way up the treacherous, winding mountain road from the lake's southern shores, breaking through the Syrian defenses at Tuwafik. IDF ground forces took the positions of Fiq, El Al and Boutmiya along the way to Rafid Junction, deep in the Golan. Some Israeli naval commandos, anxious to get in on the action, joined in this part of the operation. Ground forces cleared out areas on the southern axis into the Heights. Paratroopers were landed behind

Syrian lines by helicopter, but for the most part they found only isolated pockets of Syrian resistance. Other infantry units mopped up posts scattered throughout the sector, taking large numbers of prisoners.

The Syrian defenses had not collapsed completely. Earlier in the day, reinforcement convoys had headed towards what was becoming a rapidly receding front, and the situation was deteriorating. An IDF infantry and armored force had crossed the Jordan River and taken the lower and upper Customs House positions, and was now moving on Kuneitra from yet another direction. The Syrians tried to slow the Israeli advance by mining the roads, but there was no stopping the Israelis' momentum, and they arrived at Kuneitra's southern outskirts.

Within hours of the renewed Israeli operations that Saturday morning, the Syrians were fleeing the entire Golan. Speeding their retreat was a Radio Damascus report, meant either to motivate its soldiers to fight with greater resolve or to speed the UN into bringing about a cease-fire, announcing that Kuneitra had fallen—hours before the IDF arrived. The plan backfired as Syrian units still in Golan, fearing they would be encircled, beat a hasty retreat, leaving behind all sorts of weapons and equipment, down to boots and socks.

Kuneitra was surrounded and Mandler's 8th Armored Brigade moved in to complete its conquest. As a precautionary measure against Syrian snipers, only tanks entered at first. Finding the town all but deserted, Golani infantry went in to mop up and Kuneitra was securely in Israeli hands by 15:00.

Later, a force from the Golani's Gidon Battalion was flown by helicopter from Kuneitra to the southern face of Mount Hermon. Landing on the lower peak of the mountain, the Golani troops raised the national flag and determined Israel's new border. Perched high above the approaches from Damascus, that position would become a vital intelligence post for Israel.

The Golan Heights' 480 square miles had been captured in 27 hours, and the IDF was on the road to Damascus when a cease-fire went into effect at 18:00 on June 10. The Israelis then pulled back to a defensible line—a string of extinct volcanic cones commanding strategic views into Syria. For Syria, just as for Egypt and Jordan, the war was a humiliating defeat that left it seething for revenge. The final cease-fire was signed the following day in Kuneitra by Israeli and Syrian officers, overseen by UN military representatives.

The Battle for the Golan Heights had cost Israel 115 men killed and 306 wounded; Syrian casualties were estimated to be 10 times greater, along with about a third of its tank force and half its artillery. "Fortress Golan," as it was sometimes called, had been broken. While much of Israel was euphoric at the sudden end to its claustrophobia, with new borders far away from the Israeli heartland, the people of Israel's north finally had reason to be hopeful that after two decades of regular use, their protective shelters would become a thing of the past.

Notes

1.*Olei Britannia.*
2. William Stevenson. *Strike Zion!* (New York: Bantam Books, 1967), p.86.
3. Moty Har-Lev. *Golani Sheli [My Golani]* (Aviv Publishers), p.103.

CHAPTER 16

SACRIFICIAL STAND IN THE GOLAN HEIGHTS

1973 YOM KIPPUR WAR

Defeat seemed imminent. The Syrians' Soviet-style massive frontal assault was too much to bear, and the Israeli front lines had already collapsed. The Israeli general in charge of the entire front had abandoned his nearly surrounded headquarters and retired to a makeshift command post a few kilometers away. With two Syrian brigades advancing on the headquarters and no Israeli reserves in sight, defending the headquarters—left in the hands of infantrymen supported by only two trackless tanks mustered from the camp's repair depot—seemed almost futile.

On October 6, 1973, during Yom Kippur, the holiest day of the Jewish calendar, a Syrian armored force of 1,400 tanks backed by more than 1,000 artillery pieces and supporting air power began a coordinated assault along the Israeli–Syrian border in the Golan Heights in the north of Israel. The attack coincided with a similar onslaught by Egyptian forces along the Suez Canal, suddenly forcing Israel to fight a two-front war.

Israeli defense doctrine relies on the standing army to hold the line with air support while the reserves are mobilized. Therefore, the two

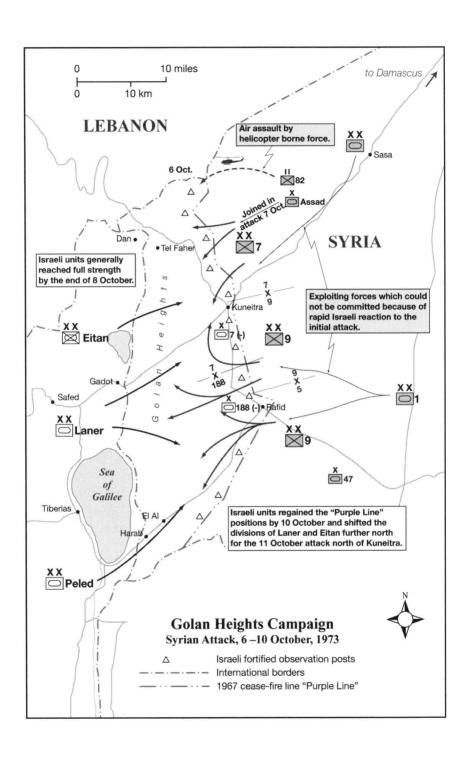

0   10 miles

0   10 km

LEBANON

to Damascus

Air assault by
helicopter borne force.

• Sasa

XX

6 Oct.

△

II ⊠82

△

Joined in
attack 7 Oct

X ⊡ Assad

Dan •

△

XX ⊠ 7

SYRIA

• Tel Faher

△

Israeli units generally
reached full strength
by the end of 8 October.

Golan Heights

7
X
9

△

• Kuneitra

Exploiting forces which could
not be committed because of
rapid Israeli reaction to the
initial attack.

XX ⊠ Eitan

X ⊡ 7 (-)

△

XX ⊠ 9

Gadot •

7
X
188

△

9
X
5

XX ⊡ 1

• Safed

X ⊡ 188 (-) • Rafid

△

XX ⊡ Laner

XX ⊠ 9

*Sea
of
Galilee*

△

X ⊡ 47

Tiberias •

El Al

△

Harab •

Israeli units regained the "Purple Line"
positions by 10 October and shifted the
divisions of Laner and Eitan further north
for the 11 October attack north of Kuneitra.

XX ⊡ Peled

N

Golan Heights Campaign
Syrian Attack, 6 –10 October, 1973

△   Israeli fortified observation posts
—·—·—   International borders
——·——·— 1967 cease-fire line "Purple Line"

Israeli brigades that stood in the Syrians' way in the Golan had to hold off the onslaught long enough for Israel's reserve mobilization to kick in. The 7th Armored Brigade's epic defense of the northern Golan has come to be widely regarded as one of the finest defensive stands in military history. Less is known about the heroism of the shattered fragments of the 188th (Barak) Brigade in slowing the Syrian advance in the south. In some respects, however, the Barak Brigade's story is more incredible, considering the fact that hundreds of Syrian tanks had overrun its sector and were held off by only a handful of tanks.

The 1973 conflict was about honor. In the Six Day War of June 1967, Israel had seized the Golan Heights, sweeping out the Syrian defenders and putting an end to the harassment that the Syrians had inflicted on civilians in the Hula Valley and the villages of the north. The loss of the Golan Heights had been humiliating to Syria, and between 1967 and 1973, there had been frequent skirmishes along the cease-fire line. For months leading up to the attack, the Syrian army had been fully mobilized and on war alert. Since the Israelis were accustomed to seeing those forces at battle strength, the Syrians were able to make final attack preparations without sending noteworthy warning signals. Furthermore, with tensions escalating between the two countries, Israeli leadership feared that strengthening their de-fenses might be misconstrued as preparation for a pre-emptive strike, thus provoking the Syrians to attack.

Since the Golan Heights' geography restricted defensive mobility, Israel had continued its advance in 1967 until a defensible line was reached—a string of extinct volcano cones that commands strategic views into Syria. Post-1967, Israeli defenses were based on 17 for-tified observation posts. The Purple Line, as the 1967 cease-fire line was known, marked the end of the no-man's land separating Syria from the Golan. Lacking a true defensive barrier, the Israelis had dug a 20-mile (30-km) antitank ditch along the border from Mount Hermon to Rafid, an obstacle Syrian armor would be forced to cross under fire from Israeli tanks positioned behind ramparts. At the out-break of hostilities in 1973, the Golan Heights were defended by two armored brigades: the 7th, which had only been dispatched to the northern sector on October 4, and the 188th (Barak) Brigade, who were based in the area and intimately familiar with the local terrain, in the south. The modified Centurion and M-48 Patton tanks fielded by both brigades were fitted with the 105mm NATO gun and modern diesel engines.

Considering the faulty Israeli intelligence assessment suggested that, at most, armed skirmishes with the Syrians would break out, the 170 tanks and 70 artillery pieces in the Golan were thought to be enough to meet any Syrian threats, at least until the reserves arrived.

Against that comparatively small force, the Syrian army fielded five divisions for its attack: two armored and three mechanized infantry, including some 1,400 tanks. Approximately 400 of those tanks were T-62s, the most modern Soviet-bloc tank at the time, equipped with a 115mm smoothbore gun and infrared night-fighting capability. The balance of the tank force consisted of T-54s and T-55s armed with 100mm guns. The Syrian plan called for its 5th, 7th and 9th mechanized infantry divisions, in BTR-50 armored personnel carriers (APCs) supported by 900 tanks, to breach the Israeli lines, opening the way for the 1st and 3rd armored divisions to move in with their 500 tanks to capture the entire Golan Heights before Israel had a chance to mobilize.

At 14:00 on October 6, Syrian gunners opened up a tremendous barrage along the entire front as a prelude to their two-pronged attack—a northern one in the vicinity of the Kuneitra–Damascus road and one in the south where Rafid bulges into Syria.

7th Armored's Legendary Stand in the Northern Golan Heights
Facing Colonel Avigdor Ben-Gal's 7th Armored Brigade in the Golan's northern sector were the Syrian 3rd Armored Division under Brigadier General Mustapha Sharba, the 7th Mechanized Infantry Division and the Assad Republican Guard. When the Syrian assault began, mine-clearing tanks and bridge-layers led the way to overcome the Israeli obstacles. Naturally, those engineering vehicles were the 7th's first targets, but Syrian infantrymen, braving intense fire from the heights, rushed forward and used their entrenching tools to build up enough earthen causeways for their tanks to negotiate the Israeli antitank ditches.

While the Israelis took out every Syrian vehicle they could get in their sights, the sheer mass of some 500 enemy tanks and 700 APCs advancing toward their lines ensured that the defenses would be over-whelmed. The number of defenders dwindled as Israeli tanks were knocked out, yet the vastly outnumbered Israelis managed to take a heavy toll on Syrian armor. Despite heavy losses, the Syrians pressed their attack without let-up, yet the overexerted 7th managed to hold its ground, throwing stopgap blocking actions wherever the Syrians were on the verge of breaking through.

When darkness fell, the Israelis had nothing to match the Syrians' night-vision gear and the enemy armor were able to advance to ranges effective for night fighting. In the close fighting, the Syrians succeeded in seizing some of the high ground, but a counterattack by the small group of persistent defenders forced them back. When some Syrian tanks did overrun the Israeli lines, the 7th's gunners rotated their turrets to destroy them and then immediately turned their attention back to other oncoming tanks. It amounted to an armored version of hand-to-hand combat.

The battle raged for two more days as the Syrians, seemingly oblivious to their heavy losses, continued their assault. By the after-noon of October 9, the 7th Brigade was down to six tanks protecting what was otherwise, for all intents and purposes, a clear path into Israel's north.

Those last few tanks fought until they were down to their last rounds. Then, just as the 7th Brigade's tanks were finally starting to pull back, they were suddenly augmented by an impromptu force of some 15 tanks. The Syrians believed the clock had run out and that the first of the fresh Israeli reservists had arrived, and the Syrian offensive ran out of steam. In fact, it was a motley force of repaired tanks that had pulled back from Tel Faris, mustered by Lieutenant Colonel Yossi Ben-Hanan, a veteran commander who, upon hearing about the outbreak of war, had hurried home from his honeymoon overseas. By virtue of its timing, that force, now manned by injured and other crewmen, proved to be the 7th Brigade's saving grace. As individual tanks began to augment the Israeli forces, the Syrians, ex-hausted from three days of continuous fighting and unaware of how close to victory they actually were, turned in retreat. Hundreds of destroyed tanks and APCs scattered about the valley below the Israeli ramparts were testimony to the horrible destruction that had taken place there, leading an Israeli colonel to dub it the "Valley of Tears."

188th Stands Its Ground in the Southern Golan

Meanwhile, the Syrians, whose objectives included seizing the bridges spanning the Jordan River—most of which could be easily reached through the southern Golan, concentrated a large part of their attack in that sector on October 6. Up against hundreds of enemy tanks, arranged in a line of armor as far as the eye could see, the Barak Brigade crews had no choice but to try to hold fast, because the terrain did not allow for much defensive maneuvering. Retreat would give the Syrians nearly free rein to seize the entire heights and move on the Israeli villages in the valley below.

The Syrian advance was initially slowed by an Israeli minefield and by deadly, accurate cannon fire. With dozens of Syrian tanks destroyed, the first few hours of the war were encouraging for the Israeli crewmen, whose intense training was paying off. Knowing they would be outnumbered in any engagement, the Israeli tank gunners had focussed relentlessly in training on gunnery skills and rapid target acquisition to ensure kills on the first shot. But the Israeli defenses could not contend with so many Syrian tanks. The Syrians' losses did not deter them, and they kept coming.

When fighter aircraft were called in to help stem the flow of Syrian armor, many of the Douglas A-4 Skyhawks and McDonnell F-4E Phantoms that responded to the plea were shot down or damaged by the Syrians' dense antiaircraft umbrella. Aware that Israeli doctrine relied on air power to even the score against their enemies' numerical advantage, Syria had acquired massive quantities of the latest Soviet missile and antiaircraft systems. With the help of Soviet advisers, they created an air defense network over the Golan that was thicker than the one protecting Hanoi during the Vietnam War.

With their air support thus limited, the Israeli tanks on the Golan were on their own—and the fate of northern Israel was in their hands. The Israeli tanks stood their ground and were knocked out one by one. Pushed beyond their limits, the defenses in the southern sector broke.

Bypassing the Israeli fortifications and pouring through gaps in the defenses, Syrian tanks pushed through the Israeli lines onto the wide-open plain that was ideal for tanks. The Israelis defending the southern Golan knew that they had to hold on at all costs to allow time for the reserves to mobilize, and in many cases the tank crews sacrificed themselves rather than give ground. As the hours passed, fewer and fewer Israeli tanks were left to stem the tide of oncoming tanks. The Syrian force split into a two-pronged advance. Colonel Tewfik Jehani's 1st Armored Division moved northward toward the Golan command headquarters of Major General Rafael Eitan, situated on the road leading down to the Bnot Yaakov Bridge, over the Jordan River and into the Israeli hinterland. The second prong of the Syrian attack, spearheaded by the 46th Armored Brigade of the 5th Infantry Division, moved south from Rafid on the southern axis road toward El Al, with units breaking off toward the north in the direction of the Arik Bridge at the northern tip of the Sea of Galilee. Some 600 tanks were now engaged in the southern Golan, against which stood 12 tanks and isolated units that had been cut off near the various fortifications along the border.[1]

Night offered no respite from the Syrian advance as they capitalized on their advantage of sophisticated night-vision equipment. The Israeli crews' long-distance firing efficiency was hampered by their lack of adequate night-fighting equipment. They did their best to overcome this obstacle by ordering illumination rounds to light up the sky, in conjunction with the xenon light projectors mounted on their tanks. Those were no match for the Syrians' infrared searchlights, so the Israelis did what they do best—improvise. They directed small tank units to carry out stopgap blocking actions against the far superior enemy forces—a tactic that may have prevented the Syrians from overrunning the entire Golan.

One of those lethal holding actions that have become legend was led by a young lieutenant named Zvi Gringold, affectionately known as "Lieutenant Zvicka," whose nighttime hit-and-run attacks on October 6–7 are credited as single-handedly holding at bay a major thrust by almost 50 tanks. His guerrilla-style tactics on the route leading toward his brigade's HQ at Nafakh caused the Syrians to believe they were up against a sizable Israeli force. After more than ten of its tanks were destroyed, the Syrian column withdrew, its commander deciding to hold off and deal with the Israeli force in daylight. Gringold continued to engage the Syrians throughout the night and following day, destroying upward of 30 tanks, until injuries, burns, and exhaustion caught up with him and he was evacuated. Gringold recovered and was subsequently awarded the *Itur haGvura,* or Medal of Valor, for his heroic defense of Nafakh.

Another blocking force operating in the south, albeit attached to the 7th Brigade, was "Force Tiger" under Captain Meir Zamir. Force Tiger's seven tanks were sent to block a column of some 40 Syrian tanks that had broken through at Rafid and was heading north—a move that threatened to cut off and isolate the 7th Brigade. Force Tiger laid an ambush that succeeded in destroying half the Syrian tanks during the early hours of Sunday morning, October 7. When 20 tanks escaped, Zamir prepared a second ambush that succeeded in finishing off the Syrian battalion just after dawn the next morning.

Yet another Syrian thrust by two brigades was advancing rapidly on the southern access road in the wide-open southern sector and inexplicably stopped short in its tracks just before reaching El Al. While some of its units fanned off toward other objectives to the north, a large part of the Syrian force failed to press its advantage, meaning that in effect the Syrians just waited for the Israeli reserves to arrive and engage them. A number of theories abound as to why the Syrians would halt their advance in the midst of their momentum, including fear of an ambush on what certainly should have been a heavily defended route, lack of flexibility and initiative once their objectives had been achieved, overextended supply lines and the more far-fetched fear of an Israeli nuclear reprisal in that critical hour. Whatever the true reason, their lack of initiative at a critical moment robbed the Syrians of the chance to reach the Jordan River—and perhaps beyond—virtually unopposed.

In the morning of October 7, the Syrians pressed their attack yet again. The few remaining defenders of the Barak Brigade pleaded for air support, which again suffered heavy losses. Ironically, the Syrians helped solve the problem of the antiaircraft missile threat for the Israelis. After the Syrians fired rockets at Israeli civilian areas, the Israeli Air Force responded with reprisal attacks on Syrian infrastructure in Damascus and beyond. To defend against these attacks, the

Syrians pulled back some of their missile batteries from the Golan front. Overall, it took the IAF several days to develop tactics and gain experience in defeating Syrian air defense systems, and 27 Israeli aircraft were lost on the Golan front in ground-support missions, as well as scores of others suffering various degrees of damage.

On October 7, Minister of Defense Moshe Dayan toured the Golan front and recognized how critical the situation truly was. Not only were the access routes into the Golan threatened, but also the entire north of Israel. Grasping the very real prospect of a Syrian breakthrough into integral Israel, the minister of defense considered a retreat to a line just forward of the escarpment overlooking the Jordan Valley for a major defensive stand—in effect putting his forces' backs against a wall. Israel prepared to destroy the bridges over the Jordan River to prevent a Syrian breakthrough.

The Syrian 1st Armored Division was advancing up the route toward the Golan HQ at Nafakh. Colonel Yitzhak Ben-Shoham, commander of the Barak Brigade, realized his brigade was for all intents and purposes destroyed. He therefore organized and led a small group of surviving tanks in a holding action that slowed the Syrian advance on his HQ for several hours until he and the rest of the group were killed. With the brigade commander dead, no reserves in sight and two Syrian brigades advancing toward the Golan HQ—and with some units having bypassed the base on both flanks—the situation at Nakakh could only be described as grave. Lead elements of the Syrian brigades actually reached Nafakh and broke through the base's southern perimeter. One Syrian T-55 crashed into General Eitan's HQ, only to be knocked out by the last operational tank in Gringold's platoon.

At that point, Eitan evacuated his headquarters to an improvised location farther to the north. Those left to defend the base manned two trackless Centurions from the camp repair depot and fired bazookas in a final stand that knocked out several Syrian tanks until those last Israeli tanks were destroyed.

The 188th Barak Brigade was no more. The Syrians were poised to overrun the Golan headquarters at Nafakh and, seemingly, the entire Golan. That final stand, however, had been enough to buy a few crucial additional minutes. While the Syrians paused to regroup after their final opposition had been neutralized, the first Israeli reserve units began reaching what had become the front lines. Finding Syrian tanks milling about their command headquarters, the Israelis immediately opened fire and attacked, dispersing the Syrians.

The arrival of the Israeli reservists spelled the beginning of the end for Syria. For both sides, the war had been about time—the Israelis doing all they could to buy time until their reserves arrived, and the Syrians racing against the clock to achieve their objectives before the Israeli mobilization. While many more bloody battles would take place, those first reserve units coming up the Golan and engaging the Syrians at Nafakh meant that the tide had turned.

The reservists found the Syrians enjoying nearly free rein in the Golan's southern sector. With Syrian tanks advancing along the routes down toward the Jordan River, the critical situation allowed no time to organize divisions and brigades. Instead, platoons and companies of tanks and other units rushed off to battle as quickly as the forces were mustered, at times being thrown in against Syrian battalions and even brigades. The fresh Israeli reserve units halted the near—and, in some cases, actual—retreat and began to check the Syrian advance. By midnight on day two of the war, the reserves had managed to stabilize what had been a disintegrating front.

The Syrians had managed to penetrate to areas a mere 10-minute drive from the Jordan River and Sea of Galilee and to less than a kilometer from El Al on the southern access road. Those gains had not come easily. In spite of their superior numbers, the Syrians' supply lines, extending great distances from their rear areas to points deep into the Golan, had been decimated by the Israeli defenders, and they could no longer replenish and support their forces. Convoys of supplies and reinforcements were under constant attack by the IAF, as well as IDF armor and other ground forces, severely hampering the Syrian advance.

While the Syrians dug in to consolidate their gains, the Israelis went on the offensive. Brigadier General Moshe Peled led a division up the Ein Gev road into the center of the southern sector while Major General Dan Laner's division moved up the Yehudia road farther to the north—a parallel advance that boxed in the 1st Syrian Armored Division and effectively brought the Syrians' brief conquest to an end. The Syrians fought viciously to free themselves from that pincer movement. A major confrontation near Hushniya camp, which the Syrians had captured the previous night and turned into a forward supply base, ended with hundreds of wrecked, burning and smoldering Syrian tanks, armored vehicles, and other vehicles littering the landscape.

By October 10, the Israelis had forced the Syrians back to the antebellum cease-fire line in the southern sector. Well aware of the strong Syrian defensive preparations in the south, Israel chose the northern Golan, with its more difficult, less-defended terrain, as the launching area for its counterattack into Syria itself. Among the units joining the counterattack was the reincarnated Barak Brigade. Since 90 percent of its original commanders had been killed or wounded, Barak's remnants were joined by replacements, reorganized and returned to fighting strength for the counteroffensive that penetrated deep into Syria.

Syria clamored for assistance from ally Egypt to relieve pressure on its now embattled forces. After initial successes at the beginning of the war, when its forces crossed the formidable barrier of the Suez Canal, overcame Israeli defenses and secured a significant foothold, the Egyptians now ventured out from their defensive deployment at the behest of Syria. Massive tank battles of a scale not seen since World War II were fought in which Egyptian forces were decimated. The IDF had turned the tide, which they capitalized upon when Israeli forces crossed the Suez Canal into Egypt proper, trapping an entire Egyptian army in the Sinai Desert.

A United Nations-sanctioned cease-fire came into effect on October 23, officially ending hostilities. Although the war ended with Israeli forces on the move toward the Syrian capital and entrenched in Egypt proper, the Yom Kippur War—or Ramadan War, as it is known to the Arabs—shattered the myth of Israeli invincibility. The Syrians' success in maintaining the element of surprise and its forces' discipline in executing its attack helped that country regain much of the honor it had lost in the debacle of 1967. The victorious Israelis, on the other hand, had won a Pyrrhic victory. Horrible losses had been suffered, epitomized by the obliteration of the 188th Barak Brigade. While the war reaffirmed the Israeli defense doctrine of relying on the reserves to defeat a numerically superior enemy force, there was no time for celebration as the country buried the 2,222 soldiers who had paid the ultimate price for their country's survival, and attended to its 7,251 wounded.

Notes

1.Chaim Herzog. *The War of Atonement* (Jerusalem: Steimatzky's Agency, 1975), p.87.

CHAPTER 17

TURKEY SHOOT OVER THE BEKAA VALLEY

1982 LEBANON WAR

A s Israeli Air Force (IAF) pilots flew their aircraft home and began to contemplate what they had been through, some were overcome with nervous excitement. It was not only isolated cases where pilots failed on their first landing attempts. Once the aircraft were safely back on the tarmac, ground crews saw that the launching rails, pylons and bomb racks were now largely empty. Mission tapes removed from the aircraft revealed the unprecedented feat the IAF had just pulled off—a mission nearly a decade in the making. Minister of Defense Ariel Sharon remarked that "the exemplary control, incredible accuracy, and precise planning displayed by Israel's pilots would be studied in military academies around the world."[1]

During the October 1973 Yom Kippur War, more than 40 Israeli aircraft, mostly McDonnell F-4E Phantoms and Douglas A-4 Skyhawks flying ground support and attack missions, had been shot down by Soviet-built Egyptian and Syrian surface-to-air missiles (SAMs). Stung by such heavy losses, Israel acted to ensure that its next contest against Arab SAMs would have a more successful outcome. The IAF's opportunity to implement plans based on the lessons learned from the 1973 war was Israel's 1982 invasion of Lebanon, called Operation *Peace for Galilee.*

In the spring of 1981, as part of the Israeli–Syrian power struggle over Lebanon, Syria moved SAM batteries into eastern Lebanon's Bekaa Valley, which stretches nearly 120 miles (200km) between the Lebanon Mountains and the Anti-Lebanon Mountains, from Mount Hermon in the south up to Zahla. Over the course of the next year, Syria built up an overlapping network of 19 SAM batteries, 15 of which were SA-6 sites, and a pair each of SA-2 and SA-3 for medium- and high-altitude aircraft, protected from attack by ZSU-23-4 radar-controlled antiaircraft artillery (AAA) and SA-7 Strela ("Arrow" in Russian) shoulder-launched missiles. With these capabilities, Syria could sweep the Bekaa Valley's airspace clean of Israeli aircraft.

Syrian involvement in Lebanon runs as long as Lebanon's history. As Lebanon's territory had been cut from Syria by European colonialists, Syria considered Lebanon part of its territory and never recognized its independence. Syrian troops entered the country in 1976 ostensibly in a peacekeeping role in the aftermath of Lebanon's 1975–76 civil war, their presence serving the dual purpose of blocking an exposed flank should Israel decide to invade Syria through Lebanon. Israel, however, felt equally threatened by Syria's apparent permanence in Lebanon.

Before the country erupted into civil war, Lebanon had been the "Paris of the Middle East"—a country rich and diverse both ethnically and culturally, yet held together in a delicate balancing act. Then, in 1970, when Palestinians became too cozy using Jordan as a base for terror operations against Israel and the West, King Hussein expelled them from his country. Weak and divided Lebanon became their refuge. Palestine Liberation Organization (PLO) terrorists established a state-within-a-state in Lebanon's mountainous territory. "Fatahland," as the area was known to Israel, became an armed PLO camp used to launch guerrilla infiltrations into Israel and to terrorize Israel's northern towns and villages with harassing rocket and artillery attacks.

In March 1978 the IDF launched a six-day ground incursion against the PLO in Lebanon called Operation *Litani*, but the PLO quickly recovered from that blow and continued its indiscriminate firing of Katyusha rockets and artillery salvos into Israel from south Lebanon. Overseas, an escalation in terror attacks against Israeli and Jewish sites culminated in the attempted assassination of the Israeli ambassador in London by a Palestinian terror group on June 3, 1982. In immediate retaliation for the assassination attempt, Israeli jets bombed PLO ammunition dumps and training bases in Lebanon. The PLO responded with a massive rocket and artillery bombardment against Israel's northern communities. Israel implemented its contingency plan to clear a 25-mile (40-km) security zone north of the Lebanon–Israel border that would push PLO artillery beyond range of Israel's northern settlements.

On June 6, 1982, Israeli units advanced into Lebanon along three axes, destroying PLO bases along the way. IAF fighters and attack helicopters bombed PLO strongholds, clearing the way for the ground forces. By the third day of the war, Israeli troops had achieved their goal of reaching a line 25 miles (40km) from the border. With its army in a favorable position vis-à-vis Syrian forces in Lebanon, Israel saw its chance to rid Lebanon of its Syrian foe as well. But support for its ground forces necessitated air superiority, and that was threatened by the Syrian missiles. The SAMs had to go.

Knowing that SAMs would remain a force to be dealt with in future warfare, over the years since the Yom Kippur War, Israel had developed special weapons and tactics to take them on. Syria's missile deployment in Lebanon posed a challenge to Israel, so Israel began piecing together its plan.

Since the SAM must track its target with its own radar, the key was taking out the radar. Radar is a pulse of electromagnetic energy in a concentrated beam. When a target is "illuminated" by this beam, some of the pulse is reflected back to the radar, giving the operator information on target bearing and range. The idea behind SEAD— suppression of enemy air defenses, as engaging and destroying SAMs is known in military lingo—is to entice the enemy to light up his search radars in order to destroy them. Doing so requires locating the mobile missile batteries with precise intelligence information, disrupting tracking and guidance radar systems and communications with electronic warfare, and diverting missiles by way of deception. To pull this off, Israel concocted an intricate plan involving drones, decoys, highly developed electronic counter-measures (ECM), anti-radiation (ARM) and precision-guided missiles, and other tactics which remain classified.

The first moves of the highly orchestrated operation against the Syrian air defense network in Lebanon were actually made long before the attack. Tasked with pinpointing the location of the SAMs, Israel Aircraft Industries (IAI) "Scout" and Tadiran "Mastiff" reconnaissance mini-UAVs (unmanned aerial vehicles, or pilot-less drones) flew over the area almost daily in the ELINT (Electronic Intelligence) role, scanning the area for emissions from radars and radios. In this way, Israel was able to locate the Syrian SAM batteries and identify their radar frequencies and operational sequences—information that was then used to develop appropriate electronic countermeasures. Several UAVs were downed, but the cost was negligible when compared with the risks of sending manned reconnaissance sorties over SAM-protected areas.

Electro-optical sensors on the UAVs relayed real-time intelligence data to operators controlling the aircraft from ground control stations. Their pictures revealed that the mobile SA-6s were deployed mostly in fixed positions. But since the SA-6 batteries could be easily redeployed, UAVs loitered in the air long before, during and after the attack, maintaining a vigil on them as the aircraft's cameras recorded a steady stream of intelligence information which was collected into an overall picture of the situation on the ground.

With all this intelligence information, Israel was able to put the finishing touch on its plans. Since the attack would reveal special weapons and tactics Israel had been developing over nearly a decade, Israeli leadership decided to attack on a grand scale, taking out the entire Syrian SAM network rather than a piecemeal approach concentrating on the most threatening sites.

On June 9, 1982, the fourth day of the war, at airbases throughout Israel, air crews suited up in their G suits and squadron leaders met in briefing rooms to review final preparations for the offensive. Even as the Cabinet discussed the plan submitted by Minister of Defense Ariel Sharon, Israeli pilots headed out to aircraft shelters where ground crews strapped pilots into their seats, shut them into cockpits and made final checks of the aircraft. Jet engines roared to life and aircraft rolled out to runways. When authorization to launch the attack came at 13:30 hours, an armada of aircraft howled into the sky and sped north on its brief flight to Lebanon. The attack aircraft—once the hunted—were now the hunters.

The Israeli attack force consisted of approximately 90 aircraft: McDonnell Douglas F-15 Eagles, General Dynamics F-16 Fighting Falcons (newcomers to the IAF, having arrived only in 1980), IAI Kfir C-2s, F-4E Phantoms and A-4 Skyhawks. The F-15s and F-16s flew top cover while the attack aircraft, coming from different bases, flew at different altitudes and intervals towards the batteries they were tasked with destroying. With so many aircraft involved, precise air traffic control was required. Here Israel had the luxury of running a war close to home, with full battlefield awareness. Grumman E-2C Hawkeye command aircraft, capable of automatically and simultaneously tracking hundreds of targets and controlling multiple airborne intercepts, assisted in providing continuous air control and coordination.

Flying outside of missile range, IAF Boeing 707s and other aircraft packed full of sophisticated electronic warfare equipment overlaid new data on the information previously collected by UAVs. The Electronic Warfare (EW) aircraft's highly sensitive receivers detected Syrian radars, ran their signals through computers to amplify and filter them and, by measuring frequencies of the signals, allowed the Israelis to pinpoint the locations of threatening sources. Jammers generated and returned incorrect signals to confuse the Syrian radar and disrupt communication channels. Supplemental stand-off jamming by the attack aircraft further "blinded" the radar sites, frustrating their ability to get a reliable fix on Israeli aircraft.

SAMs are most effective when operated in concert with long-range search radars which feed data on inbound aircraft to SAM batteries' targeting radars. This allows the SAM battery to activate its radar at the last moment and fire a missile with virtually no warning. Israel had done its homework to prevent such surprises by knowing the exact location of the missile batteries and by constantly monitoring for changes. The Syrians had also been helpful in this regard by deploying their missiles in visible locations, as if flaunting their presence to the Israelis. With their frequencies blocked or jammed, the

SAM batteries had minimal early warning and communication capabilities, crucial elements in an integrated air-defense network. The Israelis had also ensured that the Syrians would not have supplemental radar by launching attacks on radar installations, including an assault by a Bell AH-1G Cobra helicopter that destroyed a radar station south of Beirut with Hughes TOW (tube-launched, optically sighted, wire-guided) missiles.

The Israeli assault on the SAM sites began with a masterful feat of deception. Objects appearing on the Syrian radar as aircraft were not really aircraft. Meanwhile, the real IAF aircraft that were en route to attack the Syrians were not showing up on the radar. And the beams sent out by Syrian radar were used by some of the Israeli weapons to guide them to target. To confuse the radars still functioning, the Israelis saturated Lebanon's skies with simulated targets. The unpowered, air-launched Samson decoy, developed specifically for the IAF by Brunswick Defense, used special lenses or reflectors to enhance its radar signature, causing it to appear on radar screens as full-scale aircraft. The slew of decoys in the air forced Syrian SAM radar operators to light up their search radars, exposing themselves to ARM strikes, while they wasted their missiles on the decoys. After firing, missile launchers are extremely vulnerable as they reload, especially after publicizing their location by firing. To add to the confusion the jamming and the false images decoys were creating on Syrian radar screens, Israeli artillery unleashed a barrage of long-range shells and rockets against the SAM sites.

With all this going on, the waves of attack aircraft headed towards their targets in a massive simultaneous attack reminiscent of Israel's destruction of the Arab air forces in the 1967 Six Day War. The IAF strike force of Phantoms and F-16s went in for the kill at 14:00, descending on the Bekaa Valley trailing flares and chaff—bundles of thin metallic strips designed to confuse the guidance systems of any missiles the Syrians might succeed in launching. Following target acquisition and lock-on, the attack aircraft unleashed supersonic Shrike AGM-45 and AGM-78 ARMs to home in on the electromagnetic waves emitted by the activated SAM radar vans.

AGM-65 Mavericks and other precision-guided missiles were also fired at the SAM radars. Equipped with coordinates and aerial photographs of the sites they were tasked with destroying, Israeli airmen acquired targets visually, put radar vans between the crosshairs of their sights and launched their missiles. From the missile-eye view appearing on small cockpit screens, the Israeli aircrews could follow the missiles' progress as they raced in on "fire and forget" mode, seeing the entire missile battery coming into view in the distance, then focus on the central radar vehicle until only that vehicle could be seen, growing in size as the missile descended towards it, and then static on the screen as the missile hit.

Syria's command centers and radars were put out of action with high-explosive, fragmentation, and shaped-charge warheads, the latter designed to defeat heavy armor. The exploding vehicles were immediately engulfed in flames and thick gray smoke. The pilots pulled away, G forces pressing them back into their seats as they gained altitude and made for home.

Despite all their protective measures, the Israelis in the air still kept a wary eye out for missiles. The 20-foot (6-m) long SA-6 missiles looked like bright colored balls as they shot up from the ground. IAF pilots reported seeing some SAM launches, but they said that the missiles seemed to lack direction and did not actually threaten their aircraft. With the Syrian radars destroyed, there were no ground command links steering the missiles. With its semi-active homing radar, the SA-6 could still be lethal—until it has flown off course and its fuze times out, causing it to self-destruct.

Israeli aircraft were equipped with radar homing and warning receivers to alert pilots with a shrill alarm in their headsets if their aircraft were tracked. Small screens displaying alphanumeric figures reflected the type, angle of arrival, relative lethality and status of threats, with special warnings for missile launch. IAF pilots had been repeatedly drilled in the ways to avoid being targeted, from chaff and other countermeasures to jinking, or evasive flying. If a missile were launched against an aircraft, the pilot had to maintain incredible concentration to avoid it. In those critical moments, panic could result in death. Even if they could safely eject, the Israeli pilots did not know what type of reception they might receive below, especially after seeing televised images of the corpse of an Israeli airman downed by ground fire earlier in the war being dragged through the streets of

Beirut. But on June 9, 1982, the missiles—confused by Israeli jamming and electronic countermeasures—failed to hit a single Israeli aircraft.

Their radars destroyed, each SAM missile battery's armored Transporter Erector Launcher (TEL), with its complement of three missiles, was not only blinded, but vulnerable. Some batteries tried to protect themselves with smokescreens, but that only served to highlight their locations. Since they are mobile, SA-6s were not dug in, making them easier to spot from the air. Dozens of F-16s, Phantoms, Kfirs and Skyhawks, their hardpoints heavy-laden with general-purpose and cluster bombs, swooped in to bomb the missile batteries' defenseless launchers and AAA sites. Fused to detonate on impact, the general-purpose bombs' cast-steel cases shattered into thousands of destructive fragments. Cluster bombs, packed full of "bomblet" sub-munitions, proved particularly effective against each battery's dispersed area targets of command vehicles, generators and other support equipment. With their fuzes set to activate at a preset altitude, the bomblets dispersed and rained down on their targets in dense concentrations.

Although the SAMs were effectively blinded, bombing the launchers required aircraft to overfly the target, exposing themselves to AAA fire and optically aimed shoulder-launched SA-7 Strela missiles. To confuse the SA-7s' infra-red homing seekers, the Israeli pilots released pyrotechnic flares when going in to drop their ordnance.

Pilots knew when they had hit their mark. The ground shook from the force of explosions. Batteries went up in infernos of exploding ordnance combined with the SAMs' solid propellant and HE warheads, causing huge fireballs clearly visible from far away.

The entire attack lasted about two hours. In the opening minutes, 10 of the 19 SAM batteries were destroyed. When reconnaissance overflights revealed that not all the batteries attacked had been fully disabled, another wave of attack aircraft went in, knocking out seven more batteries. Some SA-6 batteries kept their radars off and managed to avoid destruction. The following day, however, another wave of Israeli jets destroyed the remaining sites. Syria's missile network in Lebanon had been reduced to a smoldering mass of twisted metal. The IAF had had the misfortune of being the first air force to face the

SA-6, but the hard lessons learned in the 1973 Yom Kippur War allowed Israel to make history in Operation *Peace for Galilee* with the first-ever direct, all-out attack on an integrated missile network. Israeli defense minister Ariel Sharon declared this, "one of the most brilliant, complicated and intricate operations ever carried out."[2]

Eagles and Falcons: Birds of Prey

Surprised as they were by the Israeli move, the Syrians did not idly sit by as the IAF ravaged their missile network in Lebanon. Dozens of Syrian Air Force fighters were scrambled from nearby bases to join Syrian patrol aircraft already airborne at the time of the attack. Brown and yellow-camouflaged Mikoyan-Gurevich MiG-21 Fishbeds, swept-wing MiG-23 Flogger fighters and some Sukhoi Su-22 Fitter fighters began filling the sky.

With Israel's E-2C Hawkeye airborne early warning command and control aircraft circling high in the sky, the Israelis had a comprehensive picture of the aerial battlefield. In IAF service for only a year, the propeller-driven Hawkeye, easily identified by the large radar dish on its back, was packed with powerful computers, situational displays and secure communications capable of detecting and assessing threats from approaching enemy aircraft over ranges of about 300 miles (480km). Operators sitting at consoles tracked Syrian aircraft as they took off from their bases and vectored F-15 and F-16 fighters to deal with them.

The Eagle and Falcon pilots, whose aircraft were equipped with advanced, on-board air-intercept radar, saw the dots on the radar screens representing Syrian aircraft and prepared to engage from afar. But in the limited airspace over Lebanon, where upward of 200 aircraft were operating that day, the IAF opted for a cautious approach, specifying that all aerial engagements were to take place within visual range. "We had to differentiate between our aircraft and those of the enemy," one pilot explained.[3]

With their Boeing 707s and other electronic warfare assets, the Israelis effectively jammed radio and data communications links to the Syrian pilots, who relied on ground controllers for situational awareness. The EW efforts were so successful that, in the words of the Syrians, "the entire Syrian air response was essentially disrupted . . ."[4]

Largely unaware that the missiles meant to ensure clear skies had been destroyed, the Syrians did not expect to find Israeli aircraft over the Bekaa Valley. Many a Syrian pilot first spotted the Israelis as they maneuvered to engage in air-to-air combat. In rapid dogfights lasting 30 to 40 seconds each, F-15s and F-16s downed the Syrians that came their way, most with Israel Weapons Development Authority (Rafael) Python 3 and American AIM-9 Sidewinder air-to-air missiles.

One Israeli pilot recounted how his four-man F-16 formation was on a routine patrol over the "safe zone" of central Lebanon—away from the dangers of the Syrian missile umbrella—when their controller instructed them to fly east, towards the Bekaa Valley. Since that heading would put them in what had until then been a no-fly zone for the IAF, the pilots asked for clarification. Their instructions confirmed, the pilots turned eastward and were warned of Syrian MiGs in the area. When a pair of MiGs was picked up on radar, the F-16s moved in for visual ID. Unaware that the Syrian missile batteries had already been attacked, the pilots kept a careful lookout for the bright flash indicating a SAM missile launch.

"I spotted them first: a pair of MiG-23s," the pilot recalled. "They saw us—they knew we were there. The MiGs turned sharply and broke away, trying to maneuver. I divvied them up with my partner." Hearing the tone in their headsets indicating lock-on, each pilot fired a missile at a MiG. The Sidewinder shot out from his F-16's wing, locked onto the MiG's hot engine exhaust, and flew the two nautical miles to slam into its engine. "The MiG was hit, caught on fire, lost control and came apart slowly—all before me, like in a movie. . . . The MiG managed to fly for about another 20 seconds. The pilot ejected and the MiG fell and exploded."[5]

At the Israeli ground control center, commanders watched in amazement as young soldiers keeping track of the action made wax pencil notations on transparent Plexiglas displays, showing twenty-two Syrian fighters shot down.[6] With so many aircraft taking part in such an intricate operation, losses and other complications were anticipated. Yet, thanks to meticulous planning and execution, those setbacks never materialized. Syria later admitted that Israel's superior airborne-control network gave it a clear advantage. While this certainly played an important role in the lopsided Israeli victory in the air battles, Israeli pilots simply found the Syrian pilots unremarkable. The IAF approached aerial combat with the Syrians considering them as equals, as a cavalier attitude of superiority can lead to carelessness. However, while some Syrian pilots fought valiantly and made maximum use of their aircraft, overall they proved no match for the skilled IAF pilots flying more agile American-built aircraft.[7]

Over the next few days, Syria continued challenging Israel's dominance of Lebanon's skies with combat air patrols and attack missions. On June 10, another 26 Syrian aircraft were destroyed, while all Israeli aircraft returned safely to base. On June 11, the Syrian air force took to the air once again and lost another 18 aircraft, again without a single Israeli aircraft lost. In all, between June 7 and 11, 1982, 81 Syrian aircraft were downed in aerial combat—with no Israeli losses. The Israelis had to suspend the customary air base fly-by after downing an enemy aircraft—simply too many Syrians were being shot down and the victory laps were interfering with air operations. The Syrian air force had been routed: not only did it lose billions of dollars' worth of aircraft, but half the Syrian pilots shot down were killed—a major blow. IAF F-15s were credited with 34 Syrian kills, while the F-16s surpassed them with 46. An F-4E Phantom is credited with one kill.

With the threat of the SAMs gone, Israeli aircraft controlled the skies over Lebanon; the IAF was free to provide ground support and otherwise operate at will. Syria abandoned Lebanon's skies to the IAF at that point, leaving its forces and those of its allies at the mercy of the IAF. The Israeli Air Force had achieved its mission: clear skies over Lebanon.

Israel's incursion into Lebanon, with its rapid successes in the air and on the ground, ultimately bogged down into an 18-year occupation of a security zone in southern Lebanon meant to protect Israel's north. Despite Israel's withdrawal in May 2000, the Islamic group Hezbollah, which had been battling Israel's presence in Lebanon, continued its armed resistance. Hezbollah's increasing audacity and provocations resulted in the 2006 Second Lebanon War.

Notes

1. Raful Eitan. *A Soldier's Story* (New York: Shapolsky Publishers, Inc., 1991), p.289.
2. Conor Cruise O'Brien. *The Siege* (New York: Touchstone, 1986), p.624.
3. Lon Nordeen. *Fighters Over Israel* (London: Greenhill Books, 1990), p.172.
4. Eliezer Cohen. *Israel's Best Defense* (London: Airlife Publishing Ltd., 1993), p.465.
5. Personal interview, January 1999.
6. IDF Spokesman's Office, www.idf.il.
7. While events proved this assessment true, it is nonetheless biased as it comes from an IAF F-16 pilot who became an ace during the conflict with five kills.

EPILOGUE

*H*oly *Wars* concludes with the 1982 invasion of Lebanon—a
military operation that only ended eighteen years later, in 2000.
Since that invasion, Israel has not undertaken all-out warfare, with
aircraft dog-fighting or armored formations duking it out against peer
adversaries. But that isn't to say Israel's infantry divisions, armored
battalions and air force squadrons have been idle. Each has since
taken part in operations, incursions and war. Instead of battling formal armies, the IDF has fought non- or quasi-state actors in asymmetric warfare. Lacking military equipment or capabilities anything
remotely near those of the IDF, organizations such as Lebanon's Shiite
Muslim militant group Hezbollah, or Party of God, which grew from
resistance to Israel's occupation of Lebanon to become one of the
most powerful actors in Lebanon, and the Palestinian Islamic funda-
mentalist group Hamas, an abbreviation for Islamic Resistance Movement, that seized control of the Gaza Strip, have targeted Israel's
military or its civilian population, triggering IDF responses. Despite
the gross disparity between the two sides, these militant groups have
used clever manipulation, aided by an occasional errant Israeli
artillery round, to win the battle for international public opinion, thus
largely depriving the IDF of accolades for its military successes.

Operation Defensive Shield

On March 27, 2002, a man carrying a suitcase walked into Netanya's
Park Hotel dining room, which was packed with some 250 people
sharing a festive Passover holiday meal, known as a *seder*. The man
was a Palestinian suicide bomber or, as some term it, a homicide
bomber; he detonated his deadly load of explosives, killing 30 people
and wounding more than 140. Palestinians had been resorting to
terror attacks since the outbreak of the Second Intifada uprising in
September 2000. The Passover Massacre, as it became known, was
the eighth in a series of deadly suicide bombings that month alone in
which some 33 Israelis had already been killed, and more than 260
injured. Palestinian militant group Hamas claimed responsibility for
the Park Hotel bombing the aim of which—like the other attacks—
had been simply to kill and maim.

Israel had had enough. The IDF launched Operation *Defensive
Shield*—its largest military operation in the West Bank since the 1967
Six Day War—to root out the Palestinian terror infrastructure and
stop the wave of suicide bombings. First order of business was moving
into Ramallah, where the IDF besieged Palestinian Authority President Yasser Arafat in his headquarters compound. Arafat remained
isolated and under siege until the end of 2004, when he was allowed
out for medical treatment in Paris, where he died.

Operation *Defensive Shield* focused on the West Bank's cities and
surrounding areas. Perhaps the best known aspect of the operation
was the IDF's move on Jenin, the city from which a quarter of the
Second Intifada's 100 suicide bombers were dispatched. Jenin's narrow streets were wired with booby traps and improvised explosive
devices (IEDs) that slowed the Israeli advance. After an Israeli unit
stumbled into a Palestinian ambush in which 13 soldiers were lost, the
IDF relied heavily on D-9 armored bulldozers to clear the way for its
troops. Some areas suffered extensive damage, which Palestinians
highlighted to the media to propagate false accusations of Israeli
atrocities.

During the three weeks of West Bank incursions, Palestinian casu-
alty figures ranged from 240 to 500 (accounts vary), while Israel
suffered 30 dead. The operation dealt a major blow to the Palestinian
terror infrastructure, resulting in fewer subsequent attacks, although

Operation *Defensive Shield* did not bring an end to the Second Intifada.

2006 Lebanon War

The Second Lebanon War, as it is known in Israel, began on July 12, 2006 with an unprovoked Hezbollah cross-border attack and bombardment that resulted in the deaths of eight Israeli soldiers and the abduction of two.

Israel responded forcefully with punishing air strikes and artillery fire on Lebanese and Hezbollah targets. Even Hezbollah leader Sheikh Hassan Nasrallah admitted he did not expect such a strong Israeli response. The Shiite group answered with a barrage of rocket fire into cities and towns in the north of Israel—fire that continued throughout the war, paralyzing a huge part of Israel and forcing nearly one million Israeli citizens into bomb shelters.

Israel Defense Forces Chief of Staff Lieutenant General Dan Halutz, a former air force commander, believed that air power alone would bring about the return of the two abducted soldiers and punish Hezbollah for its actions. Israeli air strikes hit thousands of targets: Hezbollah command centers, weapon and ammunition stores and rocket launchers. Israel also struck Lebanese infrastructure—Lebanon's price for its symbiotic relationship with Hezbollah, which is part of Lebanon's government. As a deterrent, Israel has long practiced a policy of severe retribution to convey the message that attacks on its citizens or territory will not be tolerated.

The Israel Navy attacked Lebanese coastal targets and blockaded ports. Just two days into the war, Hezbollah fired a radar-guided antiship missile that hit and crippled INS *Hanit*, one of Israel's three advanced Saar 5 class corvettes. The Navy admitted not to have known this weapon was in Hezbollah's arsenal, meaning that the ship's extensive defensive systems had not been activated, an embarrassing and deadly intelligence failure.

Hezbollah continued firing rockets into Israel. Hezbollah's heavier rockets were largely destroyed, but the smaller launchers proved elusive. IAF unmanned aircraft (UAVs) and other air assets operating over Lebanon worked together to reduce the so-called sensor-to-shooter loop, meaning that when a rocket was launched, the IAF quickly responded to knock out its now-exposed launcher. Despite this, some 100 rockets were hitting Israel each day. Air power alone was not stopping Hezbollah.

When Israel unilaterally withdrew from southern Lebanon in May 2000—ending its 18-year occupation—Hezbollah moved in to fill the void. Established to resist Israel's occupation of Lebanon, Hezbollah did not limit its attacks to Israeli targets. Probably its most notorious action was its 1983 bombing of US Marine barracks in Beirut that killed 241 Americans, followed by an attack minutes later that killed 58 French troops. Both contingents were supporting a United Nations peacekeeping mission working to stabilize Lebanon.

After Israel's withdrawal from Lebanon, it was not long before Hezbollah began provocations. A particularly blatant one came after only five months, when Hezbollah fighters crossed into Israel where they abducted and killed three Israeli soldiers, revealing that their agenda was more than just expelling Israel from Lebanon. Exhausted from its 18-year Lebanese entanglement, Israel's response was lackluster, emboldening Hezbollah.

Israel and Hezbollah were now paying the price for their previous policies. Realizing that rooting out Hezbollah from southern Lebanon would require a ground invasion, IDF ground forces were sent into Lebanon, where they fought Hezbollah in villages throughout southern Lebanon's western, central and eastern sectors. IDF operations were hindered by blunders such as poor equipment, outdated maps and intelligence, and supplies not reaching the front. Unhappy with the way the war was being run, IDF leadership sidelined GOC Northern Command Major General Udi Adam.

In combat, Hezbollah proved a tenacious foe. These were not the Arab irregulars of yesteryear, but well-trained, equipped, and organized fighters who stood their ground. An illustrative example was the intense battle fought, beginning on July 24, in the central sector village of Bint Jbeil, a Hezbollah stronghold. It was here that Sheikh Hassan Nasrallah gave a famous victory speech just two weeks after Israel's May 2000 withdrawal from Lebanon where he called Israel "weaker than a spider's web." Israeli troops were now back, fighting in the town's mostly deserted streets and alleyways against a hardened core of Hezbollah fighters that resisted fiercely. Tens of

Israeli troops were killed or wounded, and Merkava Main Battle Tanks were knocked out by mines and antitank weapons. The battle caused extensive destruction to the village, which was later rebuilt with Iranian support.

Deployed along the Israeli border, Hezbollah had studied the ways of the Israeli army and devised tactics and strategies to overcome Israel's strengths. They employed modern communications and electronics equipment such as night vision goggles, and put antitank weapons to lethal use against both tanks and built-up structures, causing the bulk of Israeli military casualties. In one incident, nine paratroopers seeking shelter in a house in the village of Debel were killed by an antitank rocket. In another blow to the IDF, a dozen reservists were killed when a Hezbollah rocket struck their marshalling area near the Lebanese border.

As a United Nations cease-fire was being hammered out after nearly a month of fighting, the Israeli government decided to expand the military operation. In a final drive before the cease-fire was scheduled to go into effect on August 14, 2006, Israel suffered 33 casualties. Despite all the IDF efforts, Hezbollah continued launching rockets throughout the war; the last day before the cease-fire went into effect saw more than 250 rockets fired at Israel. In all, Hezbollah launched 3,970 rockets. The war ended with acceptance of UN Security Council Resolution 1701, in which wishful thinking called for the ineffectual Lebanese army and a United Nations force (UNIFIL) to eviscerate Hezbollah, which they failed to accomplish. The failure to disarm Hezbollah raises the question of how long the fragile cease-fire will last.

At 34 days, it was Israel's longest war, excepting the protracted War of Independence, and arguably the least conclusive. At best it can be considered a draw, an accomplishment on which Hezbollah prides itself, given that no Arab country had ever fared so well in war with the Jewish state. Israel claimed more than 500 Hezbollah fighters were killed; Hezbollah acknowledges only 65 deaths. One hundred and seventeen Israeli soldiers died in the war, as well as 39 civilians, with thousands injured. Both countries suffered losses to their infrastructure and economy. An Israeli commission of inquiry known as the Winograd Commission issued a report critical of the Israeli leadership's handling of the war, reproaching Prime Minister Ehud Olmert, hapless Defense Minister Amir Peretz, and Chief of Staff Dan Halutz.[1]

Israel had failed to destroy Hezbollah or free its two abducted soldiers; corpses of the two soldiers were returned to Israel in 2008. Hezbollah—its position strengthened by the war—has rearmed with Iranian and Syrian support.

Cast Lead Gaza Incursion

Israel reestablished some of its deterrence with its December 2008 incursion into the Gaza Strip. Operation *Cast Lead* was launched on December 27, 2008 in response to incessant rocket fire into Israel from Palestinian militant group Hamas-controlled Gaza. Israeli forces set about destroying Hamas' rocket and mortar launching capabilities and its supporting infrastructure. While Israel would be accused of overkill, the scale of the operation was perhaps a reaction to criticism from the 2006 Second Lebanon War that Israel failed to bring its might to bear. This time Israel used its power, sending a clear message that the country still knew how to fight—a message undoubtedly heard in Lebanon. In this part of the world, such a heavy-handed response to provocations is a sign of strength; restraint is for the weak. One must remember not to judge the Middle East using Western values, for very different rules are at play.

During the summer of 2005, Israel had unilaterally withdrawn from the Gaza Strip, which it had occupied since 1967. Areas in Israel bordering Gaza have been under rocket and mortar attack since 2001; some 8,000 have been fired at them, which even the UN called indiscriminate and deliberate attacks against civilians.[2] Replicating events in Lebanon, the Israeli withdrawal was followed by provocations, this time in the form of continued rocket fire. Hamas further escalated with a daring cross-border attack on an Israeli army base on June 25, 2006 during which IDF soldier Gilad Shalit was abducted and remains in Hamas custody. Hamas' next milestone came a year later when they seized control of the Gaza Strip in a June 2007 putsch. Israel declared the Gaza Strip "hostile territory" and imposed a blockade. The rocket and mortar fire continued.

Operation *Cast Lead* opened with a highly orchestrated air strike lasting three minutes and 40 seconds by tens of Israeli aircraft on more than 100 targets throughout Gaza. Undaunted, Hamas continued launching rockets against Israel. Over the course of a week, aerial operations continued against Hamas command posts, training camps, weapon stores, rocket and mortar launch sites, and smuggling tunnels.

Hamas launched rockets from among its own civilian population in urban areas, with little regard for casualties. Even the UN committee established to investigate the conflict, the Goldstone Commission, acknowledged that "Palestinian armed groups, where they launched attacks close to civilian or protected buildings, unnecessarily exposed the civilian population of Gaza to danger."[3] This was precisely Hamas' underdog strategy of getting its civilians killed, knowing that civilian casualties would turn international public opinion against Israel. To this end, Hamas is said to encourage Palestinian civilians to take risks in hopes of achieving martyrdom.

In an effort to avoid civilian casualties and minimize collateral damage, Israel employed laser-guided precision weapons, and various means including telephone calls and leaflets warning non-combatants to evacuate dangerous areas. Even special low-explosive rounds were dropped to warn civilians of impending attacks, a technique known as "knock on the roof." Despite these measures, the Goldstone Commission's report was highly critical of Israel. Even the "knock on the roof" warnings were criticized by the UN report as constituting a form of attack against the civilians in the building.

On January 3, 2009, IDF ground troops entered the Gaza Strip. Knowing Hamas would be ready with booby traps and IEDs, and would likely attempt to capture Israeli soldiers to gain leverage, the IDF ground forces took a careful approach, operating when possible with tanks and other armor.

Implementing lessons from the Second Lebanon War, Israel executed a precision air-land battle where infantry commanders on the ground directed dedicated air assets. Operating in Gaza's densely populated urban areas—a theater with limited situational awareness—ground commanders could rely on UAVs to provide over-the-hill, or next city block, view of where snipers or ambushes might be laying in wait. The IDF stopped short of a thrust into Gaza City out of concern for the potential for casualties on both sides. In all, ten

Israeli soldiers were killed during Operation *Cast Lead* versus well over a thousand Palestinians, a disproportionate outcome that led to UN accusations of Israeli war crimes such as the deliberate targeting of civilians—charges Israel rejects due to unsubstantiated claims, as well as an international diplomatic backlash epitomized by the deterioration in relations with Turkey. With the benefit of hindsight, the Goldstone Commission's chairman, Judge Richard Goldstone, reassessed the report's findings. "If I had known then what I know now," he wrote in the *Washington Post* on April 1, 2011, "the Goldstone Report would have been a different document." Goldstone noted that Israel did not intentionally target civilians, as originally claimed in the report, whereas Hamas "purposefully and indiscriminately aimed at civilian targets."

The operation ended on January 18, 2009, with Israel's unilateral ceasefire and IDF withdrawal from the Gaza Strip. Not long thereafter Hamas renewed its provocations against Israel, almost inviting Israel to respond yet again.

There seems to be no end in sight to the strife that has marred the Middle East since time immemorial. Turbulence and uncertainty continue on Israel's fronts near and far, making it appear that Isaiah's hopeful prayer will remain an elusive yearning. Only time will tell.

Notes

1. An English summary of the Committee's final report and links to the full (unclassified) report in Hebrew can be accessed via the Israel Ministry of Foreign Affairs website: www.mfa.gov.il/MFA/MFAArchive/2000_2009/2008/Winograd%20Committee%20submits%20final%20report%2030-Jan-2008 (accessed March 16, 2011).
2. Human Rights In Palestine And Other Occupied Arab Territories. Report of the United Nations Fact Finding Mission on the Gaza Conflict.
3. Human Rights In Palestine And Other Occupied Arab Territories. Report of the United Nations Fact Finding Mission on the Gaza Conflict.

BIBLIOGRAPHY

Chapters 1 and 2
The Jewish Bible: Tanakh: The Holy Scriptures (Philadelphia: The Jewish Publication Society of America, 1985).
"Jericho," http://ccwf.cc.utexas.edu/~welli/archaeology/bible/jericho.html (accessed September 29, 1999).
"Was Joshua Justified in Exterminating the Whole Population of Jericho?" www.new-life.net/joshua.htm (accessed September 29, 1999).
Baretz, Julie. "Mount Tabor," *Gems in Israel* (August/September 2002), www.gemsinisrael.com/e_article000096511.htm (accessed March 14, 2011).
Dimont, Max. *Jews, God and History* (New York: Signet, 1962).
Duncan, Andrew and Opatowski, Michel. *War in the Holy Land. From Meggido to the West Bank* (Stroud, UK: Sutton Publishing Ltd., 1998).
Grayzel, Solomon. *A History of the Jews. From the Babylonian Exile to the Present 5728–1968* (New York: Mentor Books, 1968).

Herzog, Chaim and Mordechai Gichon. *Battles of the Bible* (London, UK: Greenhill Books, 1978).

Jackson, Wayne. "The Saga of Ancient Jericho," *Christian Courier*, www.christiancourier.com/archives/jericho.htm (accessed March 14, 2011).

Jaques, Don. "The Old Testament and the Ancient Near East. Jericho," www.georgefox.edu/academics/grad/wes/bst550/djaques/Jericho.html (accessed September 29, 1999).

Johnson, Paul. *A History of the Jews* (London, UK: Dent, 1911).

Josephus (translator William Whiston). *The Complete Works of Josephus* (Grand Rapids, MI: Kregel Publications, 1981).

Lemonick, Michael D. "Score one for the Bible," *TIME* (March 5, 1990), p.59.

Pearlman, Moshe. *In the Footsteps of Moses* (Tel Aviv: Nateev and Steimatzky, 1973).

Reviv, Hanoch. "The Canaanite and Israelite Periods (3200–332 BC)," in Michael Avi-Yonah (ed.) *A History of the Holy Land* (Jerusalem: Steimatzky's Agency Ltd. 1969).

Sanders, Michael. "Jericho Part II—The Biblical Account," *Mysteries of the Bible* (1998), www.biblemysteries.com/lectures/jericho2.htm (accessed March 14, 2011).

Wilson, Ralph F. "The Battle of Jericho," www.jesuswalk.com/joshua/lesson4-ex.htm (accessed March 14, 2011).

Wilson, Ralph F. "Why the Slaughter of Jericho? Devoted to Destruction—*Herem*," www.joyfulheart.com/joshua/herem.htm (accessed March 14, 2011).

Wood, Bryant. "Is the Bible accurate concerning the destruction of the walls of Jericho?" www.christiananswers.net/q-abr/abra011.html (accessed March 14, 2011).

Wood, Bryant. "The Walls of Jericho. Archaeology confirms: they really DID come a-tumblin' down," *Creation* (21:2, March 1999), pp.36–40.

Zaharoni, Menachem. "The Battle of Deborah and Barak Against Sisera," in Irit Zaharoni (ed.). *Israel Roots & Routes. A Nation Living in its Landscape* (Tel Aviv: MOD Publishing House, 1990).

Zaharoni, Menachem. "Gideon Fights the Midianites," in Irit

Zaharoni (ed.). *Israel Roots & Routes. A Nation Living in its Landscape* (Tel Aviv: MOD Publishing House, 1990).

Chapter 3

The Jewish Bible: Tanakh: The Holy Scriptures. (Philadelphia: The Jewish Publication Society of America, 1985).

Dagan, Yehuda. Interview: December 3, 2002.

Driscoll, J. F. "Philistines," *The Catholic Encyclopedia* (New York: Robert Appleton Company, 1911) http://www.newadvent.org/cathen/12021c.htm (accessed March 14, 2011).

Duncan, Andrew and Opatowski, Michel. *War in the Holy Land. From Meggido to the West Bank* (Stroud, UK: Sutton Publishing Ltd., 1998).

Gale, Richard, General Sir. *Great Battles of Biblical History* (London: Hutchinson & Co. 1968).

Garsiel, Moshe. "Ysodot shel historiah v'realiah b'tiur haMaaracha b'Emek HaElah v'krav David v'Goliat [Elements of History and Reality in the Description of the Ela Valley Warfare and the Combat Between David and Goliath]," *Beit Mikra* (Vol. 41, 1997), pp.293–316.

Grayzel, Solomon. *A History of the Jews. From the Babylonian Exile to the Present 5728–1968* (New York: Mentor Books, 1968).

Josephus (translator William Whiston). *The Complete Works of Josephus* (Grand Rapids, MI: Kregel Publications, 1981).

Reviv, Hanoch. "The Canaanite and Israelite Periods (3200–332 BC)," in Michael Avi-Yonah (ed.). *A History of the Holy Land* (Jerusalem: Steimatzky's Agency Ltd, 1969).

Roman, Yadin. "David v'Rehavam [David and Rehavam]," *Eretz v'Teva* (July–August 1998).

Zaharoni, Menachem. "Saul's Last Stand," in Irit Zaharoni (ed.). *Israel Roots & Routes. A Nation Living in its Landscape* (Tel Aviv: MOD Publishing House, 1990).

Chapter 4

The Jewish Bible: Tanakh: The Holy Scriptures (Philadelphia: The Jewish Publication Society of America, 1985).

"Accounts of the Campaign of Sennacherib, 701 BCE," in Oliver J. Thatcher (ed.) *The Library of Original Sources* (Milwaukee: University Research Extension Co., 1907), Vol. I: *The Ancient World*; *The Bible (Douai-Rheims Version)* (Baltimore: John Murphy Co., 1914). www.fordham.edu/halsall/ancient/ 701sennach.html (accessed March 14, 2011).

"Lachish: Royal City of the Kingdom of Judah," www.israel-mfa.gov.il.

"Sennacherib's Campaign (Iron Age, 8th century BCE)," http://staff.feldberg.brandeis.edu/...a/ANET/sennacherib_inscripti on.html (accessed August 18, 1999)

Borowski, Oded. "Hezekiah's Reforms and the Revolt against Assyria," www.asor.org/BA/Borowski.html (accessed August 30, 1999).

Halverson, Rob. "The Old Testment and the Ancient Near East—Lachish," www.georgefox.edu/academic...s/bst550/ rhalverson/Lachish.html (accessed August 22, 1999).

Herzog, Chaim and Mordechai Gichon. *Battles of the Bible* (New York: Random House, 1978).

Rabinowitz, Allan. "The ghosts of Tel Lachish," *The Jerusalem Post* (May 6, 1999).

Reviv, Hanoch. "The Canaanite and Israelite Periods (3200–332 BC)," in Michael Avi-Yonah (ed.). *A History of the Holy Land* (Jerusalem: Steimatzky's Agency Ltd, 1969).

Ussishkin, David. *The Conquest of Lachish by Sennacherib* (Tel Aviv: Tel Aviv University Institute of Archaeology, 1982).

Chapter 5

The Apocrypha, or Deuterocanonical Books (New Revised Standard Version) (Cambridge, UK: Cambridge University Press, 1989).

Avi-Yonah, Michael. "The Second Temple (332 BC–AD 70)—Jews, Romans and Byzantines (70–640)," in Michael Avi-Yonah (ed.). *A History of the Holy Land* (Jerusalem: Steimatzky's Agency Ltd. 1969).

Bar-Kochva, Bezalel. *Judas Maccabaeus. The Jewish Struggle Against the Seleucids* (Cambridge, UK: Cambridge University Press, 1989).

Bar-Kochva, Bezalel. *The Seleucid Army. Organization and Tactics in the great Campaign* (Cambridge, UK: Cambridge University Press, 1979: reprinted with corrections).

Dimont, Max. *Jews, God and History* (New York: Signet Books, 1962).

Duncan, Andrew and Opatowski, Michel. *War in the Holy Land. From Meggido to the West Bank* (Stroud, UK: Sutton Publishing Ltd, 1998).

Gale, Richard, General Sir. *Great Battles of Biblical History* (London: Hutchinson & Co., 1968).

Grayzel, Solomon. *A History of the Jews. From the Babylonian Exile to the Present 5728–1968* (New York: Mentor Books, 1968).

Herzog, Chaim and Gichon, Mordechai. *Battles of the Bible* (London, UK: Greenhill Books, 1978).

Johnson, Paul. *A History of the Jews* (London, UK: Harper-Collins, 1988).

Josephus (translator William Whiston). *The Complete Works of Josephus* (Grand Rapids, MI: Kregel Publications, 1981).

Pearlman, Moshe. *The Maccabees* (New York: Macmillan Publishing Co. Inc., 1973).

Zaharoni, Menachem. "Early Scenes of Battle," in Irit Zaharoni (ed.). *Israel Roots & Routes. A Nation Living in its Landscape* (Tel Aviv: MOD Publishing House, 1990).

Chapter 6

Avi-Yonah, Michael. "The Second Temple (332 BC–AD 70)—Jews, Romans and Byzantines (70–640)," in Michael Avi-Yonah (ed.). *A History of the Holy Land* (Jerusalem: Steimatzky's Agency Ltd. 1969).

Biggs, Mark Wayne. "Forty Days at Jotapata," *Military History* (April 1999).

Dimont, Max. *Jews, God and History* (New York: Signet Books, 1962).

Duncan, Andrew and Opatowski, Michel. *War in the Holy Land. From Meggido to the West Bank* (Stroud, UK: Sutton Publishing Ltd, 1998).

Gale, General Sir Richard. *Great Battles of Biblical History* (London: Hutchinson & Co., 1968).

Grayzel, Solomon. *A History of the Jews. From the Babylonian Exile to the Present 5728–1968* (New York: Mentor Books, 1968).

Guttman, Shmaryahu. "Gamla—A Heroic Stand," in Irit Zaharoni (ed.) *Israel Roots & Routes. A Nation Living in its Landscape* (Tel Aviv: MOD Publishing House, 1990).

Johnson, Paul. *A History of the Jews* (London, UK: Harper-Collins, 1988).

Josephus (translator William Whiston). *The Complete Works of Josephus* (Grand Rapids, MI: Kregel Publications, 1981).

Mattis, Richard L. "Holy City Under Siege," *Military History* (December 1995).

Rappaport, Uriel. "How Anti-Roman Was the Galilee?" in Lee. I. Levine (ed.). *The Galilee in Late Antiquity* (New York and Jerusalem: Jewish Theological Seminary, 1992).

Rashba, Gary. "Masada—Israel," *Military History* (October 2007).

Schaalje, Jacqueline. "Gamla," *Jewish Magazine* (February 2001). www.jewishmag.com/40mag/gamla/gamla.htm (accessed March 14, 2011).

Syon, Danny. "Gamla," (Israel Antiquities Authority) www.antiquities.org.il (accessed March 14, 2011).

Syon, Danny. "Gamla—City of Refuge," in A. M. Berlin and J. A. Overman (eds.). *The First Jewish Revolt. Archaeology, History and Ideology* (London and New York: Routledge, 2002).

Syon, Danny. "Gamla: Portrait of a Rebellion," *Biblical Archaeology Review* (January/February 1992, 18:01).

Tacitus (translators Alfred Church and William Brodribb). *Histories* (London, UK: Macmillan, 1864–77) www.sacred-texts.com/cla/tac/h05000.htm.

Chapter 7

Akram, A. I. *The Sword of Allah – Khaled bin Al-Waleed.* (October 1969). www.grandestrategy.com/2007/12/sword-of-allah-Khaled-bin-al-waleed.html.

Antiochus Strategos (trans. F. Conybeare). "Antiochus Strategos'

Account of the Sack of Jerusalem (614)," *English Historical Review* (Issue 25, 1910), pp.506–508. www.fordham.edu/halsall/source/strategos1.html (accessed March 16, 2011).

Bischoff, Bernhard and Lapidge, Michael. *Biblical Commentaries from the Canterbury School of Theodore and Hadrian* (Cambridge, UK: Cambridge University Press, 1994).

Donner, Fred. *The Early Islamic Conquests* (Princeton: Princeton University Press, 1981).

Elton, Hugh. "Review of *Byzantium and the Early Islamic Conquests*, by Walter E. Kaegi," *The Medieval Review* (Ann Arbor: University of Michigan University Library, 1994).

Gibbon, Edward. *The History of the Decline and Fall of the Roman Empire* (London, UK: Strahan & Cadell, 1776–89). www.ccel.org/ccel/gibbon/decline.html (accessed March 16, 2011).

Gichon, Mordechai. *Carta's Atlas of Palestine From Bethther to Tel Hai* (Jerusalem: Carta, 1974).

Goldschmidt, Arthur Jr. *A Concise History of the Middle East* (Boulder: Westview Press, 1979).

Kaegi, Walter E. *Byzantium and the Early Islamic Conquests* (Cambridge, UK: Cambridge University Press, 1992).

Kaegi, Walter E. *Heraclius. Emperor of Byzantium* (Cambridge, UK: Cambridge University Press, 2003).

Kennedy, Hugh. *The Armies of the Caliphs* (New York: Routledge, 2001).

Lewis, Bernard. *The Arabs in History* (Harper Torchbooks, 1966).

Nicolle, David. *Armies of the Muslim Conquest* (Oxford, UK: Osprey Publishing, 1993).

Nicolle, David. *Yarmuk AD 636: The Muslim Conquest of Syria* (Oxford, UK: Osprey Publishing, 1994).

Norwich, John Julius. *Byzantium—The Early Centuries* (London: Viking Penguin Inc., 1988).

Ostrogorsky, George. *History of the Byzantine State* (New Brunswick: Rutgers University Press, 1957).

Sharon, Moshe. "The History of Palestine from the Arab Conquest until the Crusades (633–1099)," in Michael Avi-Yonah (ed.). *A History of the Holy Land* (Jerusalem: Steimatzky's Agency Ltd. 1969).

Vasiliev, A. A. *History of the Byzantine Empire, Volume 1, 324–1453* (Madison: University of Wisconsin Press, 1958).

Chapter 8
"The Horns of Hattin," www.web-site.co.uk/knights_templar/templar4_7.html (accessed March 3, 1998).

Czech, Kenneth P. "City Taken and Retaken," *Military History* (February 1994).

Dafoe, Stephen. "The Battle of Hattin—July 4th, 1187," (March 31, 2010) www.templarhistory.com/hattin.html (accessed March 14, 2011).

Ernoul, a Frank. "Battle of Hattin, 1187," www.hillsdale.edu (accessed April 6, 1998).

Goldschmidt, Arthur Jr. *A Concise History of the Middle East* (Boulder: Westview Press, 1979).

Hallam, Elizabeth (ed.). *Chronicles of the Crusades* (London: Weidenfeld & Nicolson, 1989).

Hamblin, William. "Saladin and Muslim Military Theory," in B. Z. Kedar (ed.). *The Horns of Hattin: Proceedings of the Second Conference of the Society of the Crusades and the Latin East* (London, UK: Variorum, 1992), pp.228–38. www.deremilitari.org/resources/pdfs/hamblin.pdf (accessed March 14, 2011).

Hildinger, Erik. "Mongol Invasion of Europe," *Military History* (June 1997).

Kedar, Benjamin Z. "The Battle of Hattin Revisited" in B. Z. Kedar (ed.). *The Horns of Hattin: Proceedings of the Second Conference of the Society of the Crusades and the Latin East* (London, UK: Variorum, 1992). www.deremilitari.org/resources/articles/kedar.htm (accessed March 14, 2011).

Prawer, Joshua. *The World of the Crusaders* (London: Weidenfeld & Nicolson, 1972).

Rabinowitz, Allan. "Twin peaks in the lower Galilee," *The Jerusalem Post* (May 17, 1998).

Riley-Smith, Jonathan. *The Crusaders. A Short History* (London: The Athlone Press, 1987).

Robinson, John J. *Born in Blood: The Lost Secrets of Freemasonry, Vol. I.* (M. Evans, 1989).

Rozenberg, Silvia (ed.). *Knights of the Holy Land. The Crusader Kingdom of Jerusalem* (Jerusalem: The Israel Museum, 1999).

Runciman, Steven. *A History of the Crusades. Volume II. The Kingdom of Jerusalem and the Frankish East 1100–1187* (Penguin Books, 1952).

Saunders, J. J. *A History of Medieval Islam* (Routledge and Kegan Paul Ltd, 1965).

Sivan, Emmanuel. "Palestine During the Crusades (1099–1291)," in Michael Avi-Yonah (ed.). *A History of the Holy Land* (Jerusalem: Steimatzky's Agency Ltd. 1969).

Stevenson, Joseph (ed.). *De Expugatione Terrae Sanctae per Saladinum*, [*The Capture of the Holy Land by Saladin*], Rolls Series (London: Longmans, 1875), translated by James Brundage, *The Crusades: A Documentary History*, (Milwaukee, WI: Marquette University Press, 1962), pp.153–159, at www.fordham.edu/halsall/source/1187hattin.html (accessed March 14, 2011).

Chapter 9

"Baybars," http://www.web-site.co.uk/knights_templar/templar4_9.html (accessed October 17, 1999).

"Islam and Islamic History in Arabia and The Middle East. The Mongols and the Mamluks." http://islam.org/mosque/ihame/Sec11.htm (accessed March 14, 2011).

"The Mamluk Empire," http://library.advanced.org/17137...History/Other_Empires/mamluk.html (accessed October 25, 1999).

"The Mamluk Period (1250–1517 CE)," http://jeru.huji.ac.il/eg1.htm (accessed September 21, 1999).

"The Mongol Hordes," www.armouries.com/mongols.htm (accessed October 17, 1999).

Amitai-Preiss, Reuven. "Ayn Jalut Revisited," *Tarih—Papers in Near Eastern Studies* (Vol. 2, 1992).

El-Halaby, Br. Muhammed. "The Battle of 'Ayn Jaloot', A Turning Point in History," *Nida'ul Islam* (December–January 1996–7).

Goldschmidt, Arthur Jr. *A Concise History of the Middle East* (Boulder: Westview Press, 1983).

Hallam, Elizabeth (ed.). *Chronicles of the Crusades* (London: Weidenfeld & Nicolson. 1989).

Hildinger, Erik. "Mongol Invasion of Europe," *Military History* (June 1997).

Housley, Norman. *The Later Crusades 1274–1580* (Oxford, UK: Oxford University Press, 1992).

Ludolph of Suchem (trans. Aubrey Stewart). *Description of the Holy Land and of the Way Thither* (London: Palestine Pilgrims' Text Society, 1895), XII, 54–61. www.fordham.edu/halsall/source/1291acre.html (accessed March 16, 2011).

Riley-Smith, Jonathan. *The Crusades* (London: The Athlone Press, 1987).

Saunders, J. J. *A History of Medieval Islam* (Routledge and Kegan Paul Ltd, 1965).

Sharon, Moshe. "Palestine under the Mameluks and the Ottoman Empire (1291–1918)," in Michael Avi-Yonah (ed.) *A History of the Holy Land* (Jerusalem: Steimatzky's Agency Ltd. 1969).

Smith, John Masson, Jr. "Ayn Jalut: Mamluk Success or Mongol Failure?" *Harvard Journal of Asiatic Studies* (Vol. 44: 2, December 1984).

Thorau, Peter. "The Battle of 'Ayn Jalut: a Re-examination," *Crusade and Settlement—Papers read at the First Conference of the Society for the Study of the Crusades and the Latin East and presented to R. C. Smail* (University College Cardiff Press, 1985), pp.236–241.

Tschanz, David W. "History's Hinge Ain Jalut" *Saudiaramco World* (Volume 58: 4).

Chapter 10

Ayalon, David. *Gunpowder and Firearms in the Mamluk Kingdom: A Challenge to Mediaeval Society* (London: 1956).

Cook, M. A. (ed.). *A History of the Ottoman Empire to 1730* (Cambridge: Cambridge University Press, 1976).

Gichon, Mordechai. *Carta's Atlas of Palestine From Bethther to Tel Hai (Military History)* (Jerusalem: Carta, 1969).

Goldschmidt, Arthur Jr. *A Concise History of the Middle East* (Boulder: Westview Press, 1979).

Housley, Norman. *The Later Crusades, From Lyons to Alcazar* (UK: Oxford University Press, 1952).

Petry, Carl. "The military institution and innovation in the late Mamluk period," in Carl Petry (ed.). *The Cambridge History of Egypt. Volume I: Islamic Egypt, 640–1517* (Cambridge: Cambridge University Press, 1998), pp.462–89.

Petry, Carl. *Protectors or Praetorians? The Last Mamluk Sultans and Egypt's Waning As a Great Power* (New York: State University of New York Press, 1994).

Petry, Carl. *Twilight of Majesty. The Reign of the Mamluk Sultans Al-Ashraf Qaytbay and Qansuh Al-Ghawri in Egypt* (Seattle: University of Washington Press, 1993).

Sharon, Moshe. "Palestine under the Mameluks and the Ottoman Empire (1291–1918)" in Michael Avi-Yonah (ed.). *A History of the Holy Land* (Jerusalem: Steimatzky's Agency Ltd. 1969).

Twain, Mark. *The Innocents Abroad* (Signet Classic, 1980).

Winter, Michael. "The Ottoman Occupation," in Carl Petry (ed.). *The Cambridge History of Egypt. Volume I: Islamic Egypt, 640–1517* (Cambridge, UK: Cambridge University Press, 1998), pp.490–516.

Winter, Michael. Interview: April 23, 2002. Tel Aviv, Israel.

Chapter 11

"Bonaparte's despatches from Egypt, parts IV and V," from *Pièces diverses et correspondance relatives aux opérations de l'armée d'Orient en Egypte* (Imprimée en exécution de l'arrêté du TRIBUNAT, en date du 7 Nivose an 9 de la République française. Paris, Baudouin . . . Messidor an IX). www.napoleon.org.

Berman, Ariel. Lecture on May 2, 1999 at the conference commemorating 200 years since Napoleon's Syrian Campaign (Akko, Israel).

Chandler, David. *Campaigns of Napoleon* (Weidenfeld & Nicolson, 1966).

Charles-Roux, F. *Bonaparte: Governor of Egypt* (London: Methuen & Co., Ltd. 1937).

Feinberg, Herb. "North to Palestine: Napoleon Marches Against the Turks," *Napoleonic Scholarship* (Vol. 1: 2, December 1998), pp.16–22.

Gichon, Mordechai. *Carta Atlas of Palestine From Bethther to Tel Hai* (Jerusalem: Carta Publishers, 1974).

Gichon, Mordechai. "Jaffa 1799," *Napoleonic Scholarship* (Volume 1: 2, December 1998), pp.23–32.

Godechot, Jacques. *Napoleon* (Paris: Editions Albin Michel. 1969).

Grant, A. T. *Europe in the Nineteenth Century (1789–1914)* (London: Longmans, Green & Co., 1929).

Klebanoff Allon Lecture on May 2, 1999 at the conference commemorating 200 years since Napoleon's Syrian Campaign (Akko, Israel).

Nafziger, George. "Bonaparte's Egyptian Campaign," *First Empire* (Issue 10) http://firstempire.net/samples/napegy.htm (accessed March 14, 2011).

Raveh, Kurt. Lecture on May 2, 1999 at the conference commemorating 200 years since Napoleon's Syrian Campaign (Akko, Israel).

Runyan, Cory. "Napoleon in Egypt or egomaniac on the loose," (1996) http://www.napoleon-series.org/military/battles/c_egypt.html (accessed March 14, 2011).

Shosenberg, James. "Napoleon Saves the Day at Mount Tabor," *Military History* (April 1999), pp.43–48.

Tulard, Jean. *Napoleon ou Le Mythe du Sauveur* (Fayard 1987).

Wachsmann, Shelly and Raveh, Kurt. *An Encounter at Tantura with Napoleon.* (Pamphlet, undated)

Chapter 12

Allan, Steven. "Gaza: The Unsurrendered City," *ERETZ Magazine* (Issue 49, November–December 1996), pp.36–41, 63.

Allenby, Sir Edmund. "The Fall of Jerusalem," in Charles F. Horne (ed.). *Source Records of the Great War, Vol. V* (National Alumni, 1923), www.firstworldwar.com/source/jerusalem_allenby1.htm (accessed March 14, 2011).

Allenby, Sir Edmund. "The Battle of Megiddo," in Charles F. Horne (ed.). *Source Records of the Great War, Vol. V* (National Alumni, 1923), www.firstworldwar.com/source/megiddo_allenby.htm (accessed March 14, 2011).

Bodart, Gaston. "Report on the Fall of Jerusalem, 9 December

1917," in Charles F. Horne (ed.). *Source Records of the Great War, Vol. V* (National Alumni, 1923), www.firstworldwar.com/source/jerusalem_bodart.htm (accessed March 14, 2011).

Bodart, Gaston. "The Fall of Turkey," in Charles F. Horne (ed.). *Source Records of the Great War, Vol. V* (National Alumni, 1923), www.firstworldwar.com/source/turkey_bodart.htm (accessed March 14, 2011).

Bowman-Manifold, Sir M. G. E. *An outline of the Egyptian and Palestine campaigns, 1914 to 1918* (Chatham: W. Y. J. Mackay & Co., 1922).

Brown, John. "Horsemen with Bayonets," *Military History* (April 1992).

Bullock, David L. *Allenby's War: The Palestine-Arabian Campaigns 1916–18* (Blandford Press, 1988).

Duncan, Andrew and Opatowski, Michel. *War in the Holy Land. From Meggido to the West Bank* (Stroud, UK: Sutton Publishing Ltd., 1998).

Grey, Jeffrey. *A Military History of Australia* (Cambridge: Cambridge University Press, 1990).

Gullet, H. S. *The Australian Imperial Force in Sinai and Palestine—1914–1918.* (Queensland: University of Queensland Press, 1923).

Massey, W. T. "Allenby's Progress," in Charles F. Horne (ed.). *Source Records of the Great War, Vol. VI* (National Alumni, 1923), www.firstworldwar.com/source/allenby_massey.htm (accessed March 14, 2011).

Masterman E. W. G. "The Fall of Jerusalem," in Charles F. Horne (ed.). *Source Records of the Great War, Vol. V* (National Alumni, 1923), www.firstworldwar.com/source/jerusalem_masterman.htm (accessed March 14, 2011).

Meinertzhagen, Colonel R. *Middle East Diary* (London: The Cresset Press, 1959).

Hill, A. J. *Chauvel of the Light Horse* (Melbourne: Melbourne University Press, 1978).

Hughes, W. S. Kent. *Modern crusaders: an account of the campaign in Sinai and Palestine up to the capture of Jerusalem* (Melbourne: Melville & Mullen, 1919).

Jones, Ian. "Beersheeba: The light horse charge and the making of myths," *Journal of the Australian War Memorial* (No. 3, October 1983).

Lawrence, T. E. *Seven Pillars of Wisdom* (Penguin Books, 1926).

Spach, John Thom. "Allenby and the Last Crusade," *Military History* (March 1996).

Turnbull, Paul et al. *Pictures of health: War's Cruel Scythe: The Health of Australian Soldiers in the First World War* (Australian History WWW Project & Centre for Flexible Learning). http://nla.gov.au/nla.arc-13025 (accessed March 14, 2011).

Zakai, Abraham. "In the Footsteps of the ANZAC Warriors—The Battle for Beer Sheva During World War I." (Beer Sheva Municipality).

Zumbro, Ralph. *The Iron Cavalry* (New York: Pocket Books, 1998).

Chapter 13

"1948: The War of Independence," www.idf.il/English/UNITS/ IAF/iaf2.htm (accessed April 6, 1999).

"The Battle for the Roads," www.idf.il/English/HISTORY/ fiftyago.htm (accessed April 6, 1999).

Brandvein, Munio. Interviews on January 18, 2002 and September 24, 2002.

Brandvein, Munio (editor and compiler). *B'Mabat M'haHutz [A Look from the Outside. Listings of the Yad Mordechai Battles from May 19–23, 1948]* (Yad Mordechai: 1984).

Dupuy, Trevor. *Elusive Victory: The Arab-Israeli Wars 1947–1974* (Hero Books, Greenhill Books, 1984).

Elon, Amos. *The Israelis: Founders and Sons* (Holt, Rinehart and Winston, 1971).

Larkin, Margaret. *The Six Days of Yad Mordechai* (Yad Mordechai Museum, Israel, 1965).

Morse, Stan. *Modern Military Powers: Israel* (New York: The Military Press, 1984).

Nordeen, Lon. *Fighters Over Israel* (London: Greenhill Books, 1990).

O'Brien, Conor Cruise. *The Siege* (New York: Simon & Schuster, 1986).

Robinson, Donald. *Under Fire—Israel's 20-year Struggle for Survival* (New York: WW Norton & Co., 1968).

Rothwell, Steve. "Military Ally or Liability, The Egyptian Army 1936–1942," *Army Quarterly & Defence Journal* (Vol. 128: 2, April 1998).

Sachar, Howard. *A History of Israel* (New York: Alfred A. Knopf, 1985).

Transcript of interview with Grisha Zilberstein.

Chapter 14

Adam, Avshalom. Personal Account. IDF Paratroopers History Site. www.202.org.il/Pages/Footer/eduyot/avsha.php

Bar-Zohar, Michael (ed.). *Sefer haTzanchanim* [*The Book of the Paratroopers*] (Tel Aviv: Levine-Epstein, 1969).

Ben-Uziel, David. Interview: August 4, 2008.

Dayan, Moshe. *Diary of the Sinai Campaign* (New York: Schocken Books, 1965).

Dayan, Moshe. *Story of My Life* (Jerusalem: Steimatzky's Agency Ltd, 1976).

Duncan, Andrew and Opatowski Michel. *War in the Holy Land. From Meggido to the West Bank* (Stroud, UK: Sutton Publishing Ltd, 1998).

Eshel, Aharon. Interview: August 6, 2008.

Eshel, David. *Chariots of the Desert* (London: Brassey's Defence Publishers, 1989).

Gilai, Arieh. www.202.org.il/Pages/kadesh/sinai/jump.php

Katz, Samuel M. *Follow Me! A History of Israel's Military Elite* (London: Arms and Armour Press, 1989).

Maroz, Muni. Personal Account. IDF Paratroopers History Site. www.202.org.il/Pages/Footer/eduyot/muni.php

Milstein, Uri. *Milchamot haTzanchanim* [*The History of the Israel Paratroopers*]. *Book 2* (Tel Aviv: Schalgi Ltd, 1985).

Morse, Stan. *Modern Military Powers: Israel* (NY: The Military Press, 1984).

Nordeen, Lon. *Fighters Over Israel* (London: Greenhill Books, 1990).

Oren, Amir. "38 soldiers killed. Who approved the action?" www.haaretz.com. (accessed October 29, 2006).

Oren, Michael B. "The Second War of Independence," *Azure Magazine* (Winter 2007).

Rapoport, Meron. "Into the valley of death," www.haaretz.com (accessed February 13, 2007).

Sachar, Howard M. *A History of Israel* (New York: Alfred A. Knopf, 1985).

Sharon, Ariel and David Chanoff. *Warrior: The Autobiography of Ariel Sharon* (New York: Simon & Schuster, 1989).

Shavitt, Matti. *On the Wings of Eagles: The Story of Arik Sharon, Commander of the Israel paratroopers* (Tel Aviv: Olive Books of Israel, 1970).

Zur, Avi. Interview with Micha Ben-Ari (Kapusta). www.inz.org.il/article.php?id=330 (accessed May 19, 2008)

Chapter 15

"The Six Day War—The Syrian Front," IDF Spokesperson's Office. http://www.idf.il/English/HISTORY/sixday5.htm (accessed June 25, 1998).

Armored Corps. *HaHativa Shelanu b'milchemet Sheshet Yamim* [*Our Brigade in the Six Day War*] (Israel Ministry of Defense Publishing House, 1969).

Associated Press. *Lightning Out of Israel: The Six Day War in the Middle East* (USA: The Associated Press, 1967).

Bashan, Raphael. *The Victory* (Chicago: Quadrangle Books, 1967).

Batelheim, Avi. *Golani—Mishpachat Lohemim* [*Golani—Family of Fighters*] (Golani Brigade Publishing, 1980).

Bennett, Michael. "From the Fighting Front," *Olei Britannia* (UJIA, July 1967).

Chesbiah, Arieh. *Hel haShirion. Tsahal b'Chilo. Encyclopedia l'Tsava u'l'bitachon.* [*The Armored Corps. Zahal and its Soldiers. Encyclopedia of the Army and Security*] (Rivivim Publishing, 1981).

Churchill, Randolph S. and Churchill, Winston S. *The Six Day War* (London: Heinemann, 1967).

Donovan, Robert. *Israel's Fight for Survival* (New York: Signet, 1967).

Duncan, Andrew and Opatowski, Michel. *War in the Holy Land.*

From Meggido to the West Bank (Stroud, UK: Sutton Publishing Ltd., 1998).

Eshel, David. *Chariots of the Desert* (London: Brassey's Defence Publishers, 1989).

Har-Lev, Moty. *Golani Sheli* [*My Golani*] (Aviv Publishers).

Herzog, Chaim. *Arab-Israeli Wars* (New York: Vintage Books, 1982).

IDF. *Anashei haPlada* [*Men of Steel*]. (IDF Armored Corps, Ministry of Defense Publishing House, 1983).

IDF. *Egrof haBarzel.* [*Iron Fist*] (IDF Armored Corps Command, 1969).

Katz, Samuel M. *Follow Me! A History of Israel's Military Elite* (London: Arms and Armour Press, 1989).

Marshall, S. L. A. *Swift Sword* (American Heritage Publishing Co., 1967).

Michelsohn, Benny. "A History of the IDF Through Four Decades. Part IV: Six Day War, June 5–10, 1967," www.idf.il/English/HISTORY/born4.htm (accessed June 4, 1999).

Morse, Stan. *Modern Military Powers: Israel* (New York: The Military Press, 1984).

Sachar, Howard M. *A History of Israel* (New York: Alfred A. Knopf, 1985).

Stevenson, William. *Strike Zion!* (New York: Bantam Books, 1967).

Chapter 16

Eshel, David. *The Yom Kippur War* (Israel: Eshel-Dramit Ltd, 1978).

Eshel, David. *Chariots of the Desert* (London: Brassey's Defence Publishers, 1989).

Herzog, Chaim. *The War of Atonement* (Jerusalem: Steimatzky's Agency, 1975).

Katz, Samuel M. *Fire and Steel* (New York: Pocket Books, 1996).

Katz, Samuel M. *Follow Me! A History of Israel's Military Elite* (London: Arms and Armour Press Ltd, 1989).

Nordeen, Lon. *Fighters Over Israel* (London: Greenhill Books, 1990).

Ostrinsky, David. Interviews: 1997.

Sachar, Howard. *A History of Israel* (New York: Alfred A. Knopf, 1985).

Zaharoni, Irit (ed.). *Israel—Roots & Routes* (Israel: MOD Publishing House, 1990).

Chapter 17

Barrie, Douglas. "The Future of Israeli Air Power," *Flight International* (supplement. 1998).

Braybrook, Roy. "Now you see me, Now you don't," *AIR International* (May 1998).

Clancy, Tom. *Fighter Wing* (New York: Berkley Books, 1995).

Cohen, Eliezer. *Israel's Best Defense* (London: Airlife Publishing Ltd., 1993).

Eitan, Raful. *A Soldier's Story* (New York: Shapolsky Publishers, Inc., 1991).

Elisra Electronic Systems Ltd. Product literature.

Eytan, Lieutenant Colonel, F-16 pilot. Interview: January 5, 1999.

Hewish, Mark, et al. *Air Forces of the World* (London: Peerage Books, 1979).

IDF Spokesman's Office (www.idf.il)

Janes' *All the World's Aircraft* (London: Jane's Information Group).

Morse, Stan. *Modern Military Powers: Israel* (New York: The Military Press, 1984).

Nordeen, Lon. *Fighters Over Israel* (London: Greenhill Books, 1990).

O'Brien, Conor Cruise. *The Siege* (New York: Touchstone, 1986).

Parmiter, James. "Israeli Air Force Tactical Development in the 1982 Bekaa Valley Campaign," www.oocities.org/paris/LeftBank/7438/iaf.html (accessed March 23, 2011).

Sachar, Howard Morley. *A History of Israel. Volume II* (Oxford, UK: Oxford University Press, 1987).

Epilogue

Human Rights In Palestine And Other Occupied Arab Territories. Report of the United Nations Fact Finding Mission on the Gaza Conflict (United Nations, 2009)

www2.ohchr.org/english/bodies/hrcouncil/specialsession/9/docs/U
NFFMGC_Report.pdf (accessed March 14, 2011)
Goldstone, Richard. "Reconsidering the Goldstone Report on Israel
and War Crimes," *The Washington Post.* April 1, 2011.
"The Second Lebanon War (2006)" (Israel Ministry of Foreign
Affairs)
www.mfa.gov.il/MFA/History/Modern+History/Israel+wars/Hizbu
llah+attack+in+northern+Israel+and+Israels+response+12-Jul-
2006.htm (accessed March 14, 2011)
Zidoni, Ofer and Aloni, Shlomo. *Israel Air Force Yearbook. IAF At
War (*Israel: Wizard Publications, 2007).

INDEX